Spirit Hunter

THE HAUNTING OF AMERICAN CULTURE BY MYTHS OF VIOLENCE: SPECULATIONS ON JEREMY BLAKE'S WINCHESTER TRILOGY

Spirit Hunter

THE HAUNTING OF AMERICAN CULTURE BY MYTHS OF VIOLENCE: SPECULATIONS ON JEREMY BLAKE'S WINCHESTER TRILOGY

Philip Monk
Art Gallery of York University

Art Gallery of York University
4700 Keele Street, Toronto, ON Canada M3J 1P3
www.yorku.ca/agyu

Library and Archives Canada Cataloguing in Publication

Monk, Philip, 1950-
Spirit hunter: the haunting of American culture by myths of violence: speculations on Jeremy Blake's Winchester trilogy/Philip Monk.

Published in conjunction with an exhibition held at the Art Gallery of York University, May 12–June 27, 2004.
Includes bibliographical references.
ISBN 0-921972-44-X

1. Blake, Jeremy. 2. Winchester House (San Jose, Calif.)–In art. I. Blake, Jeremy II. York University (Toronto, Ont.). Art Gallery III. Title.

N6537.B522M66 2005 778.59′092 C2005-903052-6

The Art Gallery of York University is supported by York University, the Canada Council for the Arts, the Ontario Arts Council, and the City of Toronto through the Toronto Arts Council.

Canada Council for the Arts Conseil des Arts du Canada
Ontario Arts Council Conseil des Arts de l'Ontario
torontoartscouncil An arm's length body of the City of Toronto

Edited by Alison Reid
Designed by Lisa Kiss Design, Toronto
Photography courtesy of Feigen Contemporary, New York
Printed and bound in Canada by C.J. Graphics Inc., Toronto

Available through D.A.P./Distributed Art Publishers
155 Sixth Avenue, 2ND Floor, New York, N.Y. 10013
TEL 212.627.1999 FAX 212.627.9484

CONTENTS

Oh, god said to Abraham, "Kill me a son"
Abe said, "Man you must be puttin' me on!"
God said, "No," Abe said "What?"
God said, "You can do what you want Abe but
The next time you see me comin' you better run"
Well, Abe said "Where do you want this killin' done"
God said, "Out on highway 61."

—Bob Dylan, "Highway 61 Revisited"

Cowboys and Indians

[In 1967], American troops would be describing Vietnam as "Indian country" and search-and-destroy missions as a game of "Cowboys and Indians"; and Kennedy's ambassador to Vietnam would justify a massive military escalation by citing the necessity of moving the "Indians" away from the "fort" so that the "settlers" could plant "corn."

—Richard Slotkin, *Gunfighter Nation*

TWENTYNINE PALMS, SEPTEMBER 22, 2001 A few days after 9/11, I wait in the desert evening for the mock drive-in screening of Douglas Gordon's *5 Year Drive-By*, a work based on John Ford's Western *The Searchers*. As the sun declines in the California desert to commence the overnight projection, a close-up image of a crazed John Wayne is slowly exposed in the diminishing light. Gordon's screening is ideally set with our desert viewing repeating Ford's desert drama of abduction and rescue—a classic American "captivity narrative." Could Gordon possibly have imagined the pertinence to current events that would be less uncanny coincidence than reminder of historical repetition? Then the abyss looms threateningly in this desert site in the uncanny division of my attention when someone mentions that Twentynine Palms is a Marine training base for desert fighting. Right, I think, and the kidnapping Comanche are Arab or al Qaeda terrorists; we've seen *this* movie before. At the screening of *The Searchers* that same night at the local drive-in, pickup trucks full of Marines cheer on John Wayne's relentless, mad, vengeful hunt.

Cut to New York City earlier in the week where Jeremy Blake is in residence in lower Manhattan watching George W. Bush and his hawkish administration declare their fierce determination to hunt down Osama Bin Laden, rounding up their posse on television in the iconic language of Hollywood Westerns: "wanted dead or alive." He thinks to himself, Here we go again. So began the stirrings of Blake's *Winchester Trilogy*, an unlikely attempt to revive history painting through the temporal medium of video projection.[1] Unlike Gordon's coincidence, Blake would seek the source of the uncanny in its repetitions. The uncanny always comes back to haunting.

That week in September, on the two coasts of that imperial nation, current events made both of us speculate on the origin and terminus of a drive that swept across the land like an irresistible force over two centuries. Native impediments to that drive, whether American Indians or seas of buffalo, were eliminated, almost magically without agency, as if by railroad and rifle alone. While this integration of technology united individuals to corporations and national interest, something else was needed to justify devastation. The *telos* of the American spirit demanded an ideology that was as well a myth. The manifest destiny of a people could then guide the acts and ideals of its future, here and beyond. In this future, the inheritors of "the winning of the West" could celebrate its foundational past, time and again, as John F. Kennedy evoked its virtues in 1960 in the political-platform rhetoric of his call for a "New Frontier." Or it could invoke it in the just cause of revenge, as had President Bush, hastily preparing a cross-border reprisal that would camouflage invasion as the export of what was, after all, a universal *telos*: American democracy. The posse was divided on two fronts: settling an old score, a second border crossing later would launch a gold rush as a bonanza of reconstruction contracts.

Ideology did not justify the centuries of killing, but from the start the means-ends ratio of killing rationalized itself as a logic of extermination. This unofficial, covert policy continued long after the frontier ended—and was implemented elsewhere than on the American continent. The exterminating tactics of the Indian Wars between the first settlers and displaced native inhabitants were ruthlessly administered to any insurrection against imperial ambitions, whether in the drive across the wide American continent or the hunt in the deserts and jungles of the Third World—in the Philippines during the Spanish-American War at the beginning of the twentieth century or in Vietnam sixty years later.

Spirit Hunting

> *[While it is] a trite saying that "the pen is mightier than the sword," it is equally true that the bullet is the pioneer of civilization, for it has gone hand in hand with the axe that cleared the forest, and with the family Bible and school book. Deadly as has been its mission in one sense, it has been merciful in another; for without the rifle ball we of America would not be to-day in the possession of a free and united country, and mighty in our strength.*
>
> —"The Rifle as an Aid to Civilization,"
> program copy from "Buffalo Bill's Wild West"

Some thought expiation due. Sarah Winchester, widow of the heir to the Winchester Repeating Rifle fortune, was one. Believing herself, after the death of her one-month old daughter in 1866 and her husband, William, in 1881, haunted by spirits of people killed by the "gun that won the West," she consulted a medium in Boston. The medium urged moving west and perpetually constructing a house to confound these spirits. Building sounds, rather than rifle reports, would drive evil spirits away. So on that far coast, having duplicated the passage that opened the West with the help of her family's manufacture, Sarah Winchester built her mansion in San Jose, California, obsessively creating an armature to escape the persecuting haunting that persisted around her. Between 1884 and 1922, she spent a considerable part of her $20 million inheritance in expiation, this wasteful expenditure a parody of Thorstein Veblen's notion of "conspicuous consumption" invented to explain the behaviour of America's ruling class at the end of the nineteenth century. Except that Sarah Winchester's twenty-four hours, seven-day-a-week building program was a non-stop theatre played to the spirit, not material, world.

The construction of the luxury mansion incorporated all the up-to-date mechanics that we would expect for this class of business and manufacture nobility—and then some. Yet nothing about the relentless project was rational or put to any practical use. In fact, the construction was deliberately irrational. What would one expect when the owner took guidance from the good spirits she summoned to advise on the architectural foiling of evil ones haunting her? Winchester house was a pratfall contraption that was deadly serious. Doors led out from upper storeys to dead drops or to interior blank walls; dead-end staircases led nowhere; windows or trap doors punctuated floors. Most remarkable was the sheer scale of the proliferating mansion, which housed only its owner: elaborated from its original six-room farmhouse, 160 chambers remain of a total perhaps of six hundred elevated, dismantled, or destroyed in the process.

That Sarah Winchester could pursue such extravagance was not just a sign of her wealth; her enterprise also speaks to the liberation Spiritualism offered women in the second half of the nineteenth century.[1] While our impression of spiritualism is likely derived more from movies (where ridicule of its scams figures in the deceptive plots of film noir or where its table-rapping seances function in horror films to visit punishment on the foolhardy) than historical recall, this outmoded belief had a profound cultural effect. An equal mix of charlatanism, entertainment, and religious sentiment, the spiritualist movement was common to all orders of society. It gave solace to the bereaved who experienced death in a new way. It gave voice to women hitherto silenced: typically female, trance speakers could both earn income and speak freely on social issues.[2] Intimately linked, Spiritualism and the suffragette movement contributed to the "feminization of American culture" as counterweight to the West's lawlessness. Sarah Winchester would seem a fellow traveller by putting inherited wealth to her own use to expiate a family's murderous complicity. Yet, her obsession was as likely to invoke more haunting as to cure her of it. Her "work of mourning" was perverted in the perpetual work ethic that others performed for her.

It was as though the technology that allowed the hunting of beings had to be countered by a technology that appeased their haunting. Thus, Sarah Winchester's folly was not merely a haunted house but a machine, like so many other inventions of the nineteenth century that demonstrate American technical ingenuity. This time, however, a woman invented and operated it.[3] Invention usually divides the sexes repeating a division between material and spiritual realms that isolates commerce from domesticity. Consider the use to which Samuel Morse's telegraphy was put. As much as railroad and rifle, the telegraph transformed the West, collapsing space and time to fit the schemes and schedules of commerce. This practical invention also stirred the imagination. Spirit rappers capitalized on its application to their domain. "Appropriately, while Morse's telegraph carried news of banking, commerce, and other concerns of the masculine sphere, the spiritual telegraph addressed issues of vital concern to women."[4] Current technologies are always ready metaphors for consciousness, as in the expression "spiritual telegraph." But as Friedrich Kittler has written, technology also invents its haunting spectres. Or social manifestations rapidly follow from industrial patents, their own inventions spirited by the new technology, through which their haunting presences and representations are metaphorically expressed and physically transmitted. Telegraphy brought forth spirit rapping; with the invention of photography, spirit photography followed.[5] (Can media haunt? In 1845, the British writer Thomas de Quincey believed so. He thought that "the brain is haunted as if by some jealousy of ghostly beings moving amongst us" brought about by the technological agitation of the age.[6] Isn't America's material success the product of this agitation—its haunting as well? "The pure products of America go crazy," poet-diagnostician W. C. Williams wrote.)

Winchester house is neither a quaint relic of a Victorian obsession fit for recycling as psychedelic kitsch nor a house haunted by a madwoman. There is reason to its madness. Paradoxically, its dysfunctionality makes the house into a machine, but not of the domestic sort invented to reduce women's drudgery. The medium Sarah in her Blue Seance Room (a lookout from which she also spied on her servants), the spirits who were on a time clock summoned between midnight and 2 AM by the bell tower, and the entrapping house construct a machine: a spirit machine. A machine for capturing and a medium for registering spectral images—is this haunted house not a camera? Or at least a prototype. When spirits animate their representations, their haunting presence calls for a new medium and a new machine to house it. Winchester house would have to imagine, rather than invent itself, the representation in film that awaited it.

Sarah Winchester's over-zealous hunt for persecuting spirits makes us wonder whether her expiation was rather a repeating in the spirit world of the slaughters of the material world that the Winchester rifle expedited. Her overbuilt, booby-trapped mansion was not merely a fortification to keep evil out; it was a frontier garrison from which she made her midnight, counterinsurgent sallies into the spirit world. We think she protested too much when she withdrew behind secure ramparts disguised as a conspicuously mannered Victorian mansion. One conjures spirits only in order to chase them away; the spiritualist hunt is the specular circle of a paradoxical pursuit: "Come so that I may chase you!" would be its rallying cry. In this chase, "the ghost does not leave its prey, namely, its hunter. It has understood instantly that one is hunting it just to hunt it, chasing it away only so as to chase after it.... This logic and this typology of the *paradoxical hunt* (whose figure, beginning before Plato, will have traversed the whole history of philosophy)" was obvious to Herman Melville who saw it motivating every spiritual and profit pursuit of his countrymen on the make: "heiress-hunters, gold-hunters, buffalo-hunters, bee-hunters, happiness-hunters, truth-hunters, and still keener hunters after all these hunters."[7] The type of hyphenated hunter that Sarah Winchester proved to be is answered by what her house intended to trap. Sophistical truth hunters that we are, can we say what Sarah Winchester's hunting cum haunting perhaps was intended to shield? We must be adept not to turn prey to what we hunt.

Fluid Mechanics: *Winchester*

> *...huge masses of agitated vapour... glowing in the unnatural light of a faintly luminous and distinctly visible gaseous exhalation which hung about and enshrouded the mansion.*
>
> —Edgar Allan Poe, "The Fall of the House of Usher"

Did Sarah Winchester know she was on the *Zeitgeist* mark with her proto-cinematic machine, one of many inventors pursuing the century's culminating technology through their own obsessions? Her ghost apparatus lacked only a medium that could fix spectral images, something that was at once technical *and* spiritual. Her neighbour to the north (in what is now Silicon Valley), the inventor Eadweard Muybridge, without wealth of his own but funded by railroad magnate Leland Stanford, similarly pursued fleeting phantoms, trying to capture the image of motion through its analytical decomposition. Motion would be the elusive prey hunted by both.

Film haunts this house. Having prepared for its arrival, the Winchester mansion had to wait for the millennium when film itself would be haunted by the telegraphing of a new electric medium, its subtle system of analog indexing of the real transformed digitally by reproduction in an electronic image. For the Winchester house, its purpose finally fulfilled by the registrations of motion pictures, film nevertheless is a traumatic return; the weeping house releases the pent-up spirits haunting it, which seep from it as if bleeding from bullet wounds, slowly ebbing into each other in the slow pace of their languorous, transforming confluence.

Jeremy Blake has understood that film might be more than a didactic tool for the cultural pathologist as it was for the physician-psychologist J.-M. Charcot, who used the new invention to persuade an audience to his theories by staging hysteria as a spectacle. Could Monsieur Charcot induce this hysterical house, contemporary to his clinical cases, to swoon like Sarah Winchester's female French counterparts in his charge—transmitting some electrifying magic through his baton? *Winchester Trilogy* is a speculation that this dysfunctional house, haunted by the history of the settlement of the West, could cure itself by becoming the film apparatus it was in prototype. The house must give itself over to a haunting that would heal. It must release itself into an exorcising medium that could spirit and expel spectres, conjure them by projecting them into a movement that was proper to them. A motion picture could tell this story, not through the script of its inhabitant's talking cure, but by letting the house reveal its distress, movingly, through time in a film cure. Film work would be a work of mourning. This would be the American way—to ally technology and spirit—since it was the technical invention of a machine that animated these spirits.

Blake's *Winchester*, part one of the trilogy, opens with a ghostly black-and-white image of the Winchester house derived from a vintage photograph. The clickety-click of a film projector fades in and out of our attention as an image of the house and gardens goes in and out of focus and smoky, disembodied figures of rifle-toting cowboys float across the screen. How many simulacra other than the ghosts of cowboys are paraded here? Actually, the whole technology of film simulates itself through phenomenal connotations we associate with experiencing film projection. The sound, however, is a special effect, part of the soundtrack, not ambient to our space.

Likewise, the flickering and occasionally jerking and flashing images, with their ersatz celluloid scratches, are simulacra suggesting a print passing through a projector, nothing material. Subtly capturing us in remembrance of a displaced technology, this sleight of hand induces a state of mind ready for possession.

The uncertainty of possession, or the medium of possession, or which medium possesses which, is often at issue in *Winchester*. Can we ever say *where* it is an issue when issuing always is a dissolving? Depiction is nothing but an amorphous flow, which refuses to settle in any stable representation. All categories of form and content dissipate when the certainty of representation erodes in a mediumistic haunting of media by media. For *Winchester* is a projection where one medium is carried as transparently as light within another, film spirited within video. Having sustained an illusion through the magic trick of creating the illusion of itself, film effects dissipate like ghosts when a coloured emanation seeps from a door on an upper floor of the house. Manifesting itself as a phenomenon precisely when film illusion is complete, haunting arises through an electronic substitute for film's spectral projections.

Illusion sets the house in its time: at the birth of film, its gestation culminating in 1895 with the screening of the Lumières's *Workers Leaving the Lumière Factory*. The technical history of the origin of film—the invention of its devices for the photographic reproduction of movement—coincides with an ideological one. That the medium was quickly co-opted by a bourgeois ideology of representation coalescing in classical Hollywood cinema does not mean that initially there was consensus about its function, which rather conflated contrary desires. The technical search for analogical representation was, at the same time, an impulse that film theorist Noël Burch identifies as the Frankensteinian fantasy of the nineteenth century—using technology's resources to animate life in order to triumph over death. The motivation of this "seductive dream of total representation...[was], precisely, a *spiritualist* one."[1] At the time of the Lumières's Salon Indien presentation of their Cinématographie, a journalist predicted what quickly would become a common belief, because it already corresponded to the animated desire that technology was in part invented to fulfill: "When these cameras are made available to the public, when everyone can photograph their dear ones, no longer in a *motionless* form but in their *movements*, their activity, their familiar gestures, with words on their lips, death will cease to be absolute" [my emphasis].[2]

More than a fantasy, this profound desire propelled technology's inventions, even though some would be chanelled in the end toward fantasy fulfillment as happened with Hollywood's dream factory. All the technologies of telepresence, from the gramophone to the telephone and film, derive from a desire that these inventions be prosthetics to the other world. Science was indeed contaminated by spiritualism. Alexander Graham Bell's assistant, Thomas Watson, conducted nightly seances, and the inventor himself had a signed contract with his older brother where the first departed "was to contact the survivor through a medium demonstratively superior to the more traditional channel of spiritualism."[3] Likewise, the Wizard of Menlo Park, Thomas Edison, sought to combine technologies of sound and picture to restore departed artists to their publics and to revive loved ones for their families. Given this backstory to the important inventions of the time, shouldn't we consider Winchester house an affiliated, if unresolved and unpatented, invention?

An atmosphere of spiritualism presided over film's origin and was just as determinant on its final product as the analytic motion experiments of Eadweard Muybridge and his French counterpart Étienne-Jules Marey. If photography, then film, supported the positivist experiments of science, at the same time they uncannily created "a parallel world of phantasmatic doubles alongside the concrete world of the senses verified by positivism."[4] Parallel realities lent themselves at times to the mutual application of the tools of the positivist and the phantasmagorical to each other, at other times to their confusion. Phantomatic confusion was the "logic" of the day, haunting all orders of culture, technique, and commerce in an era of high capitalism when the phantasmagorical character of the commodity leaped from technical invention into images film technology brought forth.

Technologies linked to invent cinema but only following on contrary spectacles that were already affiliating. It seems that synthesis, which produces the technical apparatus of film, succeeds the syncretic, which expresses equally the period's deepest sentiments and its most frivolous fantasies. For example, the spectacle of spiritualism amalgamated with the magic show to create a vital theatre of illusion and then was adapted to film: *The Spiritualist Photographer*, a film by the owner of Paris's Robert Houdin Magic Theatre turned filmmaker, Georges Méliès, "traces a complex genealogy between the new technique of photography, a new spiritual revelation, a development of a theatrical spectacle, and then a further development of the technology of photography into motion pictures."[5] More than the devices of montage or double exposure economically employed to stage illusion, motion was the durational sleight of hand that performed its psychological seductions. What magic thing would motion conjure and dismayingly reveal within our seduced subject, who, paying to be distracted from routine, delights to be possessed by animations induced by the repetitive mechanisms of this lively art?

Culture tends to repress the past sentimental or fantastical ends to which a representational medium is put, conflating them as the same dated frivolities, by sublating their disappearing act to the technical supremacy of the emergent, triumphant technology. Nonetheless, we can only understand, perceive, and participate in

Blake's mediumistic conjuration of a haunted house by revisiting and reliving the contrarieties of this complex genealogy. One more amnesiac repression completes this genealogy, the repeating-action collusion that troubled Sarah Winchester: that "the history of the movie camera thus coincides with the history of automatic weapons."[6] Our heiress could never escape the vicious circle of hunter and hunted to which technology ironically condemned her.

The quaint manufacture of *Winchester*'s opening illusion is not meant merely to nostalgically evoke or place Sarah Winchester's enterprise at the birth of film. Illusion gives the image to its time by gifting time to the image. Animating a still offers its content movement but propels the image *as a whole into time*, taking us along in this stream. Film duration—not its capacity for capturing likenesses, even the mere likeness of spectral phenomena—is the *medium* of haunting here. Haunting is temporal (though ghostly visitations reanimated in the future suggest that haunting is not ordered by a temporal logic we adhere to). Movement brings spirits forth, but not in any fixed shape. The abstract movement-images that exude and morph from the upper door of the Winchester house are not representations; they are temporal flows of colour, which many have compared to Morris Louis stain paintings. An apt description of these video projections is the one Blake names them by: time-based paintings.

Calling these images durational paintings is no retreat to the nuanced language of a medium seemingly more sensitive to subjective imprint than the technical medium of film, which rather indexes the real. If a medium can haunt, or be haunted itself, it must stage these frequencies through transmission. Painting is too static a form to be phantasmal. Likewise, spirit photography could merely dream in motion pictures its wish-fulfillment there. Its dubious capture of otherworldly images is the failure of still photography to manifest motion. Hence the illusion of movement that must be imparted to *Winchester*'s opening photograph, a movement that then *really* continues as the spectral effluvia that follow.

While this movement is real, the reality portrayed is fictional: these are computer animations, not spirit emanations. Nevertheless, on the basis of illustrations in contemporary theosophist publications, we may imagine that they are adequate facsimiles, except that they are in motion. Motion defines their mode of transformation as well as their phenomenality.[7] Movement makes them *real* by making spirits phenomenal. Opposing the means of its binary making, this reality is not quantifiable in terms of space and time but can only be experienced qualitatively through duration. The fluid mechanics of movement-images reflect the fluid medium of their projection and reception: the material medium of film and the immaterial medium of consciousness. Computer morphing, film movement, and perceptual experience are one in *Winchester*, their duration characterized by "multiplicity of fusion."[8]

When we become one with the image through perception, can we trust that the medium of film does not delude us? Are we sure that it does not instead instill multiplicity of *con*fusion? At one with film for its duration, could we not be persuaded to madness, taken possession by simulacra it lets loose? As individual subjects who constitute ourselves through self-certitude, we need to think that perception is something we possess, knowing, in spite of virtual fusion, that *our* perception and *that* reality are united momentarily in *this* image. Could we imagine that perception might be split otherwise, that it might be internally *other*, belonging not to us but to a doppelgänger to whom we belong? From our *perspective*, we set an image at a distance *outside* us, protecting ourselves by guarding this fragile divide of "outside" us, so how could we be receptive to possession? What we see screened before us in continuous movement must be representation of a hallucinated consciousness that is already possessed. *Winchester* must be

Sarah Winchester's movie, a reflection of *her* deluded mind—real to her and fictional to us.

From the security of spectatorship, we witness Sarah Winchester's paranoid state of consciousness as the movie she projects outside herself from inside her house, as a realm populated by threatening spirits she imagined. Architecture and film conspire in this madness. From the garrison of her split consciousness, replicating itself in the obsessive proliferation of her mansion, she needed to patrol the frontier of her mind's divisions beyond the protective shell that architecture provided by recurrently projecting her uncanny double outside. These are the ghostly cowboys that we saw prowling her grounds, which reappear in the hallucinated, multiplying symmetries of Rorschach blots, their illustrations excerpted from forty years of Winchester print advertisements from the 1880s on, the period of her building mania.

Fusion obscures. Already several types of images in *Winchester* have been mentioned without distinguishing them. That images emerge from one another does not make them similar any more than duration strings them into a narrative. Differentiating their types, qualities, and functions, separating their zones of reference or emanation tells us the story, or rather transmits it through their disjunctive alignments or conjunctive misalignments. Within this stream of images we receive, signals are emitted from intermittent gaps but to no code we comprehend as a coherent or intentional narrative. To make these transmissions into a story, which Blake tells through images alone, means we must trace their source and address or discover "who speaks" through them.

We might start with the photograph of the Winchester house appearing as film. Already, two related image types combine here. An event within the image, however, arrives to mark the first of many distinctions. Disturbing its verisimilitude, coloured effluvia seep from the black-and-white photograph, discharging from an aperture of the house and then blossoming into a transmuting procession of computer-animated hallucinations. Is this apparition a rupture or merely a depiction within the image, within what is, after all, the closed set of a film? Can representation be disturbed by what appears within it, by what it already and only is? When it comes, the emission stains the image. It arrives in time and appears in space to confuse the image's very temporality and spatiality by distinguishing them other than themselves. (A further distinction: the event is a temporal eruption before it is a visual appearance.) An event distinguishes by its disruptions, which are no rational clarifications. Not only does this event distinguish two series of images—those that are sequenced as a series of stills animated by film projection and those that animate themselves through temporal morphing; not only does this rupture suggest an overflowing of representation by some other regime of imagining, pathological or otherwise; it also—dividing the moment as a temporal difference, delay, or desistance from the punctuating click of the shutter and instant capture of the camera—demarcates the border between inside and out by breaching an appearance rigorously maintained by representation. Demarcating, nonetheless, devastates what it distinguishes.

To account for this disruption, we can't simply make it an anomaly by suggesting, for instance, that the discharge stands for the photograph's unconscious, its leakage a depiction by means of a related medium's differing visibility. Any speculation of its source is fraught with warnings, especially criticism against attributing depth, that is, interiority or intentionality, to a statement or image. Yet an "inside" other than content is revealed here in what before was merely a facade, that is, an image only of blank exteriority. An epidermal wound opens the house to our gaze; the internal dynamics of something within overflow boundaries.

We take images for granted as record of the natural extension of our vision, which is accurately transcribed by the technical conventions of photography. Thus, the one-sidedness of a photograph, for instance of the Winchester house, positions us outside its representation, outside of what the photograph represents. While still the photograph's physical surface, the depth of the image confirms an extension beyond which vision cannot trespass. The image itself is a border: the this-side-of-a-beyond-of-no-trespass. An image thus establishes the reach of visual extension as the ground of exteriority in general, conferring, as a given, the priority of exteriority over interiority. The proper domain of our sight, the ground of our dominating vision, is a private property we securely possess. Distance would belong to us, even up to this border, to its frontier edge. If perception wanted forcibly to breach this border beyond the trajectory of its scopic protectorate, it would distinguish the other side (the interior of an absolute exteriority) from its *distant and secure* point of view.

Spatial representation cannot see what it cannot trespass and so, in turn, it jealously permits no temporal passage. Except as the retention of a past captured in the index of a spatial representation, no temporality exceeds photographic convention. The event changes perception by dissolving this convention. A temporal event alone divides inside from out by a coincident devastation of spatial boundaries. The event determines inside from out by dividing the two from a point of view inside, except that "point of view" is dispensed with when this border is divided by a temporal rupture, not a spatial crossing.

The event does not reverse the precedence of inside and out as two locales facing each other unequally across a borderline. It separates the outside from itself by a division whereby the border hovers—poised on a threshold, as spirits poise—as a spectral apparition of the outside of an inside. This uncertain border is an unstable, outdistanced projection proceeding from "within"; it is a precession, so to speak, of a preceding procession of images hallucinated from within this other "place." Our perception is unable to coincide with the event of this simulacral border, unable to see "it" because its invisibility secretes itself behind our visibility, because the event also divides inside and out by marking off space from time, in the process delegating us to different perceptions that are familiar and uncanny. While dissemblance here may be unconscious misalignment between differing regimes, dissimulation might benefit from this perceptual disadvantage.

Demarcating an illusory borderline, the event allocates modes of perception corresponding to types of images belonging to the "interior" or "exterior" of the house. Who—or what—do they *belong* to? We can account for our perception, but who owns the uncanny, hallucinated images that parade before us seeping from the flat surface of the photograph/or facade of/or from inside the house? They must belong to whoever possesses the property. These images, which we take to be reflections of Sarah Winchester's delusion, not ours, form and proceed differently, deforming and transforming otherwise. They originate from her place inside the house (and thus have a life of their own, shielded from our viewing), although whether they are Sarah's projections or those of the haunted house itself we do not at first know.

We have not yet determined, and perhaps never will, the status of what appears here as haunting. How do ghosts haunt—by the apparition they are or by their snaring diversion of simulacra or hallucinations? Beyond identifying phantomatic phenomena (the ghost possesses a "paradoxical phenomenality," a "paradoxical incorporation"), what do we call this type of apparitional figure ("if it exists, if it responds to a name and corresponds to an essence"): spirit, spectre, ghost, or phantom? Putting a name to a spectre would conjure it. Putting a name to the *revenant* might settle its spirit haunting.[9]

Throughout *Winchester* we are kept outside the house, which is as resistant to entry as the material surface of a photograph of it in our hands. As objective viewers and skeptics of the supernatural, we stay there, respectful of the conventions of both private property *and* representation. Yet, unaware, seduced into the delusion of an illusion of movement, we are passively prepared to pass through a door that will take us to another side that is an inside of perception. This trespass cannot tell us whether we—let alone perception—belong there. A perception that does not belong, an uncanny perception, is fit only to haunt a house. Nevertheless, this "perception" hovers before us, beckoning. Thus seduced by a *motion* picture, we are ready to live Sarah Winchester's psychic disorder.

Images seep, sustained in their escape, embodied and disembodied at the same time, in some medium. They do not frantically disperse, pulverized into the atmosphere as if gaseous explosions from the close confines of an airless vacuum chamber. Nor do they dissipate in infinite separation, as if from a space capsule into the airless void. They issue...mediumistically. Once outside, they are then propelled: tumbling forth, morphing in stunning configurations, seizing us in rapture, and merging, as well, with a haunting soundtrack. But lest we forget, thereby relegating it secondary, music—pure fusion of multiplicity—guides our emotions and perceptions; doppelgänger to the image, it carries us along as if within us. Haunting yet banal, music manipulates us to the conventions of a debased genre: this is a typical, though pure and wordless, horror film of the haunted house variety.[10]

Even though they fuse as part of their confounding purpose, different types of efflorescing hallucinations, we learn, can be distinguished. Deforming biomorphic configurations mutate into symmetrical, decorative fields. Symmetry associates these fields with the cowboy Rorschach tests. Yet the latter are isolated, unlike other images—we're not sure, since there are so many serried boundaries—in an internal or external stockade. Abstract images belong inside the house, or to the house, though they seep out. While they too may be disturbances of the house, the Rorschach cowboys (who likewise bleed hallucinations from their bullet holes) are instead violently expelled to wander an exterior realm of signification, because, yes, we see, they roam a landscape, but not so home on the range. Why this differing treatment for these particular images? The enemy's territory was where Sarah Winchester obsessively fled, to hold herself captive to persecuting spirits. In voluntary exile there, nevertheless, she must stand her ground. From her besieged residence she hurled her counter-accusations as abject rejections that turn these images other—though cowboys, not Indians. Expelled from belonging where they resided, are these figures guards vigilantly circulating the grounds of a psychic compound, as if a hovering palisade; scouts sent out to secretly reconnoiter Indian territory; or spectral intruders kept at bay by the security system of a camouflaged redoubt? Whatever they are, they are not alone; in its "safe room," frightful paranoia locks into a dual system of inside and out.

Categorizing the functions of images that so easily seem to dissolve together in a hallucinated consciousness (or is it our perception that is confused?), we begin to test and tamper with the redoubt's logic, which we thus learn is no secure system, merely its dissemblance. We still have to breach its security or to be invited inside this house from which even the visiting Rough-Rider president, fellow hunter, and Winchester rifle devotee, Teddy Roosevelt, was denied admission. Hunters that we are in pursuit to trap the truth—knowing Indians, too—we patiently wait to study the ways of our faceless prey. Traces of visitations to and from what she inhabits to defend are our only clues. From the exterior where we peer at its facade, at the outer edge of the reach of its protective shield, on the borderline of the exteriority of its interiority, we think we comprehend the symptoms that this house defensively embodies through its projective, protective demarcations. We recognize them because, actually, we have already been admitted inside—captured by, inducted, and implicated in the madness of the interior by our own hallucinated gaze. Because we let down our guard from the beginning, *Winchester* fuses our perception with the mad projections emanating from this haunted house.

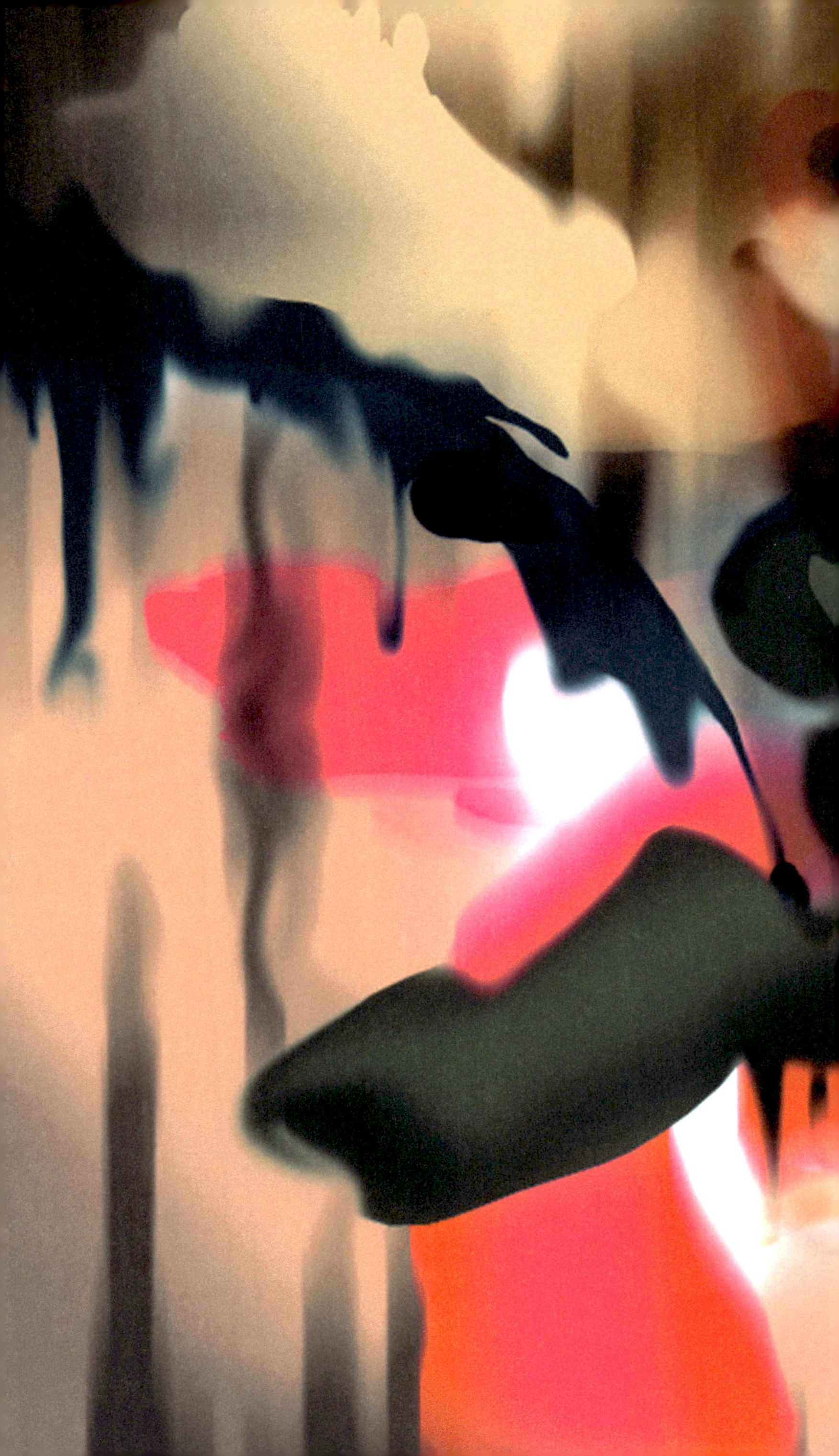

START

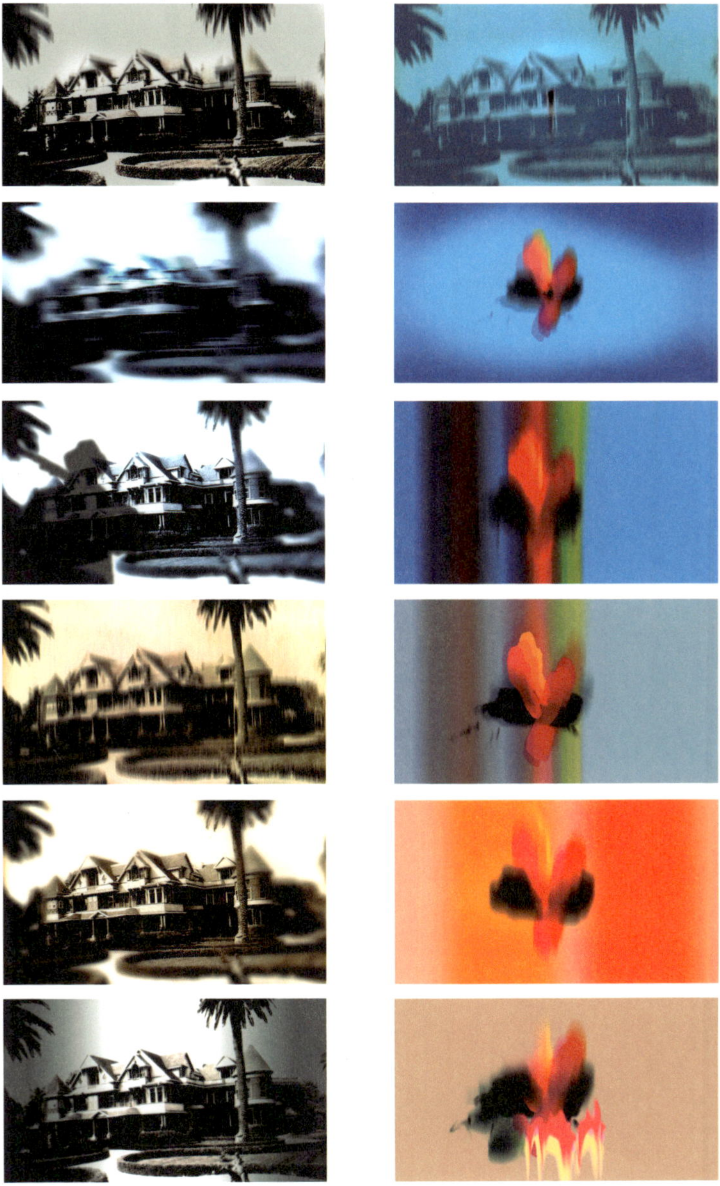

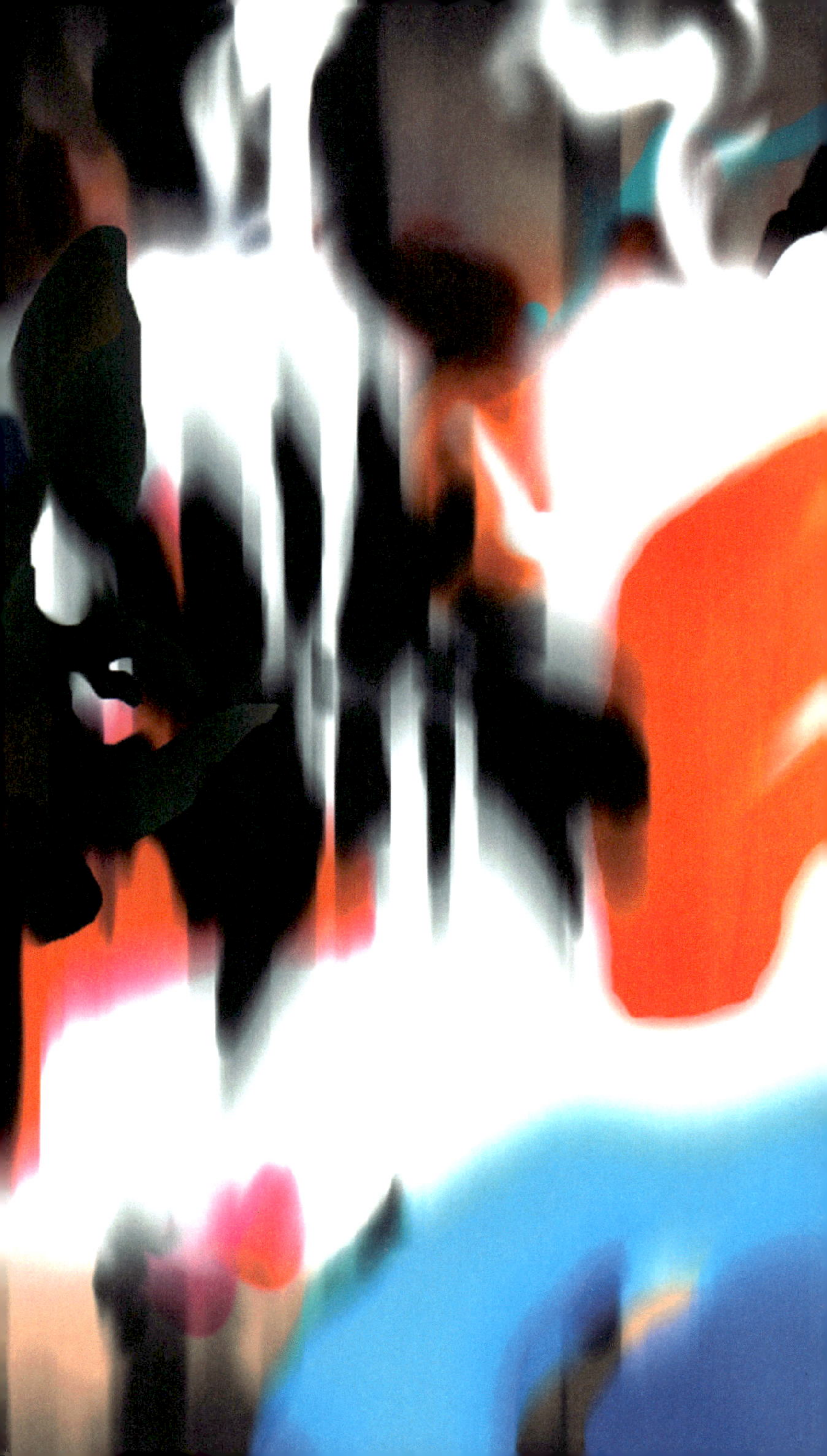

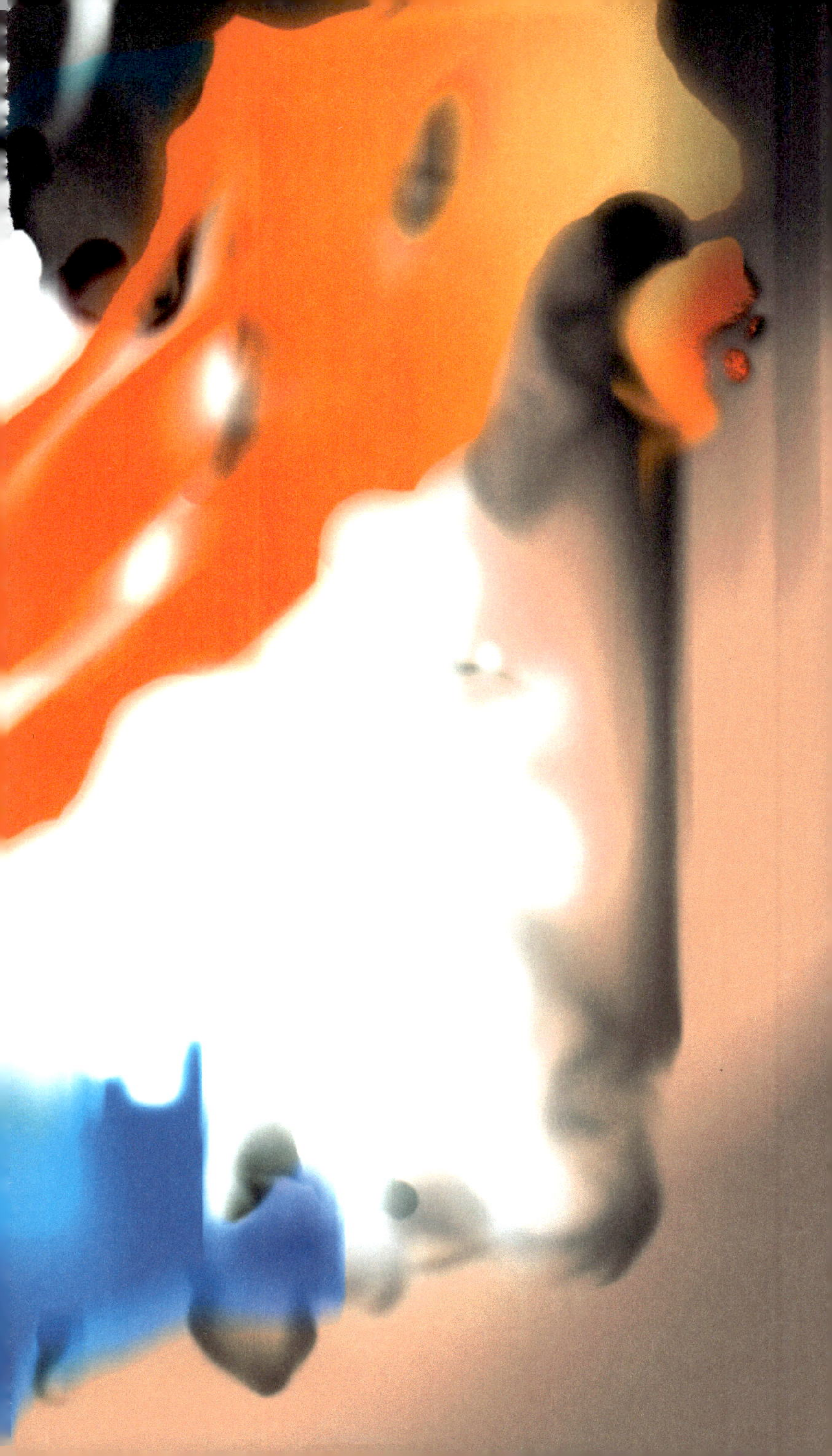

JEREMY BLAKE, *Winchester*, 2002.

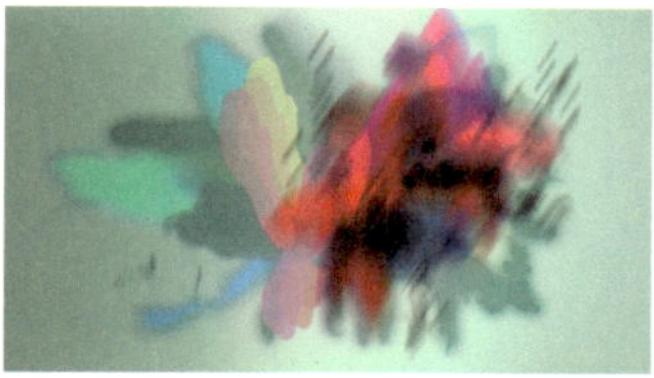
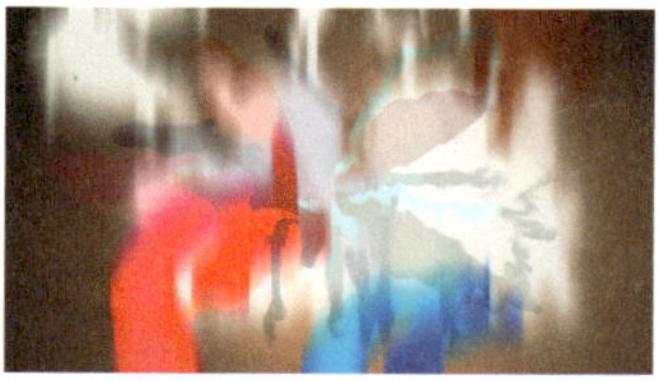
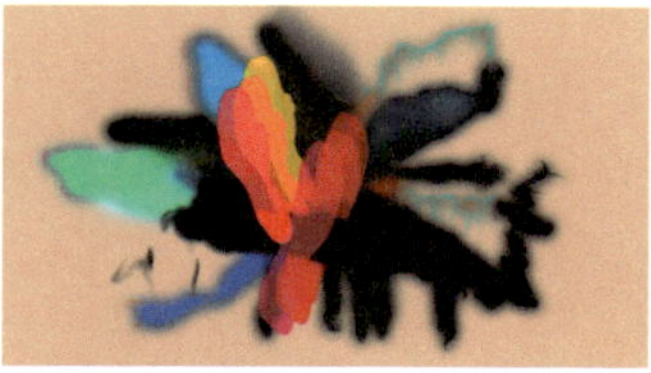
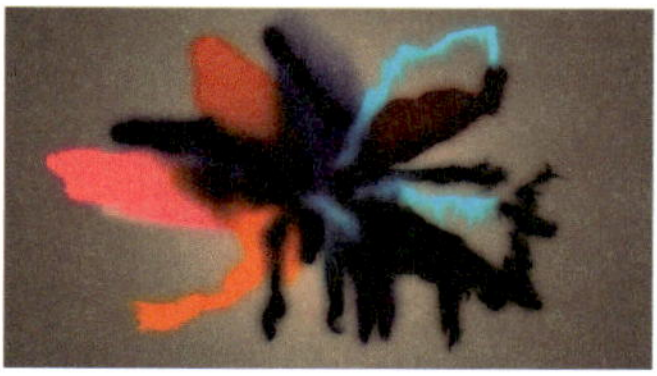
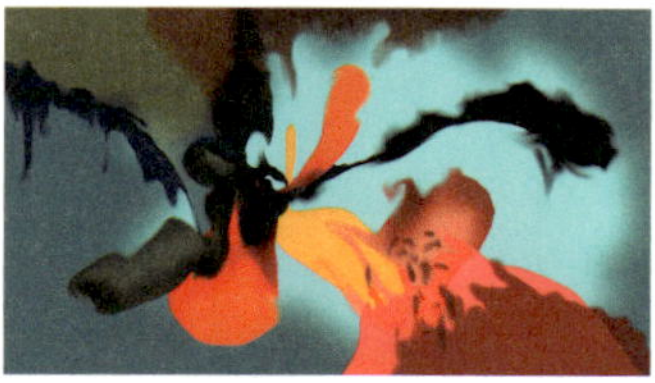
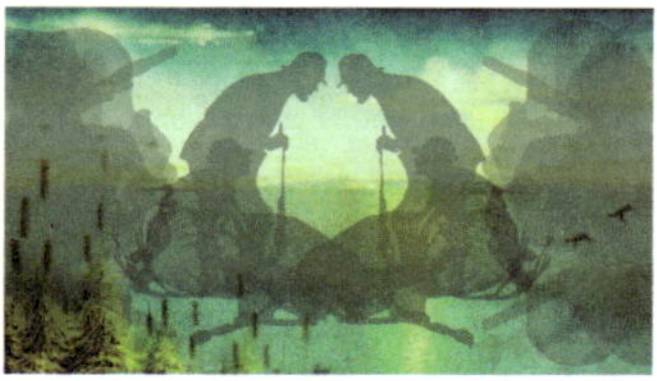
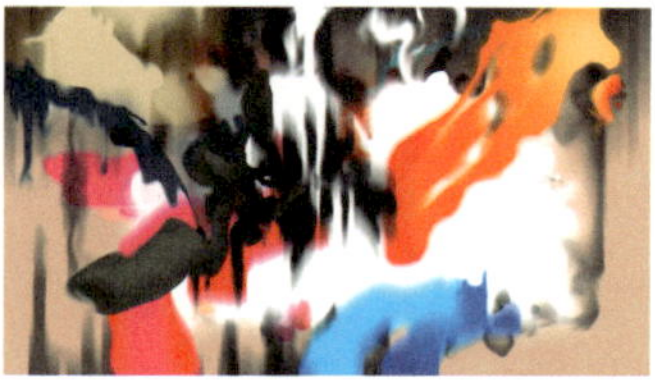
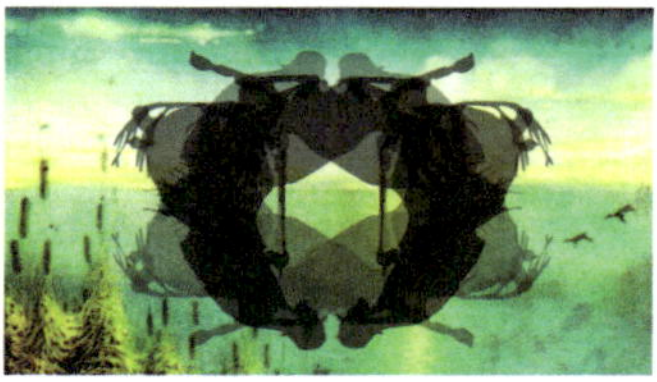
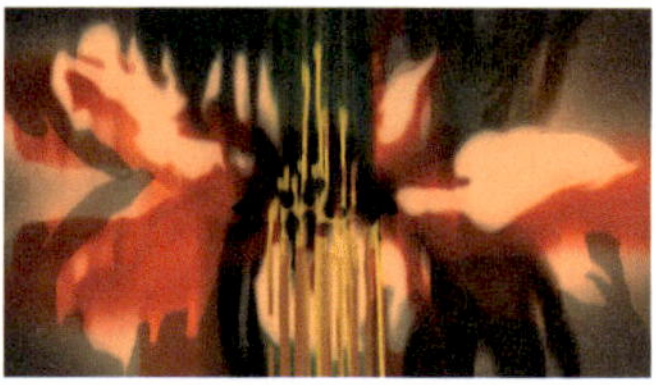
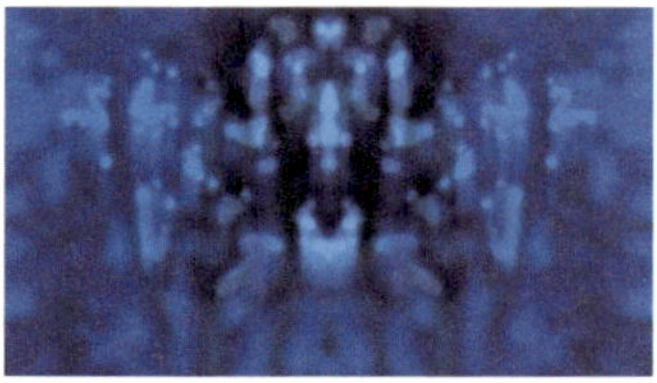
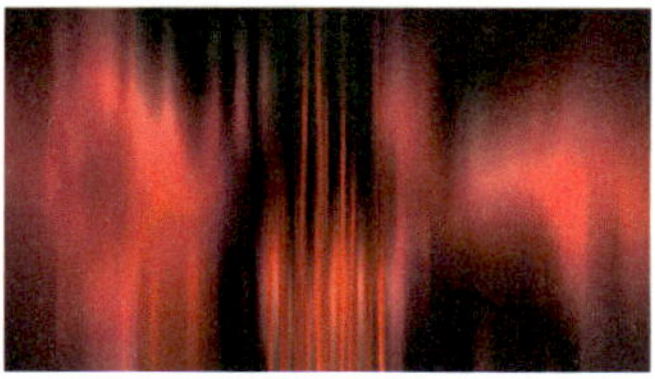
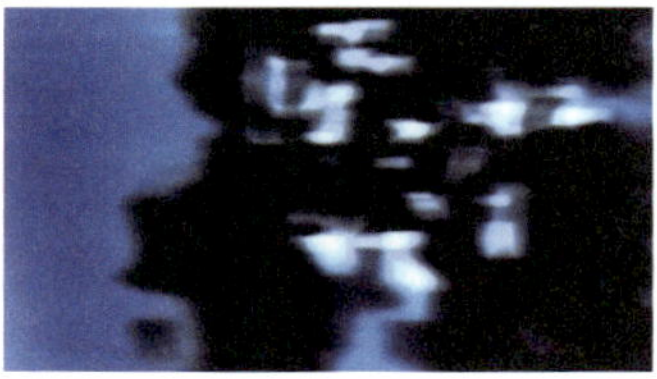

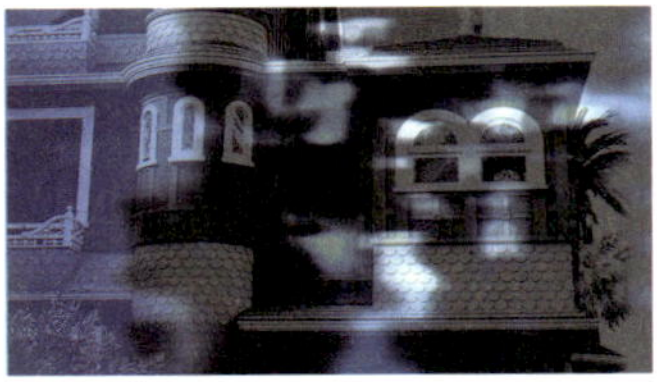
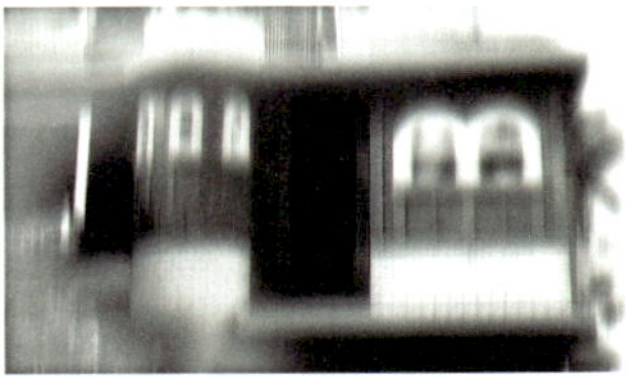
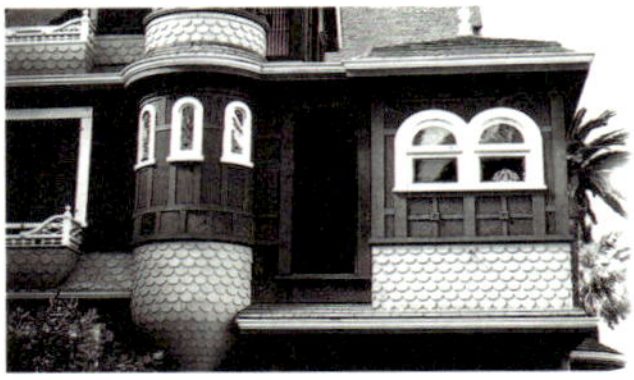
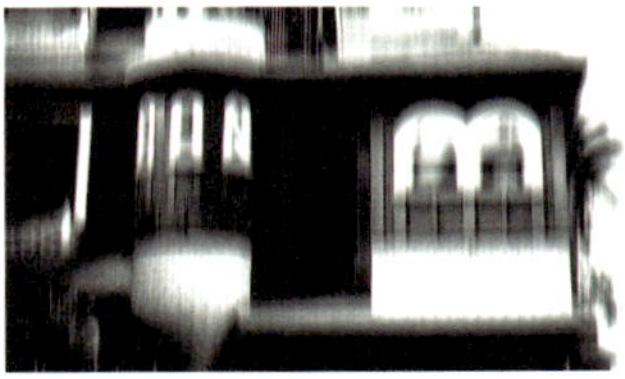
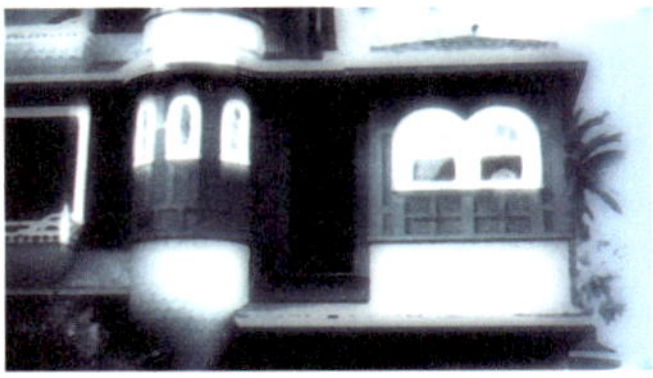
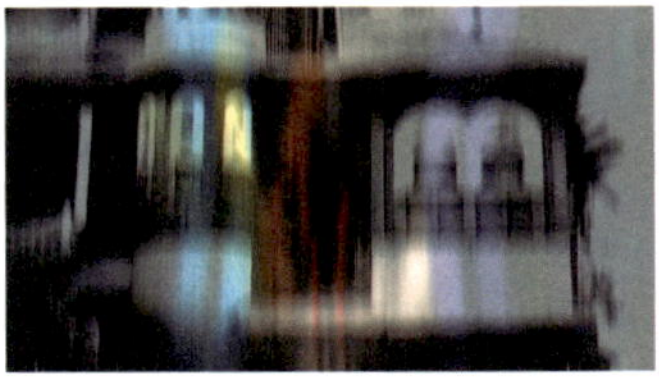
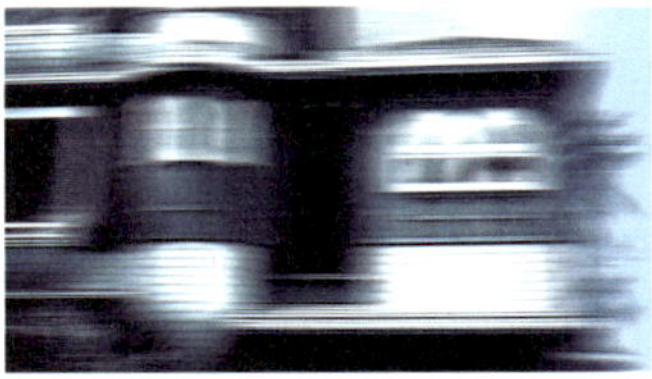
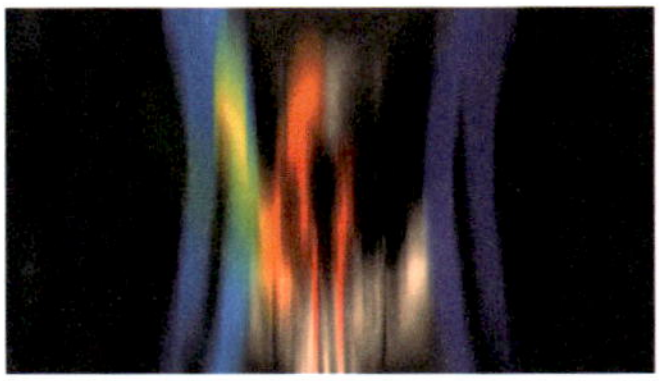
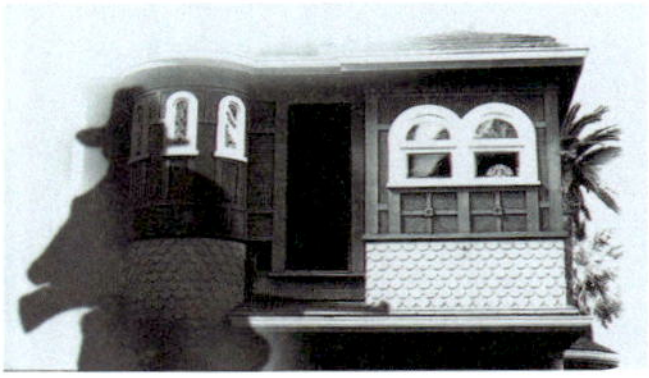
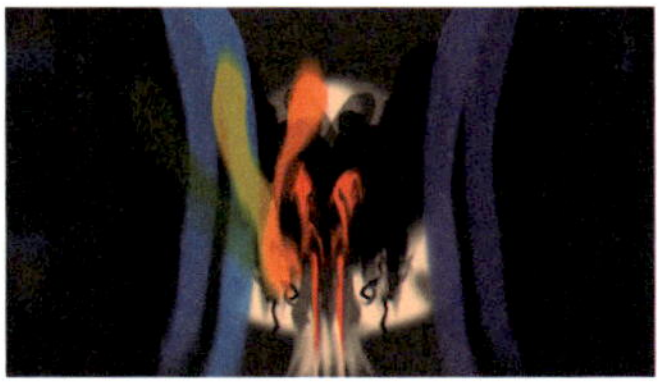
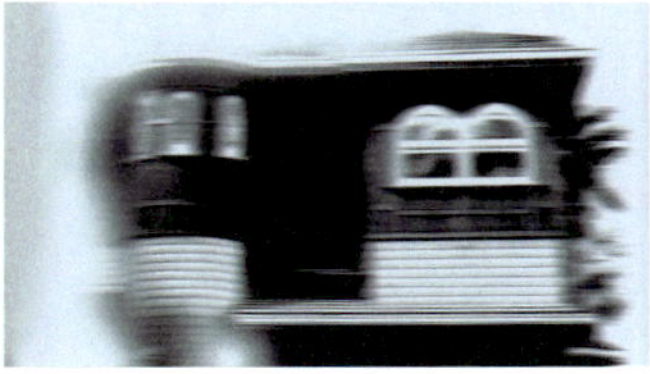
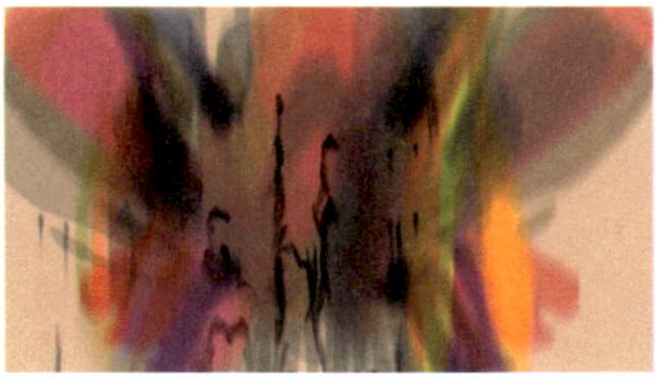

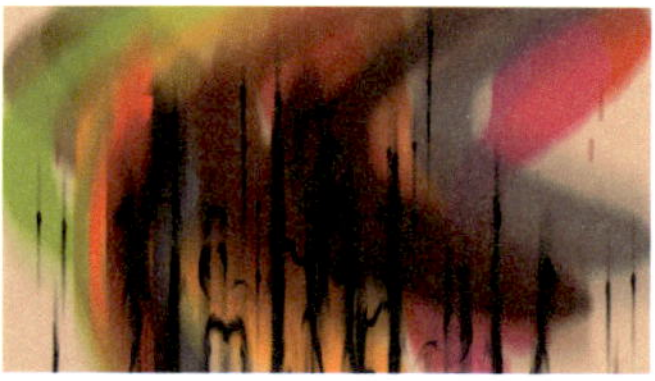
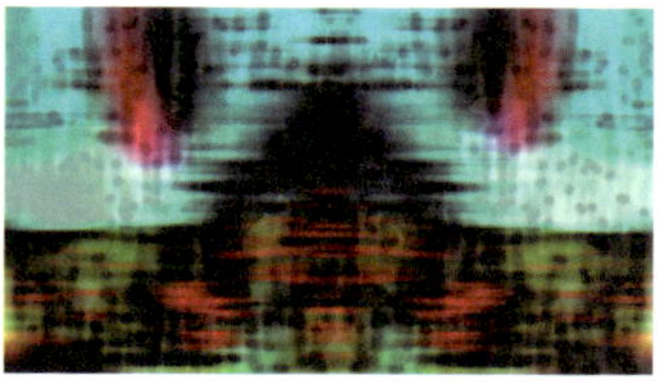
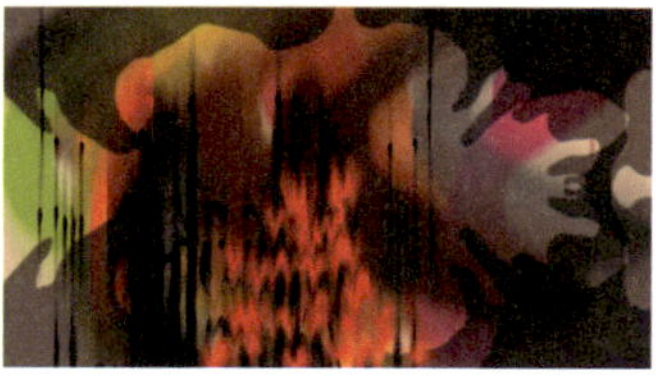
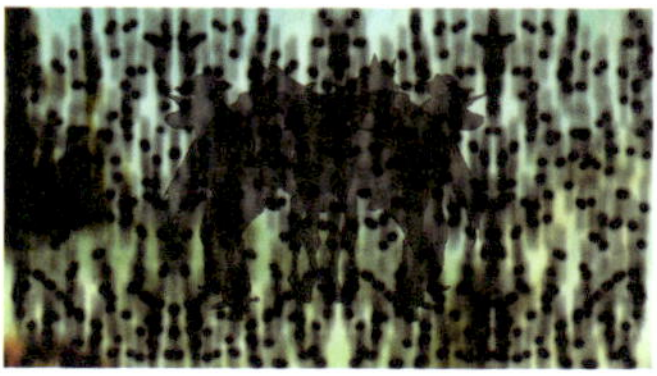
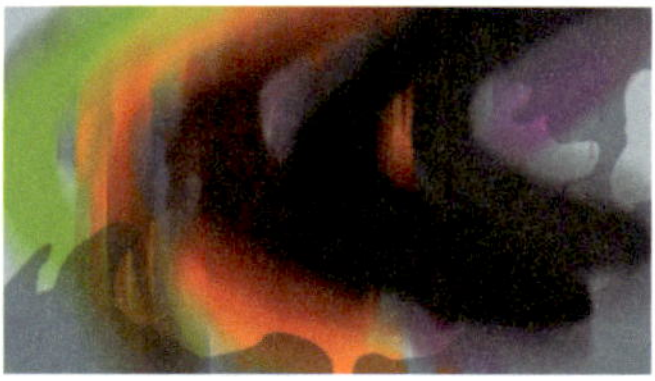
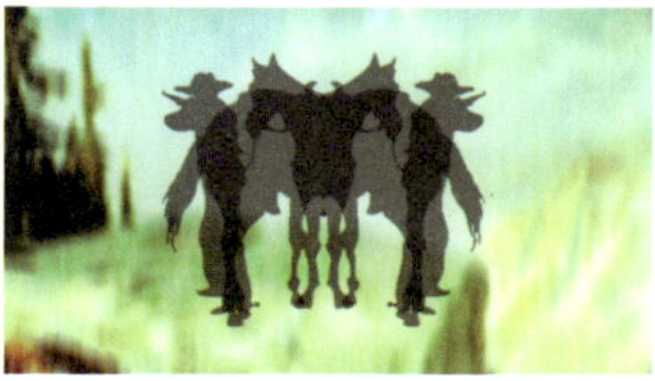
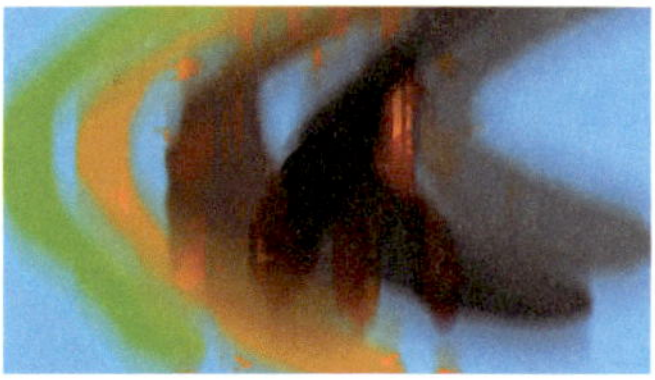
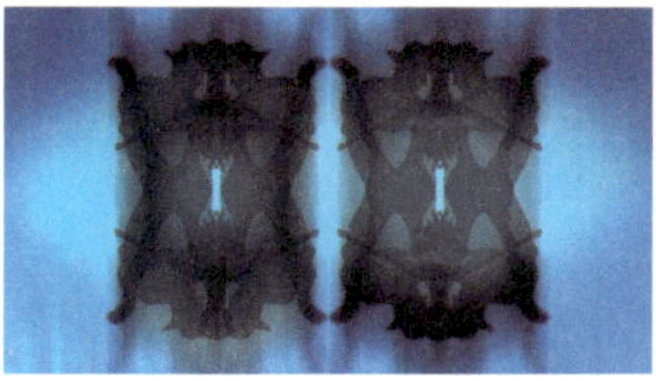
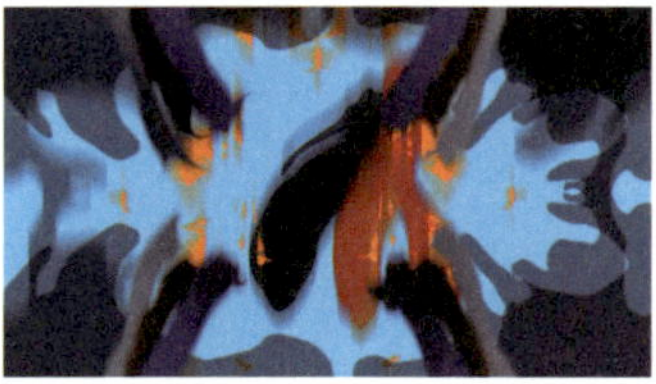
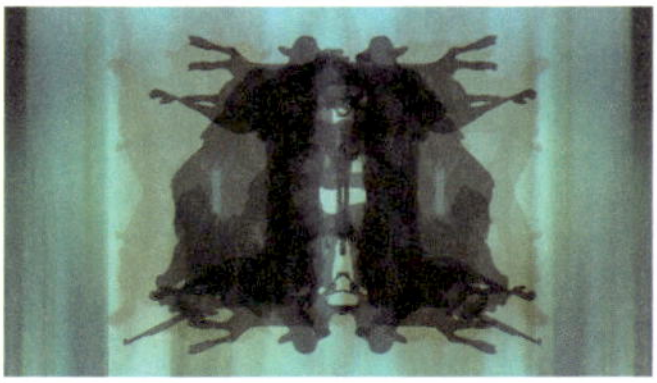
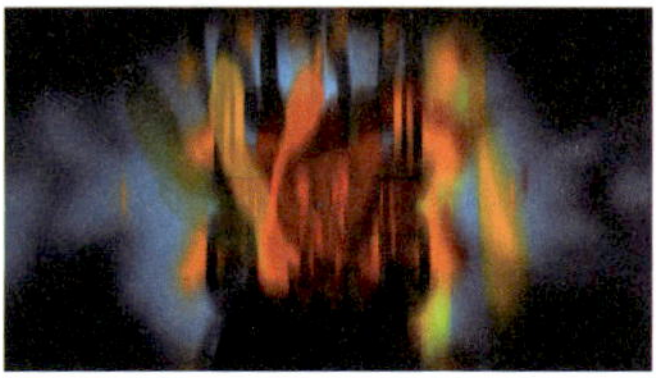
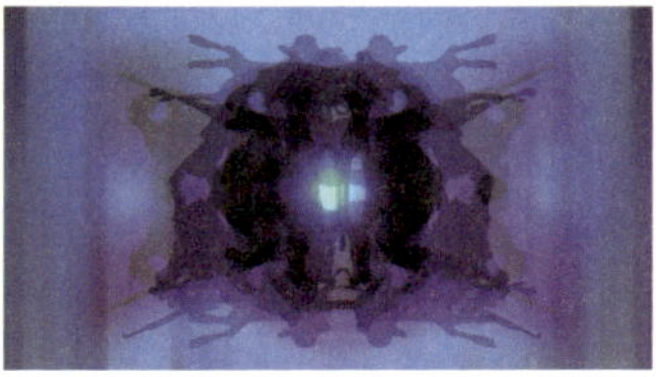

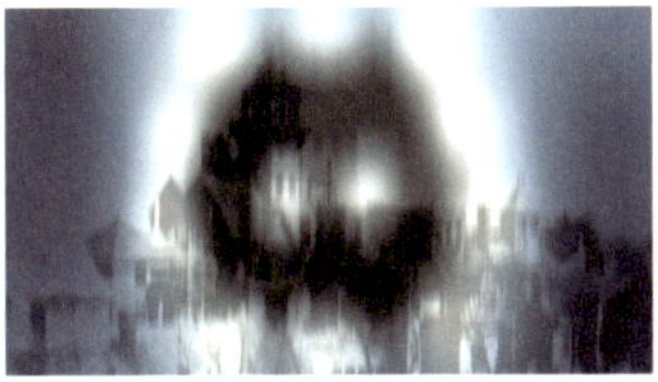
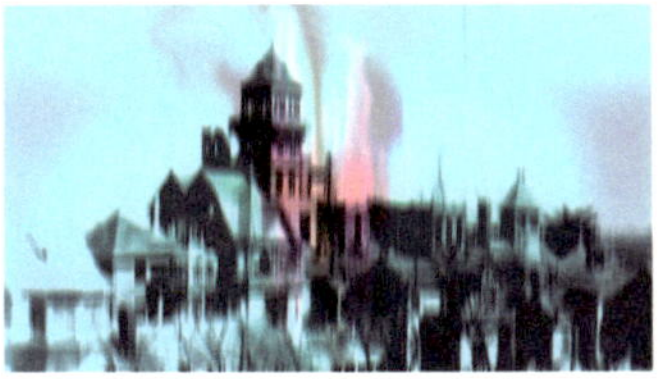
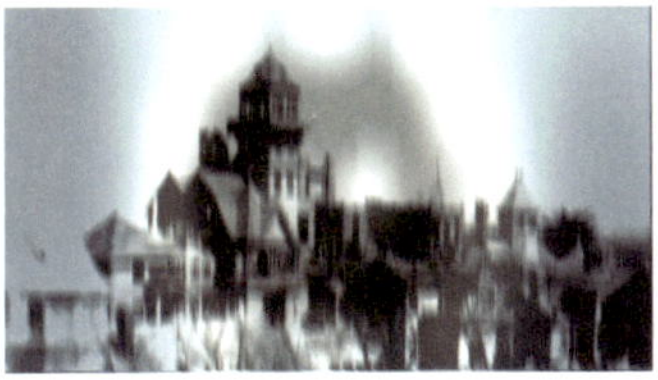
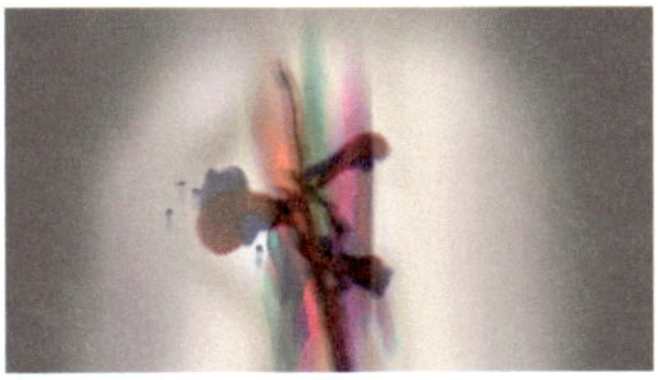
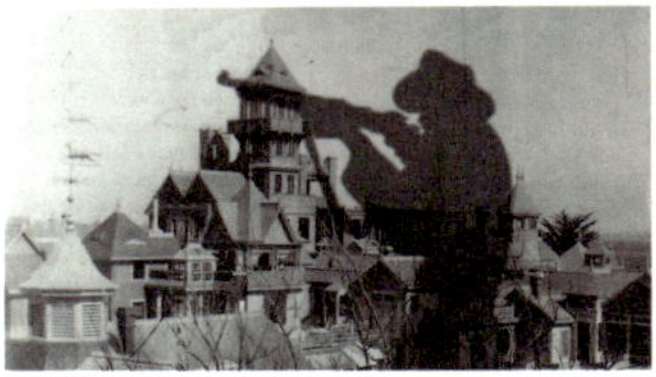
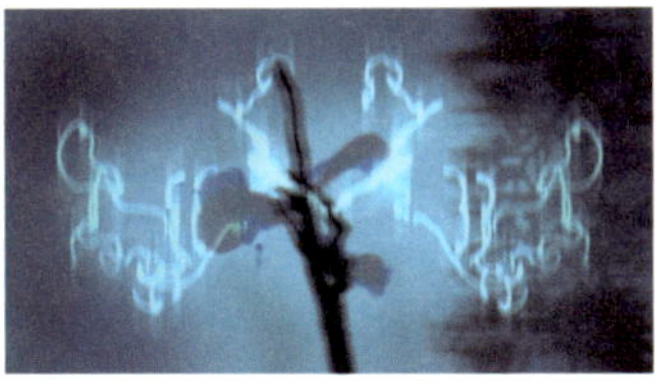
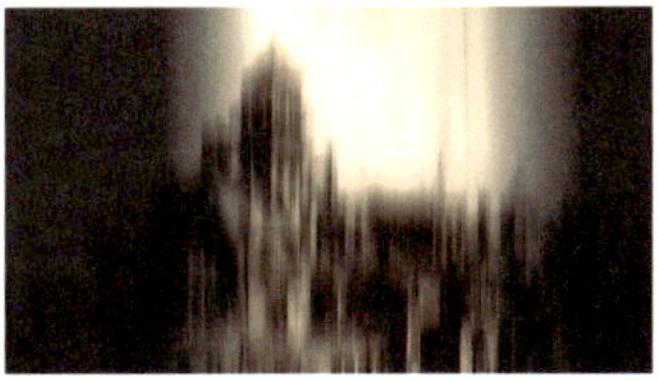
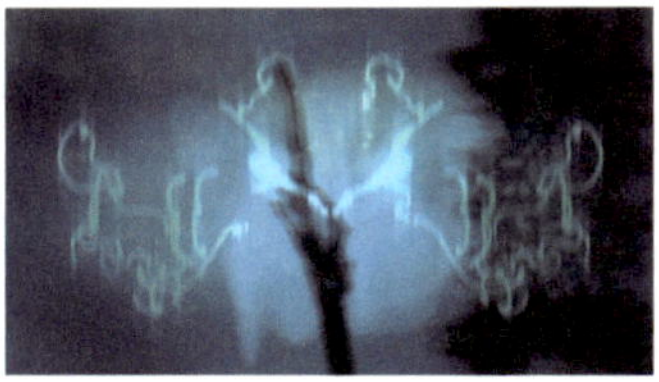
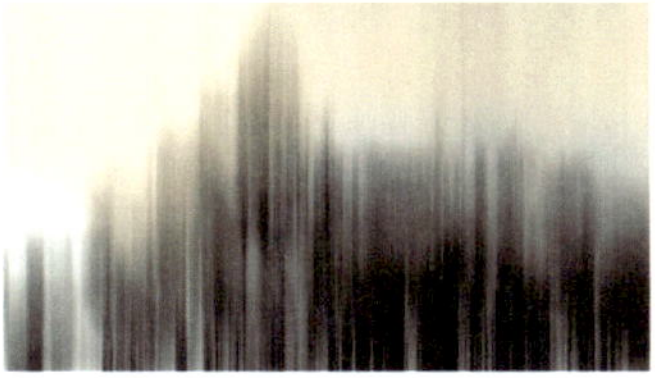
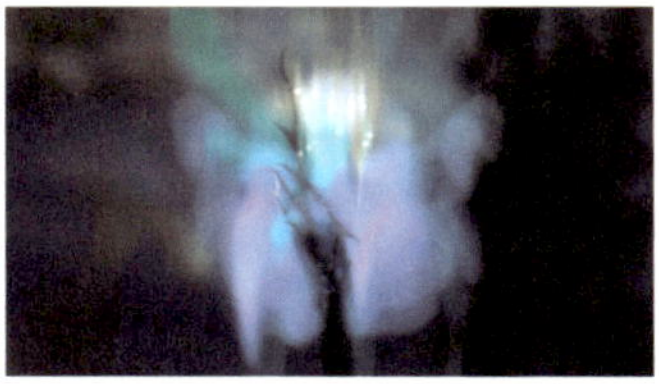
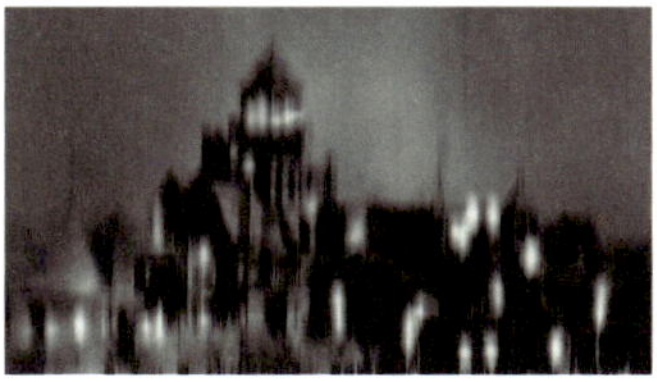
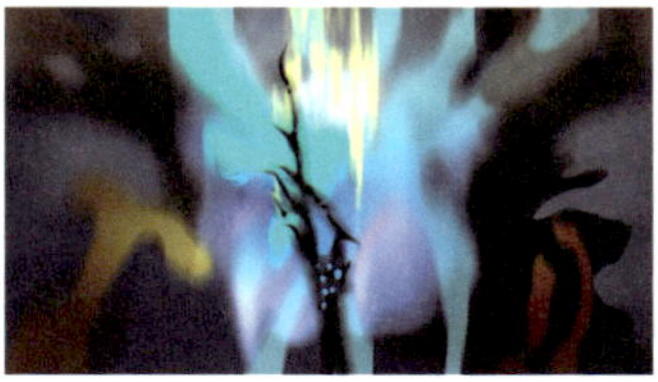

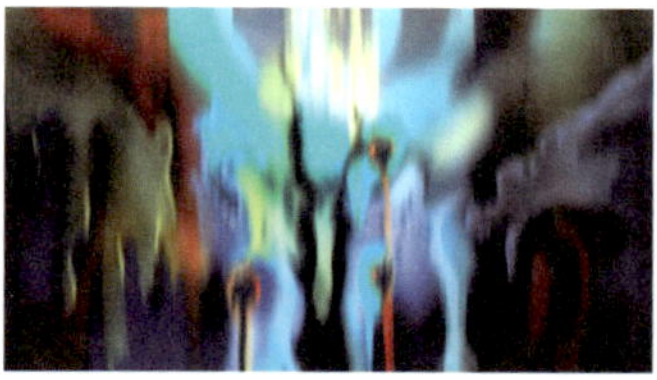
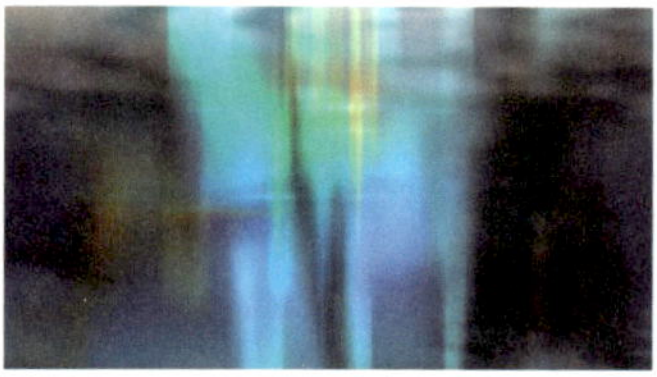
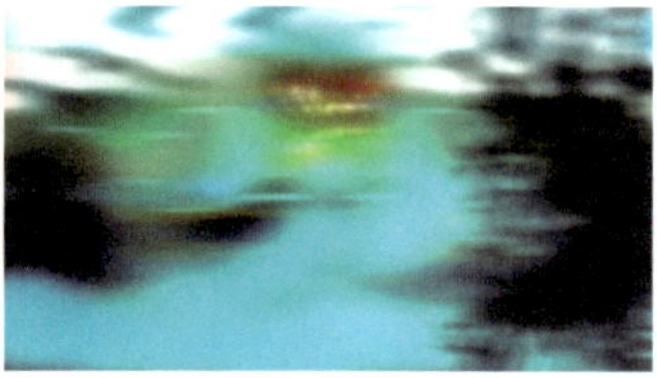
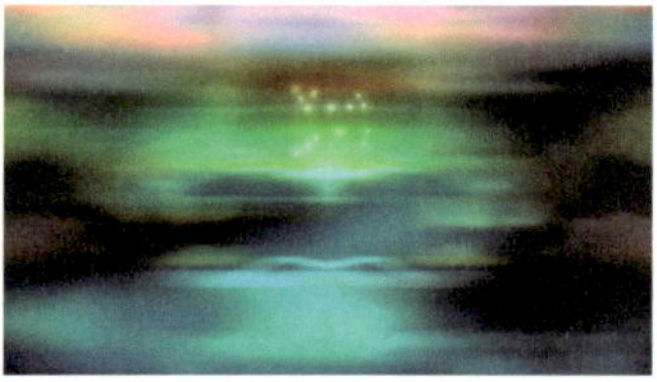
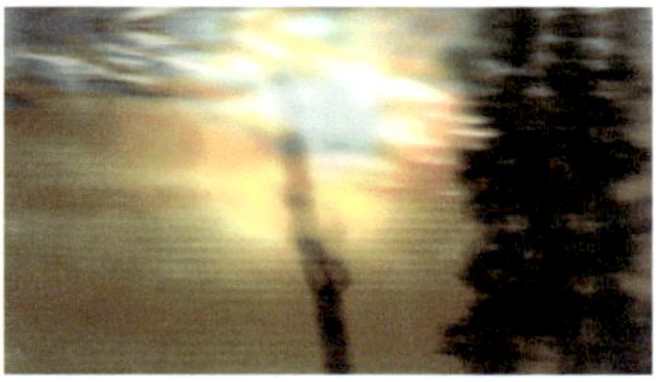
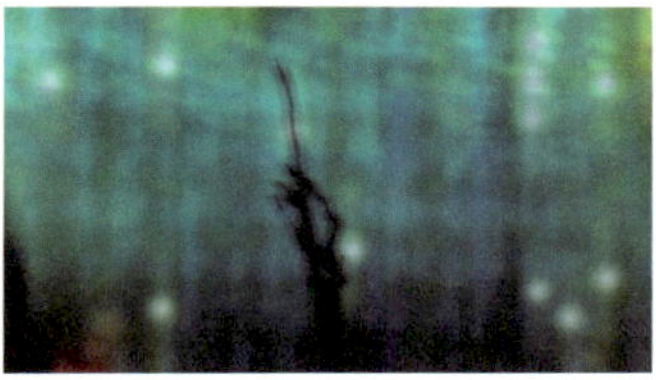
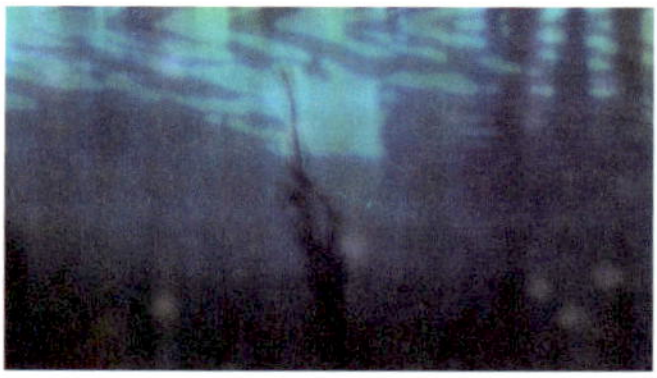
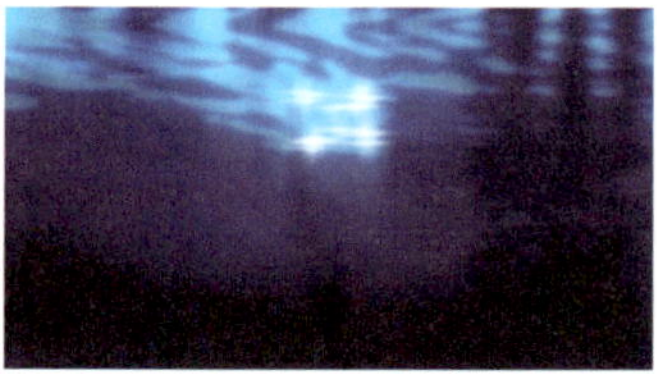
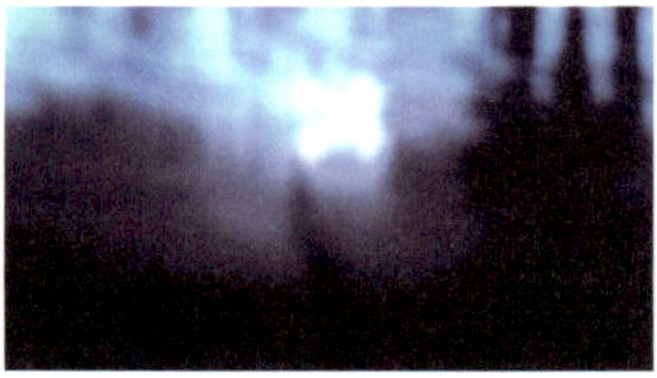
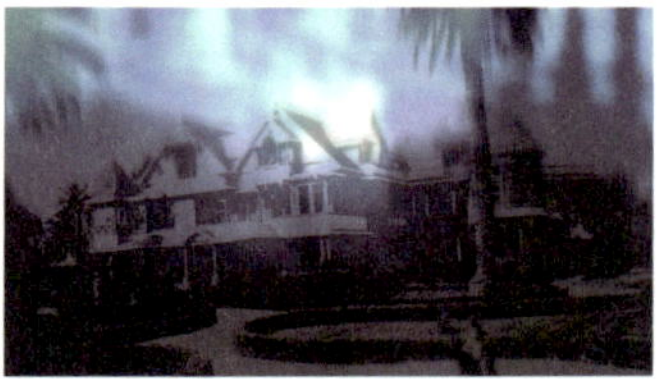
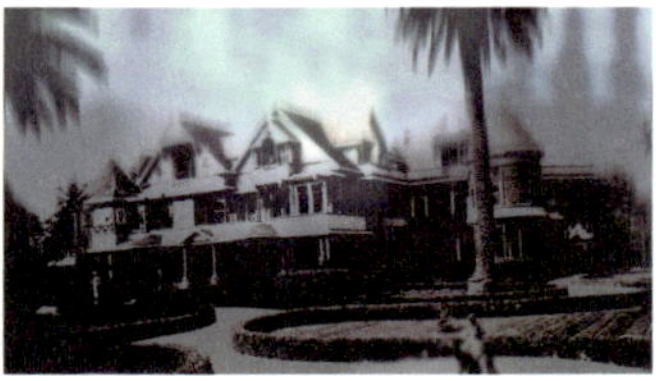
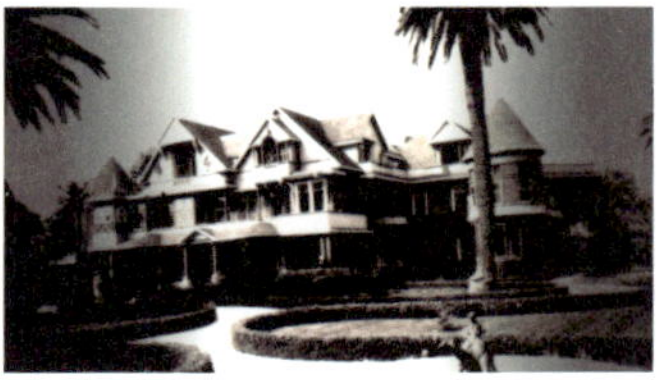

END

Interior Ruptures: *1906*

> *What is a crypt? No crypt presents itself. The grounds* [lieux] *are so disposed as to disguise and to hide: something, always a body in some way. But also to disguise the act of hiding and to hide the disguise: the crypt hides as it holds.... The crypt is thus not a natural place* [lieu], *but the striking history of an artifice, an architecture, an artifact: of a place* comprehended *within another but rigorously separate from it, isolated from general space by partitions, an enclosure, an enclave. So as to purloin* the thing *from the rest.*
>
> —Jacques Derrida, "*Fors*"

After more than twenty years of continuous construction and smooth functioning, the Winchester mansion underwent a crisis in 1906. This was the year of the great San Francisco earthquake, when the house sustained severe damage. Yet the damage was not ever cleared away—we can still see some of it in the second part of Blake's *Winchester Trilogy*—before the obsessive building program recommenced. The earthquake damage itself was not a crisis. For a moment, but long enough, the protective shield of this spirit apparatus was broken through. Not that anyone or anything took advantage, but the system momentarily failed. A momentary breakdown is no great concern if immediately remedied—except to the system's creator, who had an investment in the system itself, because in some way the system was what it was defending. Even damaged, the outer fortifications were not threatened, but only the system's inner architectonics. Return to building as usual masked the trauma: that the intricate buffer of foiling chambers or stairways leading nowhere could not disguise that a rupture of the interior had taken place. Let us repeat what was already a repetition of violence: *not a breach of the exterior but a rupture of the interior*. The house's devices, we know, were spirit traps, but they were also decoys to lead us away from some other secret—not to foil spirits, but to mislead "truth hunters." Perhaps we have too readily believed Sarah Winchester's scenario of haunting that she articulated in the architectural volume of this house. Long after she was dead, the house would entomb her secret still. Do we know what this system really was shielding?

There were always leakages in the system: that was what it was built for. The capture of spirits meant their moving about outside and inside the apparatus. Emanations from the facade that *Winchester* witnessed were no crisis. Seepage was normal: spirits seep. The crisis was a rupture that exposed the interior, but only once one was inside, not the inside as the other side of the outside—the interior of the house per se—but the inside of the inside that first set up the boundaries of the outside of the inside: the drawing board of its architectonics, the motor of its constructive machine, the site of its secret. Not that this inside is the source of it all or even something visible; it is a dark interior, unknown even to the subject, where we still have to force entry, though our way is not barred, to discover an architecture as intricately partitioned. This place, perhaps more properly a null or non-place, around which the protective guard of the house had been elaborately articulated, was now permanently exposed, fractured along the lines of its construction, a result of the earthquake. It was enough that it was exposed once for it to be permanently exposed—no need to repair the cracks in the wallcovering or gaps in the plaster and lathe through which a subtle intruder might gain entry or a secret escape in a spirited conspiracy. The earthquake's violence dislodged the house and misaligned its structure. Its discordant rupturing, however, aligned two events, two times, two places, and two forces, whereby the violence of a first event returned through the violence of a second. The quake was two crises in one.

While admitting breach and exposure, our heiress inventor could always retreat to rely on backup systems because there is more—or less—to exposure than a break-in by a breach of visibility. By exposing, one does not make visible. One hides best by showing, keeping invisible what the visible cannot see purloined in front of it. Moreover, a secret cannot be disclosed or discovered if it is not of the order of visibility. But then vision, entrained as it always has been to images, would not know this. Visibility is only grasped within the visible, which is as if to say, comprehended from the point of view of the image, in a correspondence that seemingly is clear and secure and not in any way secret. Would this not be a false or feigned security if the implicit contract between the two guarantees advantage to the image, sealed in the seductive sheen of its hard outer surface as if a stiff, glossy photographic print, the document of a contract that signifies nothing—by unsettling no thing—but a shared space? This space, exteriority itself, is a mirror effect, the convenient production of a deluded rectitude whose architecture is erected from the tautological orientation of image and self facing each other as the two reflecting walls of a propped-up illusion. Stability is its only security, the stability of convention. Could the conventions of this vision disclose a secret? Wouldn't its illusions already be a veil through which we would penetrate nothing, no thing? Wouldn't vision always be disadvantaged, deceived by visibility itself in this search for what might be invisible? The secret would be beyond seeing.

Can we place ourselves beyond seeing? Would this be possible when nothing but images are projected here, when all we see is an imaginary of images? We would at least have to abandon representation sensing that these images are nothing but ruses that we have to find a way in, around, or through by our own otherwise ruse than seeing. The realm we are about to enter through an unsettling breach is not of *visible* rending. The passage beyond seeing is not without seeing, however. We are deviating merely from the "signifying nothing" beyond visibility; only the underwriting of exposition by visibility is threatened here.[1] Vision may aid us still. Through some sense of propriety, we have lent vision a structure that instead needs to be released into motion. Not that we want an organic metaphor for vision when a crystalline one may be put to refractory purpose to refract and dazzle sight, deceive it too. The armour-like hardness of an image, which seemingly demarcates an impenetrable border, is an effective deception, especially when visibility's vision has had the foolish, vain courtesy to maintain it for us, thinking this device its own when, actually, it is conjured from its opposition. Was this not Sarah Winchester's gambit? Did she not take advantage of the conventions of vision to protect the divide of her house, recruiting them to secure the border of its facade from penetration when its divisions were instituted elsewhere? Phantasmagorical, this border marks an elsewhere-otherwise division reflected from another time and place, though it is projected now here in front of us. Projected from *there* here, the image protectively masks this invisible other place—a hidden, inner non-place we threaten to expose, though not by sight alone, or, at least, not without being aided by the disturbance of another vision. Yet these divisions have already dissipated, because, as we sense in its chill air, we are inside this house, though inside no secret, still only a mystery. If inside we find the fusion of images similar to *Winchester*, nevertheless, they belong to differing realms of imagining.

Blake's *1906* is the story of the earthquake's damage shown through evidence of its penetrative rupturing. The story must be told inside the house, through its corridors and chambers alone, since Sarah Winchester was silent on the secrets of her domicile. The distressed and punctured surfaces of its interior walls will not tell all. They too were fabricated—as a precautionary palisade inside the house but ever beyond what it knew not what it was protecting, silent to guard—to partition a secret. This internal security system would halt vision at the wallcovering, capture it in arresting patterns of intricate weavings and psychedelic swirls so that sense would be twisted in the torques of a disorienting confusion of left, right, up, down. We must scrupulously avoid these distracting snares in our investigative pursuit if we want to track the right path and reconstruct this story. We must descend deeper and deeper into the building's vaulted inner chambers rather than ascend higher and higher to the vaulted extremes of its architectural ambition—even though the apex of the building is exactly where we enter in *1906*. The vanity expressed by Winchester's overweening enterprise was struck down by an act of God when the earthquake toppled much of the upper levels of this architectural conceit with its babel of perverted functions and conflicted spaces. We descend from the zenith to the nadir following an archaeological speculation: that this architectural heap was a ruin even before the earthquake struck a violent blow that momentarily dislodged the forces supporting its crypt's construction. This crypt was always precariously upheld, like those mirrored boxes magicians dissemble on theatre stages, by a balance of illusions—though force and illusion here were of violent imagining. The walls of this near abyssal vault, verging on a fathomless pit to another place and time, were dangerously disjointed by the earthquake. Seismic violence released pent-up forces by repeating the violence that originally sealed the crypt's architectonics. So, like the professorial academics of the supernatural in films such as Robert Wise's 1963 *The Haunting*, we methodically proceed employing the camera's tracking shots to register any trace of psychic disturbance. (Who knows, we may be as lucky as Shasta Supernatural Investigator and founder, Craig S. Martin, who, in January 2001 taking the 10:30 daylight tour of what is now a commercial tourist attraction, registered a good EMF reading of 2.7 in Sarah Winchester's main bedroom.[2])

After being kept at bay at the perimeter of its private property, at the proper distance of Victorian decorum, we are now inside, accomplices to the camera's break-in. No fictional staging of the cinematic apparatus deceives us here, as in *Winchester*. We are savvy to that magic trick now, having learned a trick or two entertaining ourselves to film's progress from 1895 on, which by 1906 had already consolidated its realist mode. Not that this story will be told subtly. Rather, the camera seems to satisfy our demand for prurient entertainment and puritanical exposure at the same time. After all this sordid secrecy, we want the embarrassing truth, and the harsh lights of reality television readily comply with the camera's close scrutiny.[3]

Once we start, we are met with an even more virtuoso performance, a spirit spectacle that no longer seeps from the apertures of the building but sweeps in veils through its interior, like gusts of chill wind, overwhelming the tawdry illumination of our television realism. Rank on rank of shields of agitated vapour advance to test our determination and frighten us away. As if boastfully demonstrating the sheer profusion of their inventiveness, these spirits, horrific and beautiful at the same time, feign to startle us. But instead of dazzling us with their unyielding display, these curtains of colour and shimmering movement dissipate one after the other, falling back one by one, veil after veil, as if in a retreat, to more interior ramparts. Their bursts of energy are merely simulacra that mask the exhausted symmetry of their hunted haunting. Rushing to block our intrusion, they effuse one last gasp, as if, resident in this haunted home custom-built for their attendance, familiar with the uncanniness of their intimate habitation, they were the disconsolate, wandering, forlorn-to-be-abandoned, end-of-the-line survivors that Edgar Allan Poe so loved to write lugubriously about.

For these spirits, too, conspire. Spirits consort, and conjuration is not only a conspiracy of exorcism against them. No more than Sarah Winchester do these spectres want their secret exposed—not the secrets of incestuous crimes of dynastic old houses, the rotten core of their decrepit Gothic Revival ruins, of which ghosts are the malingering manifestation—but their secret complicity, their agreement in staging the disturbances that conjure the phantasmagorical spectacle of this architectural marvel. The spectral machinery of the mansion, which cannot exist without this party of two, is the contract closed between Sarah Winchester and her haunting spirits. Co-dependent, Sarah Winchester could not survive without her spirits, nor they without her: hunter and hunted in one specular-spectral circle.

Ironically, the earthquake trapped the trapper. Sarah Winchester attributed this table-turning retribution to the spirits' malevolence. After rescue, she promptly sealed thirty rooms and the front door, presuming this fallback, rather than an offensive of new outworks, stalled the potential advantage of unlicensed entry, to which the earthquake temporarily gave leave. The Winchester house, however, sustained new trauma through the earthquake. Its untended scars unleashed new spectral visitations, though they no longer emanated from the facade's apertures but from internal disruptions. When a delicate machine for capturing spectral effects is damaged, its architecture no longer true, its measurements out of register, the uncorrected misalignment distorts all images; in the mirror of its measurements, we no longer know if the machine is sending or receiving, inside out confused.

Blake's *1906* restages the quake as the traumatic memory of the house. At one point long into the projection, after the camera has surveyed the traces of the earthquake's malingering damage, an old drawing of the mansion's Victorian glory trembles in a cheap special effect. Revisiting the damage has triggered repressed memories. From the moment we penetrated the building from its spiritual pinnacle and tumbled down one of its dissembling staircases, we have all along witnessed this trauma's haunting: emanations are generated from the wounds of this unhappy home.

In *1906*, image-types oppose and alternate between real and imaginary, but with this significant difference: the second are now generated from the first. The camera systematically examines sites ripe, indeed overripe and bruised, for haunting, whether Winchester's constructions or the earthquake's destruction: idiosyncratic ghost traps; broken and distressed surfaces. Investigation concludes that haunting is internal; its ghost effects are no external visitation. We have the evidence before us on film. Transformations stage themselves: haunted images form before our eyes, as the camera's overexposed, high-keyed realism mutates in dissolves to computer-fabricated chimeras. The abject leakages exposed by the earthquake or stemming from its decomposing violence are the *material* source of phantoms, no more. Tricks of eyesight: "phantasms" derive from plaster seeping through lathe, congealed glue stalactites dripping below floorboards, or from cracked walls.

Such conclusive derivation is proof of one sort; but a continually decomposing devolution from objectivity to illusion should prorogue our judgement and undermine our resolution, believing that we have led ourselves to an exorcism for the house, a cure for its inhabitant, or, perhaps most important, rational reassurance for us of a superstition laid to rest. Meanwhile, the spirits spooking this house are laughing at us, shaking the mansion's foundations to rupture corridors to other haunted places. Being the "same" image differing from itself, these dissolves were no proof, only passage to other haunting. We tremble in this transition to the quaking of the slow-motion gearing-down of image and soundtrack. Distortion—the signal of an event dislocating space and disjointing time—drags us unresisting into invisible depths of the house. Or is it another consciousness irresistibly drawing us? In the event of passage, an unconscious quakes. In this house of masks, it may be a "false unconscious" that trembles to be discovered?[4]

This late discovery seems to question our a priori schema, refute our thesis, and dispute our findings; it demands publication or broadcast delay. Abandoning preconceptions and going with the flow, we might then be guided to other discoveries, startling to ourselves, unsettling conceptions. We might find that sibling spirits though they are, haunting has two different sources: the originating trauma that was sealed within this architectural contraption, erected on the lie of an external haunting: Sarah trapped her own ghosts, which were already spirited and sealed away; the secondary trauma of the earthquake that, wound upon wound, was a ghostly *revenant* haunting the original formation. Nothing—indeed, no thing, let alone a secret—has been exposed here.

Nevertheless, thinking its investigation complete, the camera ascends to the roof where it records the last departing burst of the exorcised spirits, which dissipate, dispersing their energy in a glorious fireworks display disseminated from the tip of a decorative lightning rod. We know from the conventions of horror films that ghosts always return, their defeat disguised in the last frames, awaiting a sequel to haunt another amnesiac generation. For what is the lightning rod here but perhaps an antenna that broadcasts frequencies, like signals sent from a dying star, something that we receive from the future that is buried in the past. Cunning haunting—it signals where the secret is buried but does not uncover it.

Let's halt before we proceed and repeat our passive surrender of a moment ago, when the moment itself was divided, time trembling in the aftershock of a violent quake. We tremble *before* an event that has struck us with as much force as the earthquake struck the Winchester house or its crisis shook Sarah Winchester. Not that this rupture will dislodge from us any secret we could have, as it will our host's (a repetition of a first time she fears more than mere material breach), though it will derange us terribly through its devastation: its quaking crisis collapsing rational confidence, disordering our senses, separating sight from comprehension, displacing vision to the disjunctions of time. Time is ruined; time is in ruins. The ruin of time is our break-in, our passage to and through these ruins. Obviously, this is not a time we know, through which we familiarly comprehend, grasping what is before us within the perspective of our sight. An uncanny division of the present from itself, anachronicity is the untimely rupture of the event.[5] In the ruin that dislodges space and upsets the rectitude of our perspective, time is all that can guide us by beckoning us, though we must adhere to its regime, follow its flow, and through it *spirit*, rather than space, a motion—seep into these ruins surpassing space surpassing visibility. Can we call this perception? *Our* perception? Is it ours when another possession dispossesses us of all that is proper to us, especially the certitude of a self-present consciousness? In what haunted property would this divestment take place? We would surely disinherit ourselves to remain poor there but in spirit.

This crisis was already heralded by another event, though we did not know, and could not know, as we were already swept up in it. The rupture of *Winchester* was the obverse of that of *1906*, in the sense that we began there outside. An inside was already beckoning. Inside, we follow another regime, the same, though, that ruptured the photograph of *Winchester*. Inside we learn, through a terrible disruption and division, that the outside was a delusion, a conjured demarcation. Here we see, "see" from the inside, through its regime of perception, that the outside was *our* delusion, not just another's dissemblance. The perspective of its/our images was sent from another place, "two" seeming to meet and greet face to face in a borderline that was the inside's out. Would this message come from that other source "within" or from within us? Who would be dissembling/deluding whom? Who would be dissembling projection by deluding perspective? Or what deluding projection would be dissembling perspective? Would we stand our ground for this? Fight or switch?

We cannot be certain that our categories survive this quaking when even the present is disturbed. Falling into the abyss of the quake's division, we stagger to find that division destroys divide and does nothing but ruin our safe side, jeopardize the guarantee of our perspective outside the house, and change our rules for its regime. In the trembling of categories, stable spatiality surrenders to an unhinged temporality, outside turned inside out and inside turned outside in, an anarchic knotting that may be more an underside than an other side.[6] Did we know that a still image, corresponding to our familiar regime of spatial exteriority, was all there was right from the beginning of *Winchester*, a photograph after all? Our delusion made it shimmer, an untimely collusion turning still to motion, photograph to film. Were we *ever* "outside," we wonder?

Could we think that the ruin of all that was familiar, the unsettling of all that we were happily at home with, confidently and comfortably inhabiting our perception, might deliver us to a secret? Could we comprehend that the instant of this rupture, by which we would share Sarah Winchester's crisis, would lead us, as well, to share another's perception or to see through it (by sharing, knowing that this "perception" was ours and *not* ours, familiar *and* uncanny)? Could we believe that only a haunted perception, a haunting of our perception, would open Sarah Winchester's secret, let us see through—if we would look *through* others' eyes, even though they be our own? The secret she hid was always visible, though perception would have to be made uncanny to see what was visible and invisible about it.

Would such an event make us question where we were at home? Would its terrible trauma make us wonder what would make us welcome in another's abode, even if we stumbled in through rupture? And if the house were haunted, how would we be welcome—or at home? Could we imagine that something uncanny in us would be welcome there, that some other inhabitation would be greeted at the threshold of its door? In that we were the host of another, this stranger would be welcome. That we were the host of an uncanny stranger (unless we were his or her hostage) might mean we already belonged inside, that we were at home there: familiar to others, uncanny to ourselves. There would be no secret within this familiar and uncanny home, in the intimacy of this haunted house.

When we see into this home, or look out, with whose eyes do we peer that would make us welcome and not an intruder? How would we inhabit an uncanny perception, or it us, and both be strangely welcome within this sight? Would we see through the stranger's eyes, or he through ours? Would we not fear an evil eye; that seeing through our eyes, his perception would make us merely a medium—or, worse, a machine: a *thing*? Our doppelgänger would animate or operate us through his uncanny seeing. (Not just dissembling or deceiving us, he would make us deviate in sleepwalking committal of his crimes.) Is this our secret, or shame: the *Thing* within, the thing we are within?[7] Could there be a secret within this house that we thus share, something encrypted there? The thing within, if our doppelgänger, would not be a secret, *the* secret: the doppelgänger is too uncanny to be encrypted; *he* dissembles, not others. Perhaps the secret is something we two share, my doppelgänger and I, splitting a treasure's loot as criminal accomplices? Would the thing within be conspiratorial, whereby a seeing of two, a doubled or misaligned seeing, would be a pact with an enemy—a perceptual conspiracy: secretly seeing secrecy? A misaligned seeing would tremble to open the secret of another and see within. Seeing through the other would be a secret shared, a shared secret. Only the stranger's uncanny perception would see through the other and find a secret there.

Could we ever be secure in this new possession of an uncanny perception as we were before in what we thought our own? Seeing *through* the other (without) *through* the seeing of the other (within), by means of the seeing of this inside other, is no more certain than what is hidden uncertainly within this or any other sentence comprehending the incomprehensibility of the abyss of the secret. Merely one of the "secrets" of the secret is its invisibility to visibility. Would we ever be witness to a shared secret if the secret shared were secreted in us, unknown to us? What would Sarah Winchester's secret be to us in this dilemma of our own?

There would be no secret within this familiar and uncanny home in spite of the fact that only a secret would be housed there. Could a secret be familiar and uncanny? This is the uncanny economy, or *an*-economy, Freud recognized in the terms "*heimlich*" and "*unheimlich*," that beyond their contrary meanings of "familiar," "intimate" or "homely" and "eerie," "uncanny," "ghostly," or "haunted" (of a house), they both could mean "secret"—something concealed from the sight of others.[8]

Rupture would be kept secret, as Sarah Winchester wished so as not to disturb her secret. But rupture itself would be secret. We would share this rupture with Sarah Winchester but to differing effects. In the rupturing of a crisis, we would be familiar with what was most unsettling. The crisis would be welcoming: we would welcome it. Through its devastation, derangement, and dislodging, we would be at home with Sarah Winchester, if she would be at home with herself, if she would welcome the break-in to where we belong. *Winchester* and *1906* ready us; their moving images are already this welcome. Would Sarah Winchester likewise be ready to receive us, having already received so many spectral visitations? In the comings and goings of her haunted house, where none entered or were admitted but ghosts; in the untimely transits of its disjointing threshold, would our entry-exit from phenomena to phantasmagoria make us, too, ghostly? Would it make the ghost in us two? The question of the event is the question of the ghost.[9] Poised as a threshold, this event—the ghostly event of the ghost effect—welcomes the stranger within.

START →

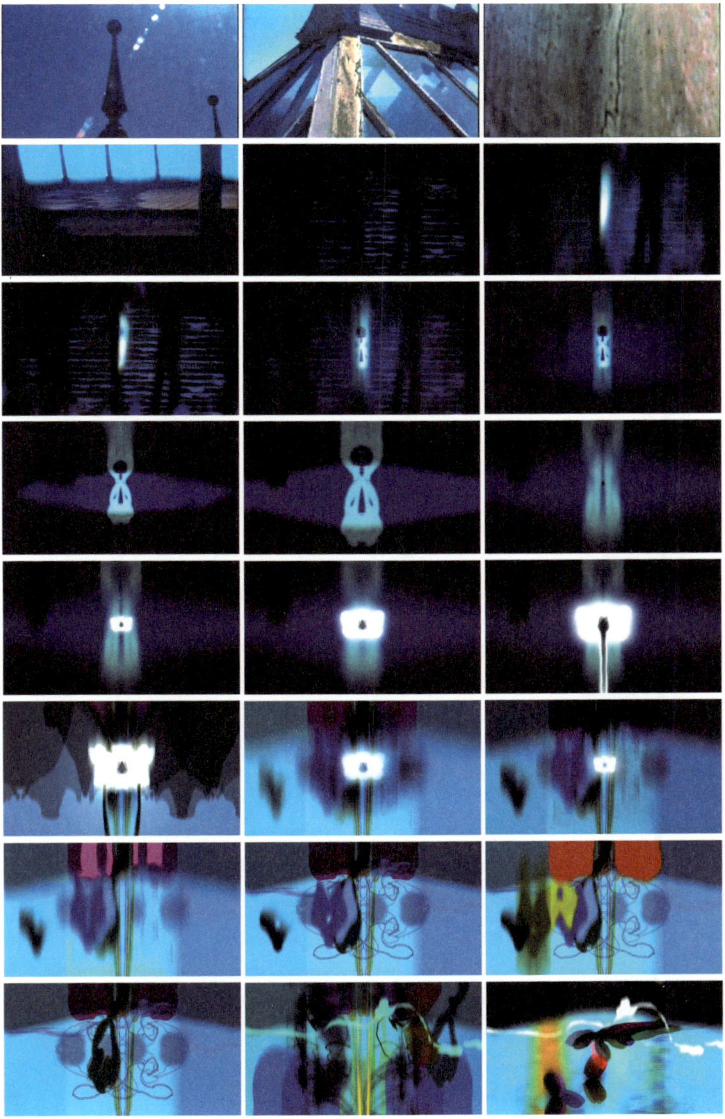

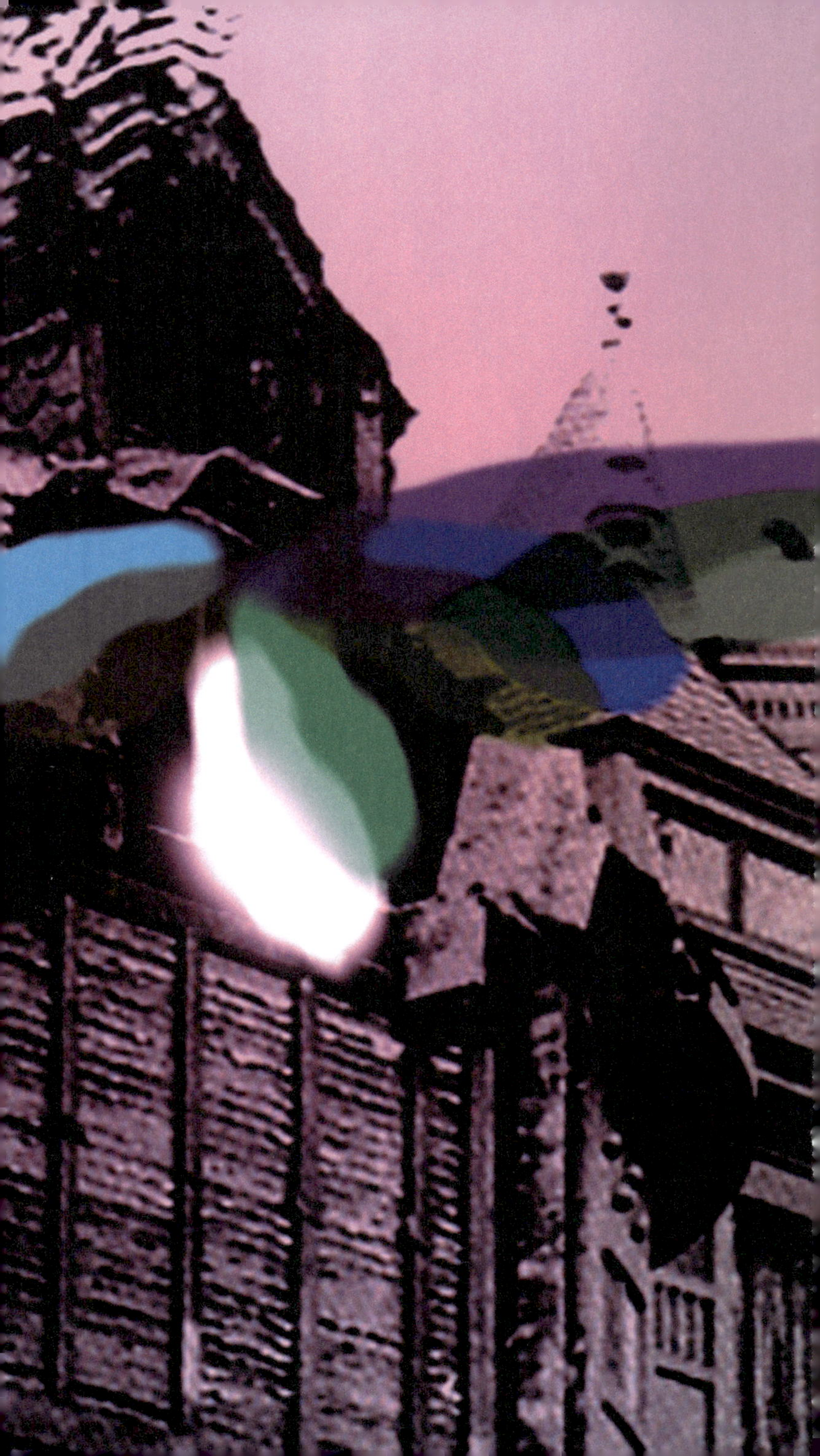

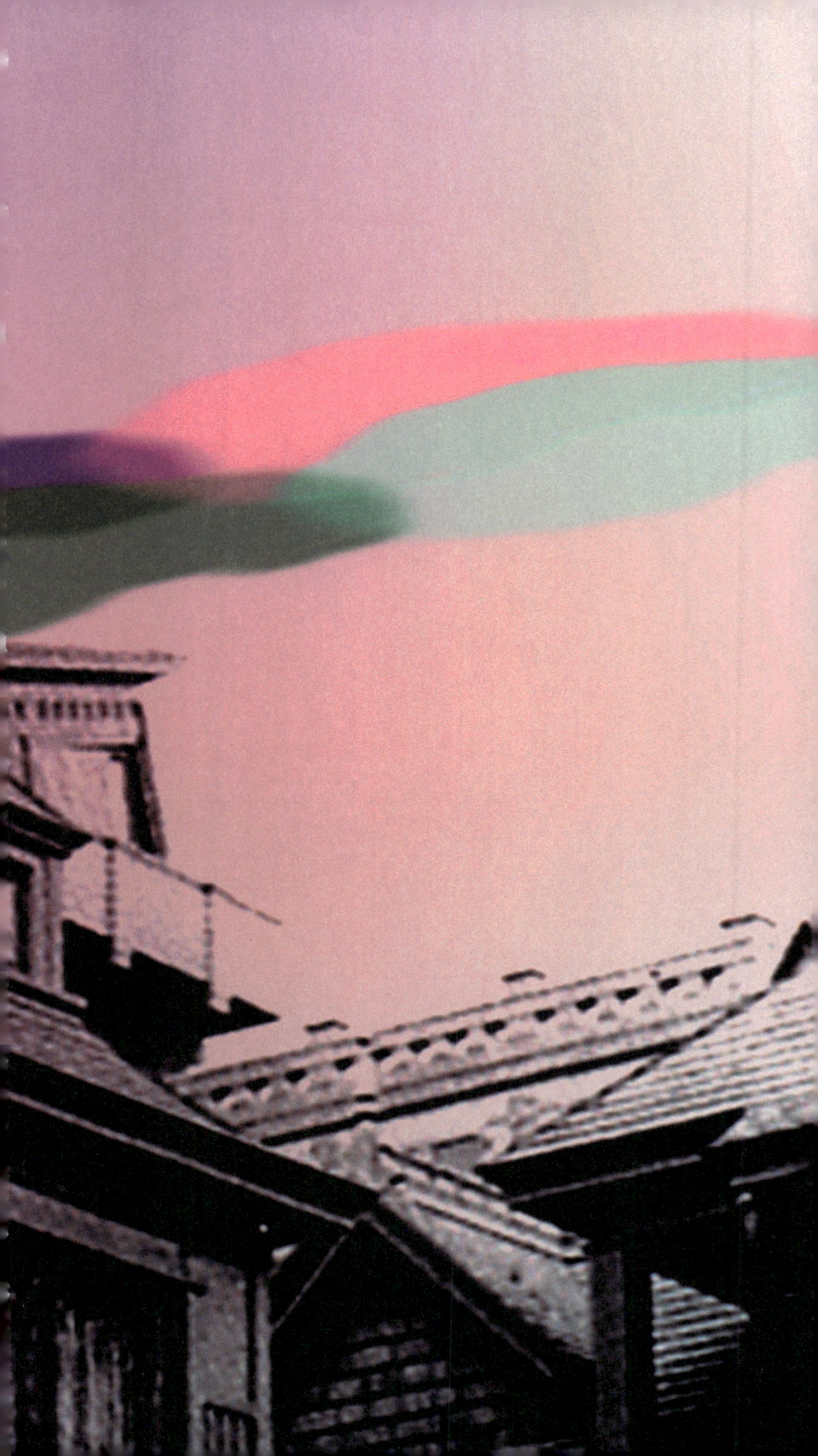

JEREMY BLAKE, *1906*, 2003.

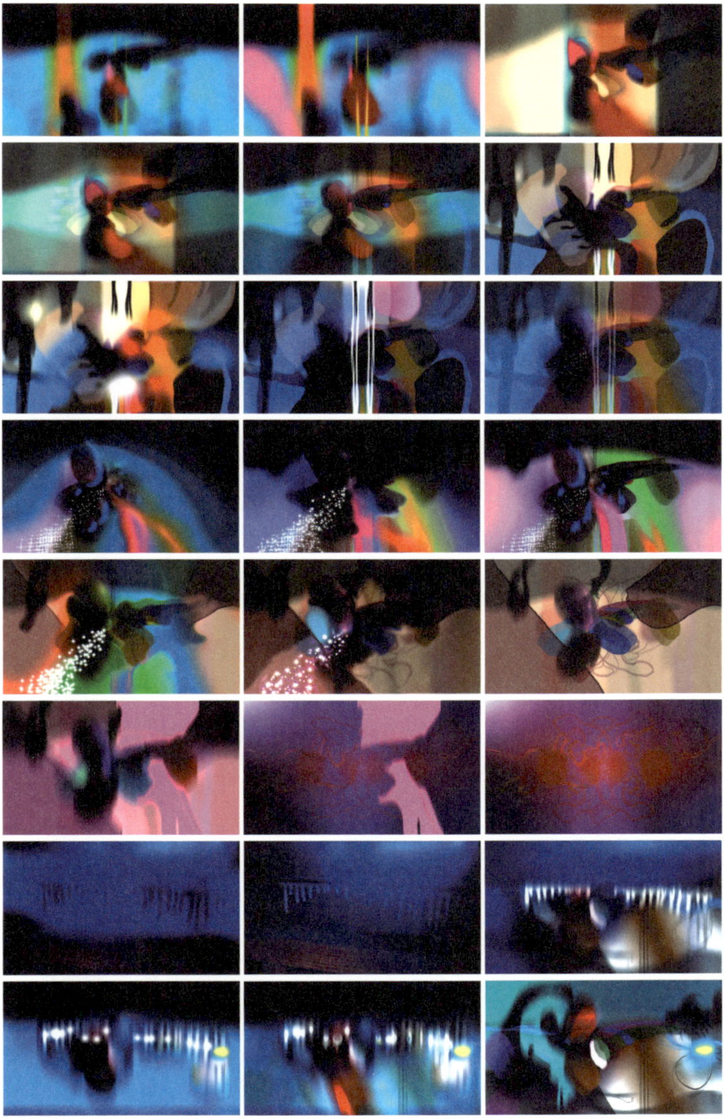

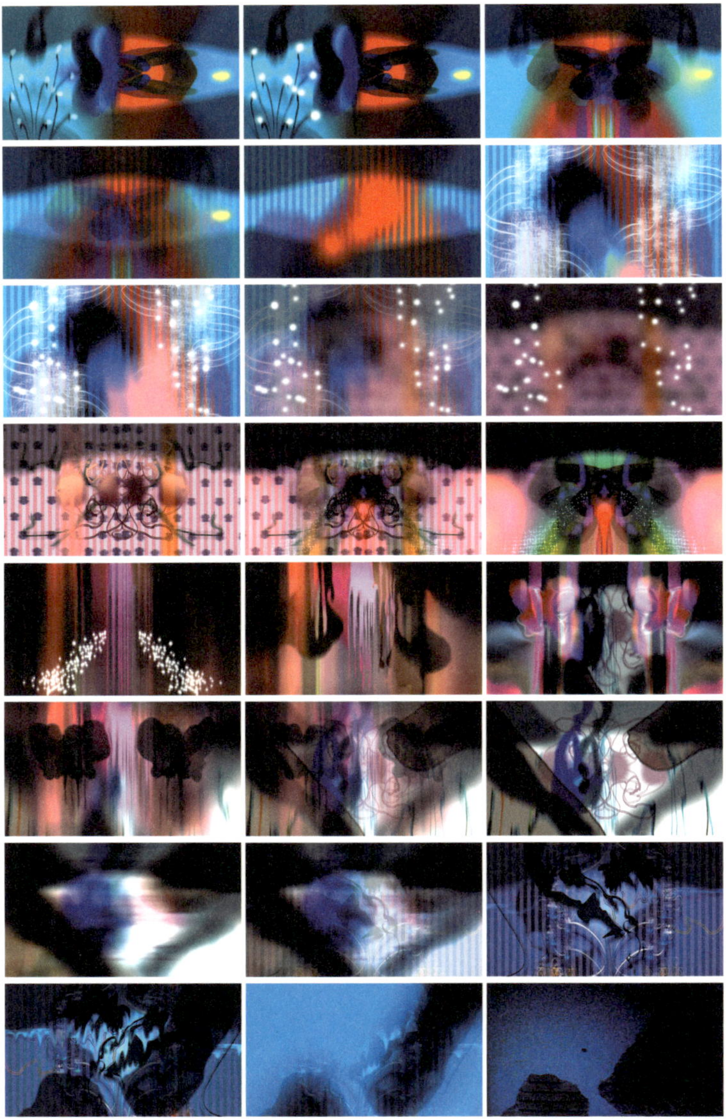

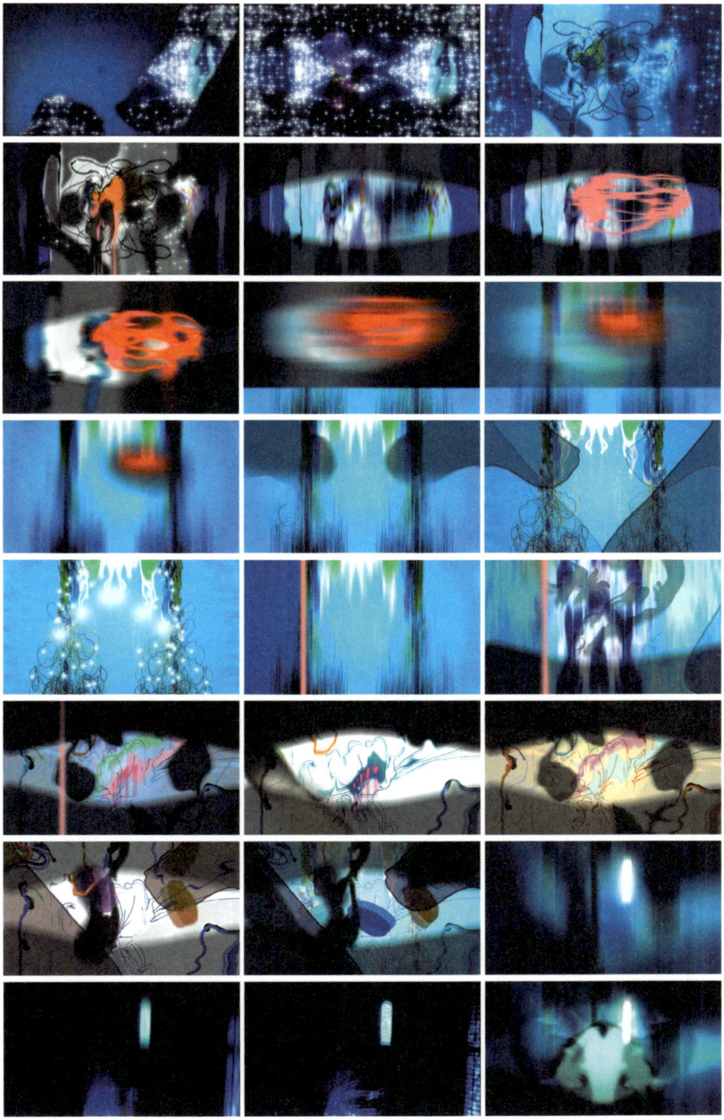

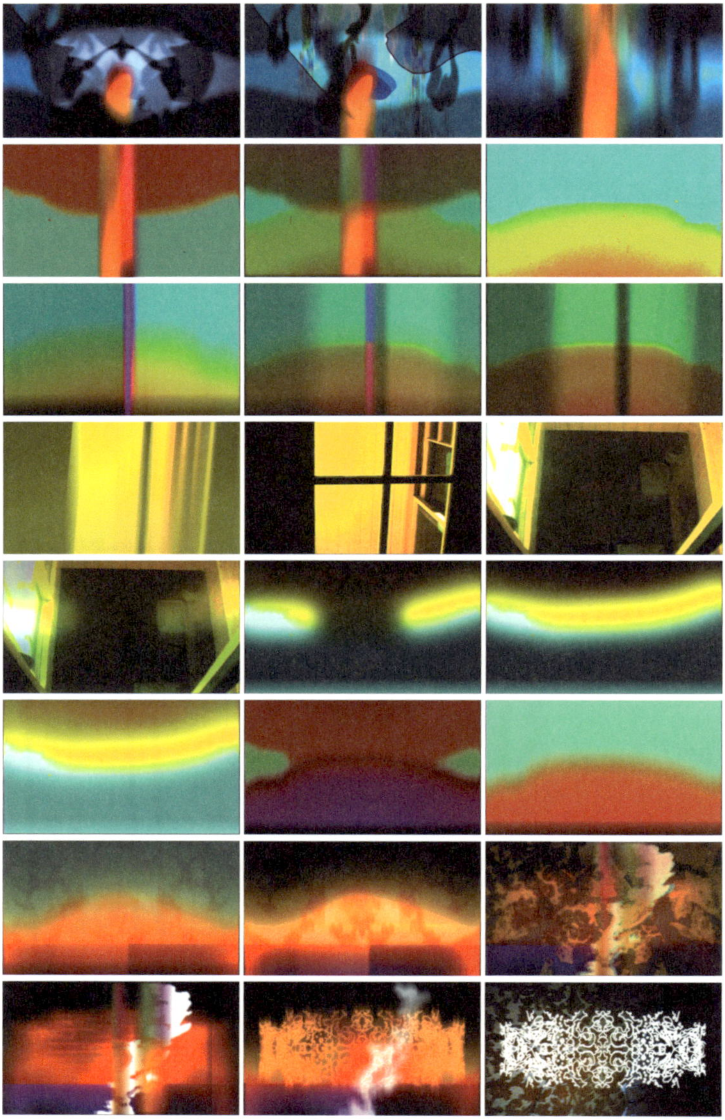

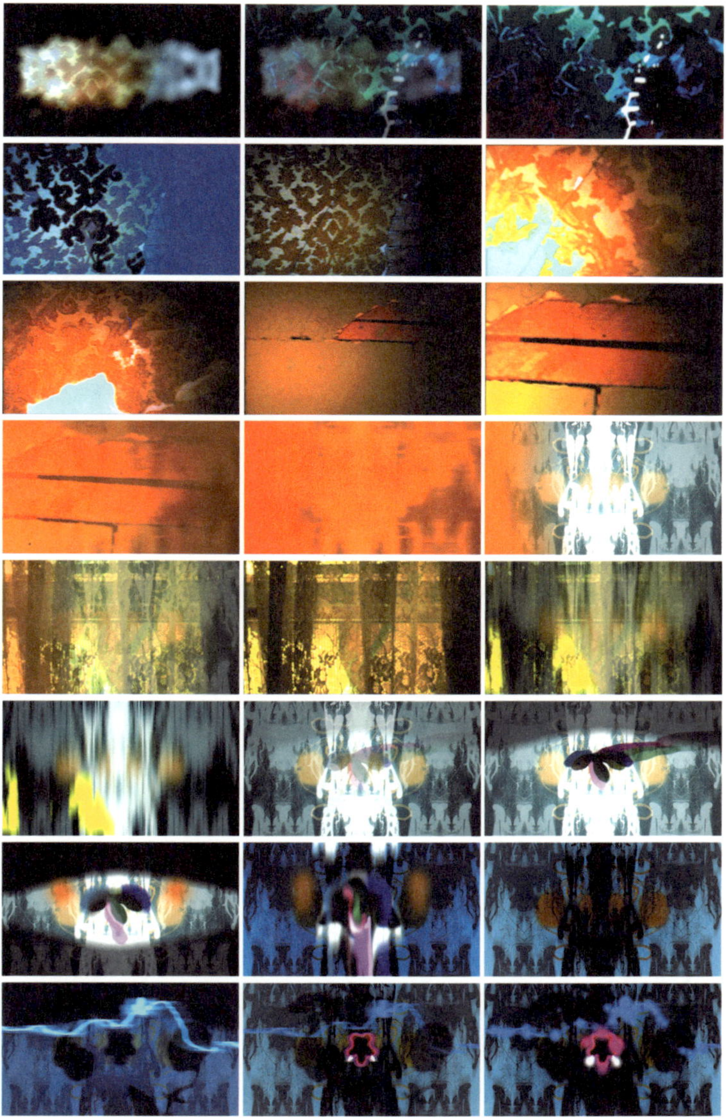

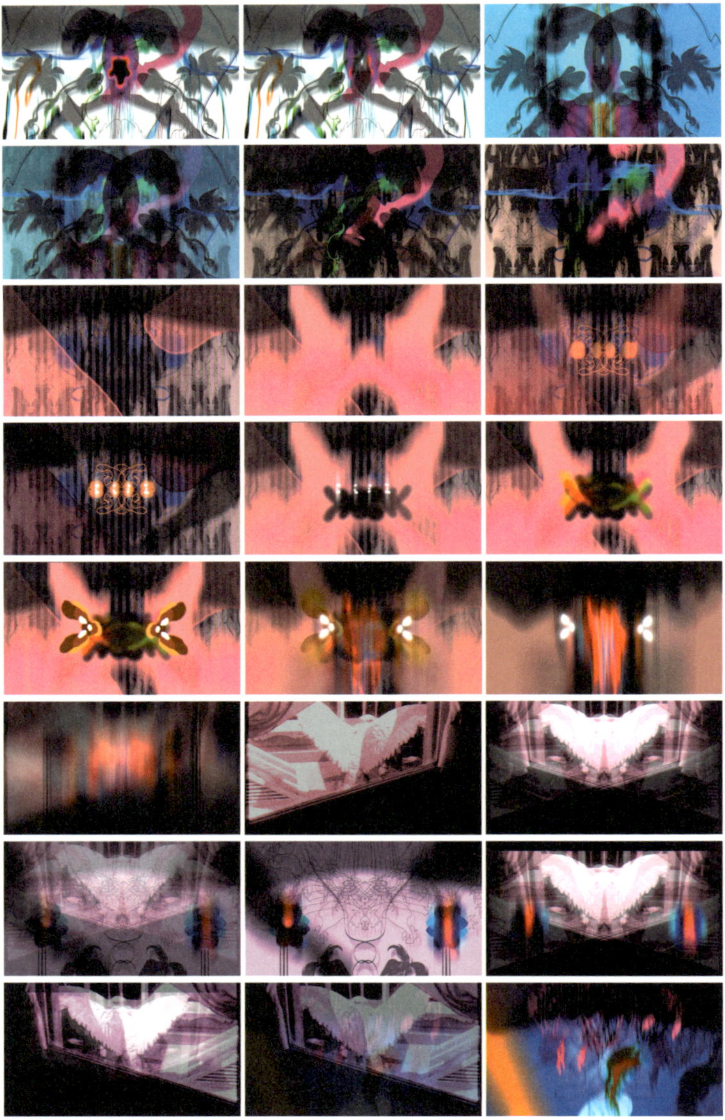

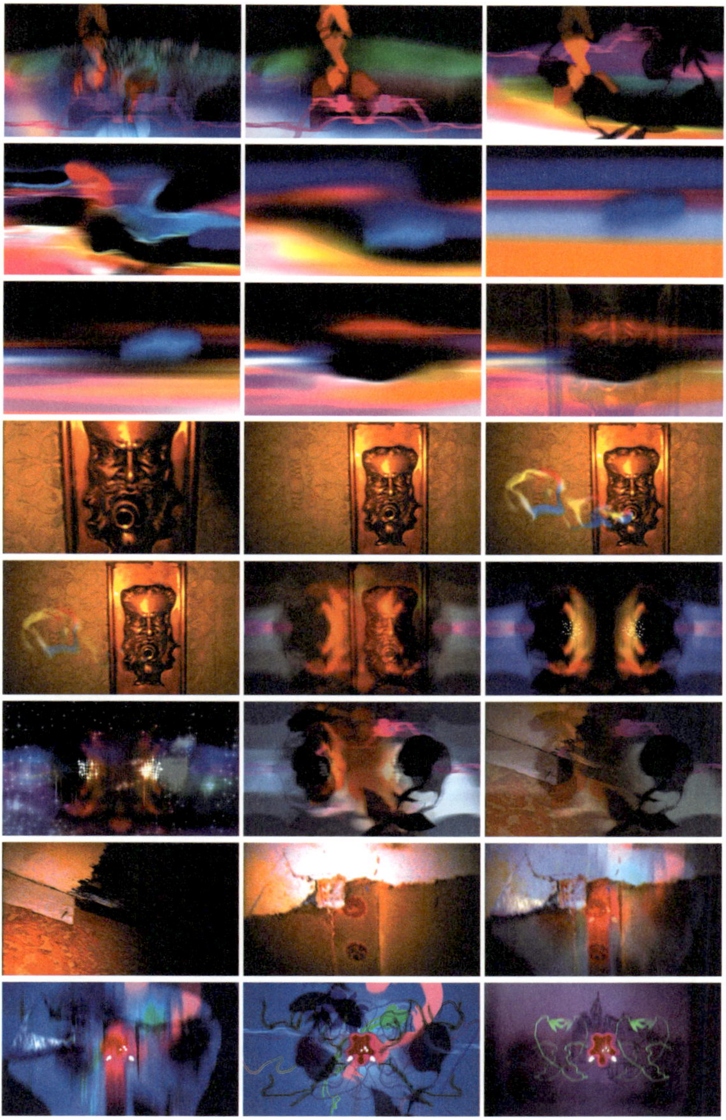

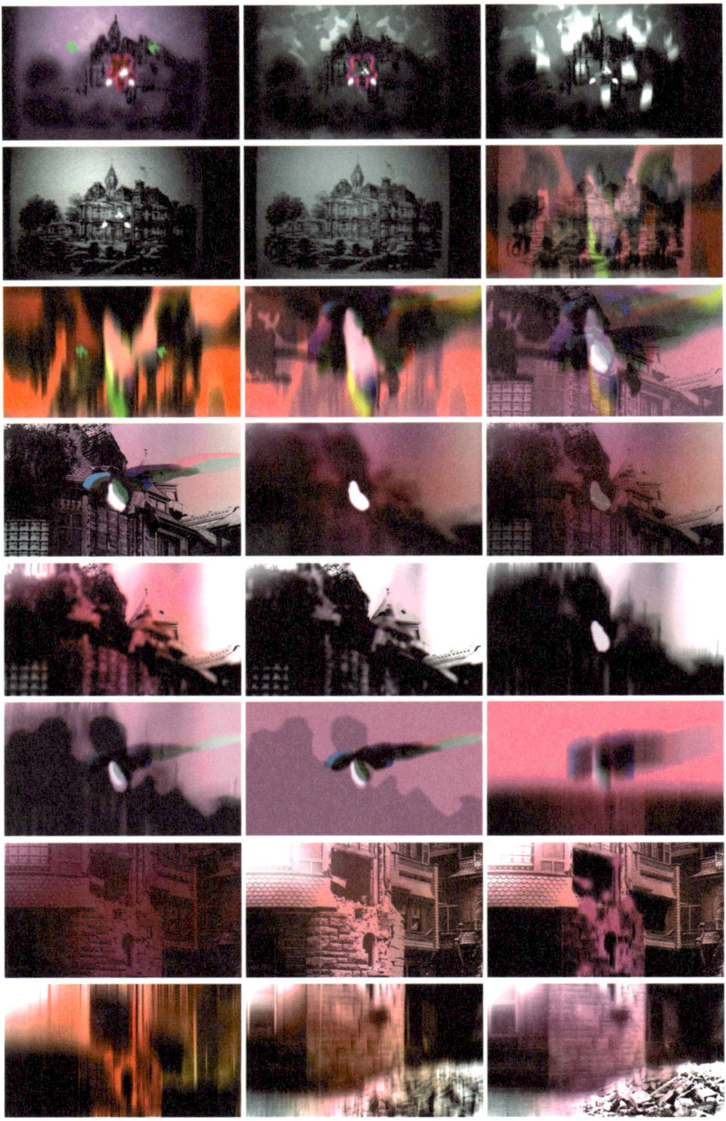

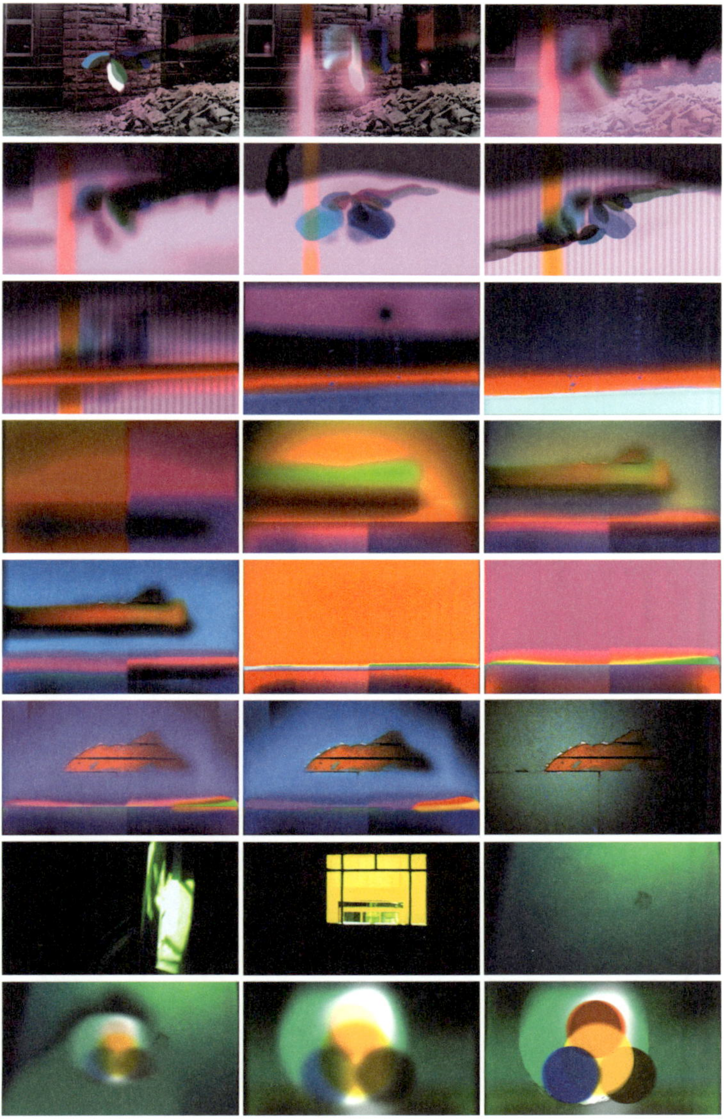

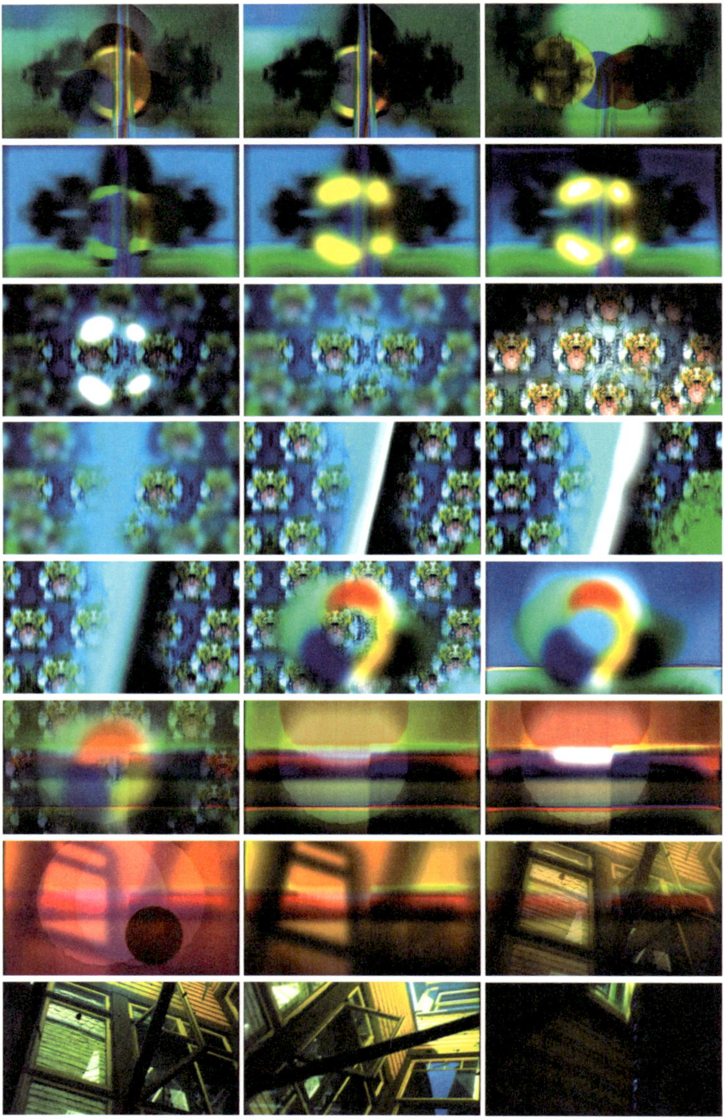

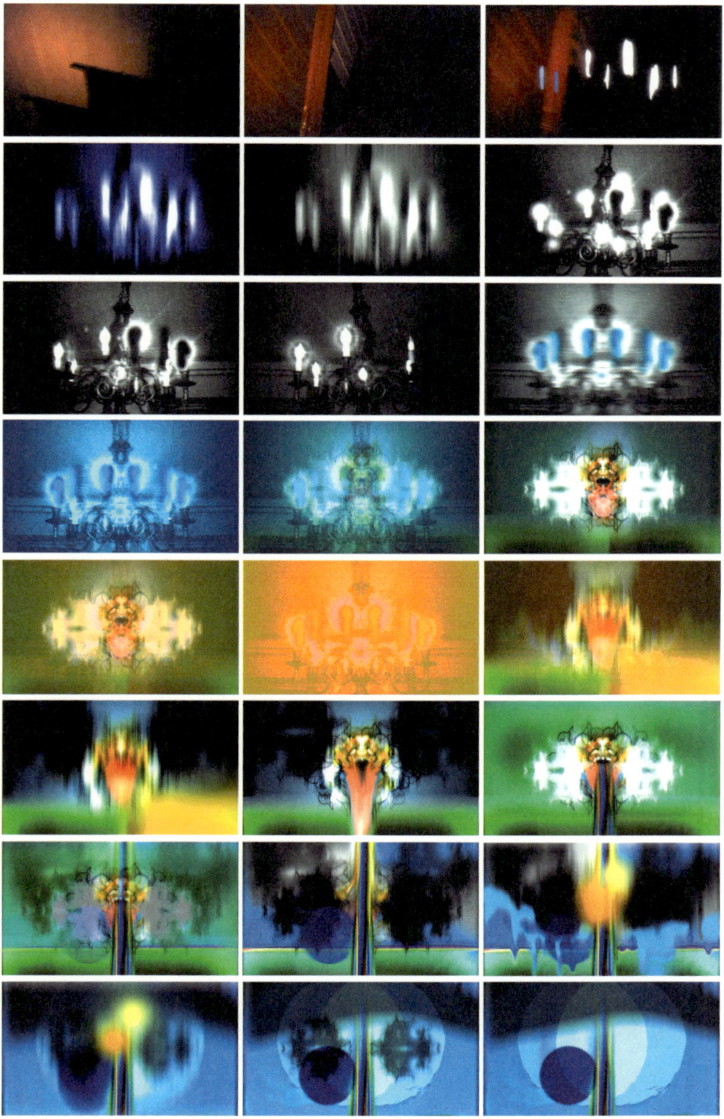

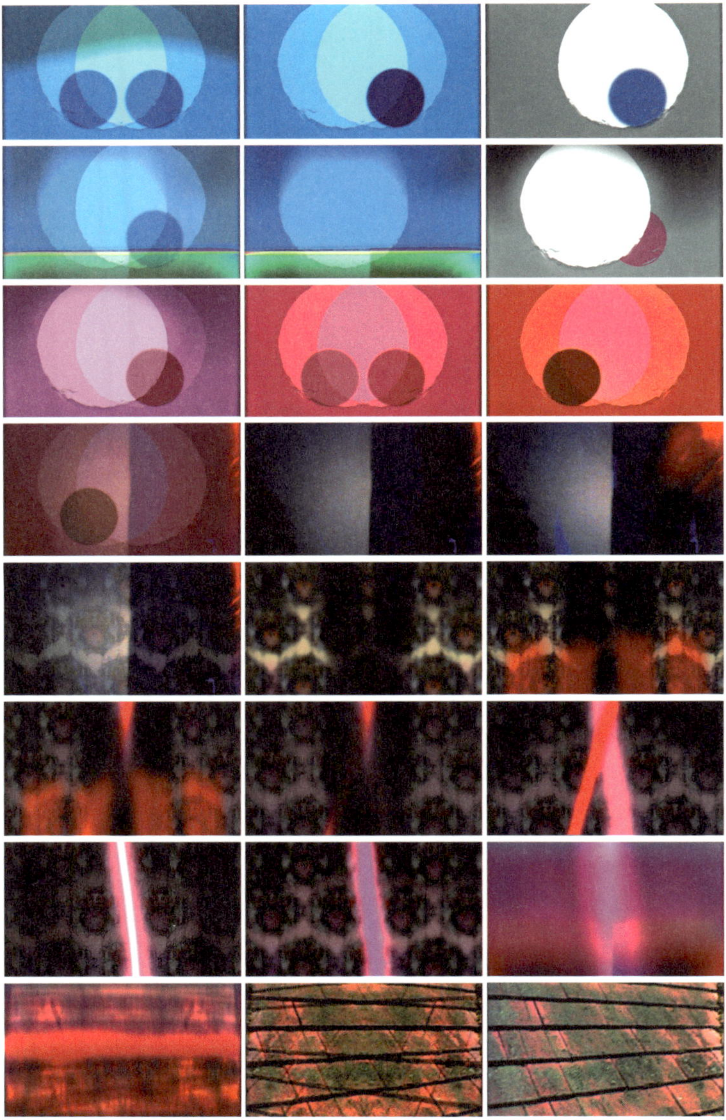

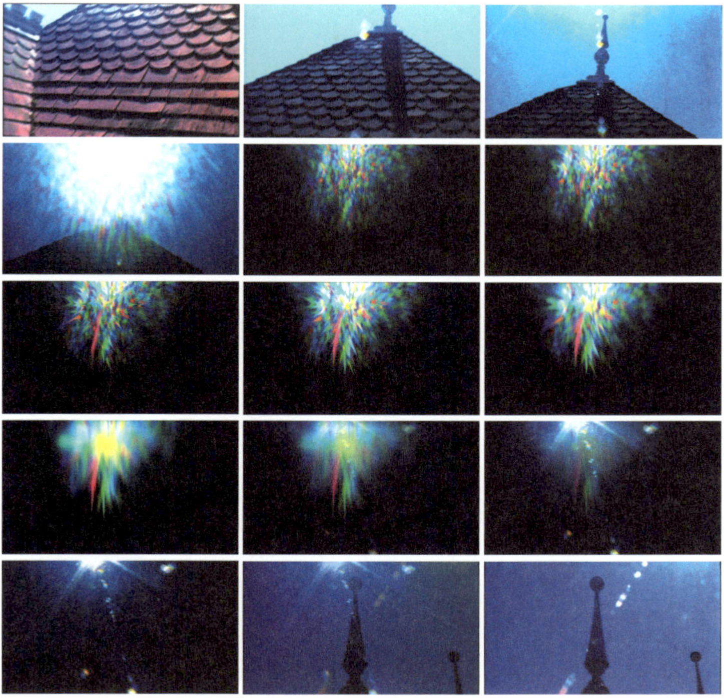

END

Symptomatological Digression 1: The Crypt

Like a commemorative monument, the incorporated object betokens the place, the date, and the circumstances in which desires were banished from introjection: they stand like tombs in the life of the ego.

—Maria Torok, "The Illness of Mourning
and the Fantasy of the Exquisite Corpse"

The crypt marks a definite place in the topography. It is neither the dynamic unconscious nor the ego of introjections. Rather, it is an enclave between the two, a kind of artificial unconscious, lodged in the very midst of the ego. Such a tomb has the effect of sealing up the semipermeable walls of the dynamic unconscious. Nothing at all must filter to the outside world. The ego is given the task of a cemetery guard.... When the ego lets in some curious or injured parties, or detectives, it carefully provides them with false leads and fake graves.

—Nicholas Abraham and Maria Torok, "The Topography
of Reality: Sketching a Metapsychology of Secrets"

Sarah Winchester's wealth accorded her a privilege not granted other women of her period. Not only did her fortune shelter her madness from scrutiny but her control of it saved her from the fate of other wives and daughters of her class. She could afford the luxury of directing her diagnosis by redirecting the interpretation of her symptoms through their dissembling displacement. (Of course, neurotics are dissemblers, but she was successfully able, through symptoms that were no longer just somatic, to deflect the course of a potential cure.) The introjected fantasies of other women of her time, when psychoanalysis was being invented, classified them as hysterics, but the hallucinated mania of Winchester house seems evidence instead of Sarah's paranoia.[1] The double patriarchal inheritance of wealth (the good object) and a curse (the bad object) acted in concert to protect her from a counter-analysis of hysteria in that together they enabled her to erect the paranoiac armour of a house that shielded her from the spirit world—as well as from the social.

The assembly of dissembling symptoms displaced to the architecture of her house made for an unstable construction. The contradictory demands of her dual inheritance were like two arcs that only gain their vaulted strength by leaning together. Perhaps we can read the symptom of Winchester's architectural disorder another way. Perhaps hysterical introjection and paranoid projection are not opposing presentations. Perhaps in this case they are disguised by an incorporation that kidnaps introjection. The earthquake dislodged a secret whose reverberations could be misread in the seismographic spirit graphs of 1906. The earthquake toppled the structure, reducing it from seven to four storeys, and shook the building to its foundation, creating a crisis. The crisis was not the momentary malfunctioning of the outer shield but the misaligning of an inner architecture, the fracturing of its lines of construction, the breaking of the seal of the inner safe of the outer safe, the jarring opening of a *crypt*. The earthquake exposed…another time and another place. Catastrophe on catastrophe: "It must first be recognized that the crypt is itself the catastrophe, or rather its monument."[2]

What secret was deposited in this crypt that safeguarded a catastrophe already having taken place? Or does the crypt mark the scene of a crime—the interment of whose body? And how many: one or likely two? We are getting ahead of ourselves; but if the crypt is fabricated to keep the other place safe in this non-place, we would have to speculate that the "crime" or contradictory desire of a forbidden pleasure housed within it would locate this other place, despite the bodies, as not here but elsewhere—in the East: the fled scene of an impossible or refused mourning. (In the age of the telegraph, could crime be fled, or would news of it precede us from one coast to another, already there when we arrive? Wouldn't its reception continue to reverberate in the transformer of the crypt, still relaying its signal to the outer reaches of a hideout's redoubt? We suspect that the solidity of the redoubt's boundary is a spectral image confusing attack and defence, a simulacrum made of the periodic pulses of signals telegraphed from the crypt whose undead victims rouse buried.)

What, then, is this story of haunting but a ruse perpetrated by Sarah Winchester in the alibi, the *elsewhere*, of her house—nothing but another table-rapping spiritualist fraud? The proliferating protrusions of the Winchester house were the outworks of a crypt, not simply a redoubt; the articulations of its confusing architecture were also decoys; the feints of its false staircases were meant to lead away from a secret that the crypt kept safe. Dissembling her symptoms, Winchester led us along a false trail. Taking advantage of our own garrison mentality, she had us peering outward with her for signs of impending Indian/spirit attacks (you know, listening with our wrong ear to the animal and bird signals deceptively employed by Indians in their invisible attack), when all we had to do was look down and follow tracks to her tomb. Dividing the senses would be a ruse to confuse, depositing a secret in the folds of the intertwining of visibility and invisibility.

We know that discovery is never this simple, because why so elaborate a ruse as this house, which has hidden its secret to today? This secret was hidden even from Sarah Winchester, who nonetheless wanted to communicate something through her mystery house—and not just to spirits. Neither hysteric nor paranoiac, Sarah Winchester combined the two as a *cryptophore*—to use Nicholas Abraham and Maria Torok's term—but she presents a unique case and challenge for *cryptonymy*.[3] Her case demands that we share a crime or at least match one of ours to hers. It would take a break-in artist to crack the combination of a simulated vault even beyond engineering entry through the dissimulating armour of its exterior housing. Perhaps because Blake identifies with Winchester as an artist, the break-in of *1906* opened a way to this mystery.

What can we know of Sarah Winchester's history when all we can glean is gathered from Internet sites or gift shop chapbooks?[4] It would be pure speculation to continue to recount her so-called secret exhumed from this crypt, as well as deviation from our narrative, so I propose to bury this impertinent analysis in a second digression where those not interested to hunt its truth can detour. This analysis would itself be a decoy (and contradict what follows it, absolving Winchester of a crime by the cure that uncovers her secret), because what are we examining here, as evidence of what symptoms: Sarah Winchester, her house, motion pictures, or American culture? Perhaps all in one entwined sickness. Then again, Sarah Winchester's was never a particularized case where speculation could be thrown out of court by the evidence of incontrovertible facts, when they are already nothing but mystification. From the opening of the enveloping illusions of *Winchester*, we were already in myth. The danger of this pursuit is regression into myth. But only through the resonating sympathies of hallucinations engendered by myth, could an artist, sympathetic to the plight of his subject, pursue an obscure mystery whose wounds are the foundation and grounds of a tourist attraction. Only through his communicating artifact of wavering simulacra, itself as silent as its subject, could my analysis—a speculative fiction of a fiction—possibly be made.

Symptomatological Digression 2: The Thing

The ultimate aim of incorporation is to recover, in secret and through magic, an object, that, for one reason or another, evaded its own function: mediating the introjection of desires. Refusing both the object's and reality's verdict, incorporation is an eminently illegal act; it must hide from view along with the desire of introjection it masks; it must hide even from the ego.

—Maria Torok, "The Illness of Mourning"

To make a joke before I foolhardily enter its graveyard, cryptonymy is as well trodden an academic path as that to Jim Morrison's Père Lachaise grave. So I am not inventing anything here. A problem immediately presents itself: namely that cryptonymy, though it expresses its metaphors of the construction of a "crypt" through the terminology of architecture, searches for something that is silent while still linguistic—the secret, mute *word*. Leaving no diaries and offering no interviews, the reclusive Sarah Winchester remained silent about her obsession, which is ghostwritten in the abstract volumes of architecture, not words. This architecture is evidence, at the least, that she was not afraid to expose herself in a spectacle, as long as her monstrous monument kept silent. We are departing from a strict cryptonymic investigation such as posthumously pursued by Abraham and Torok through the rich dossier of the Wolf Man's case, which consisted of a number of case studies and the subject's autobiography. This is not to suggest that "magic words" may not have existed secretly for Sarah; they are buried with her, never to be exposed. Though they may be entombed, the Winchester house is the effect of their magical encryption; the cover of its shelter is both a defensive mechanism and a "hallucinatory fulfillment of desire."[1] The "text" of its architecture and the hallucinated images that emanate there are the only means by which we can speculate on the thing that the house contrarily attaches itself to and so cleverly detaches itself from.

Stories offer more myth than clinical facts. Buying a ticket to tour Winchester Mystery House is our point of entry to the scene of a crime. On tour, cold clues are just an accounting of facts: a stupefying enumeration of rooms, doors, windows, and fireplaces. Beyond the fabulous stories of the haunting and construction of her mansion between 1884 and 1922, there are but a few dates in Sarah Winchester's life to recount. To reiterate: she built her house in response to a medium's guidance, consulted when distraught from the death of her husband (1881), a passing that painfully revived memories of her daughter's demise (1866, when she retired from childbearing).

Tragedy two times over: the dates 1866 and 1881 mark a double loss for Sarah Winchester. Twice disinherited of love objects, she sought solace in spiritualism as a quick purchase on the work of mourning: with proof of the afterlife of the soul, the grief-stricken survivor could reconcile herself to her catastrophic separation from the departed. Only through the long, difficult work of mourning is the subject—having included the lost object in the ego, become dead to herself—able to transform the investments attached to the love object in order finally to conform to this new reality. Freud wrote in "Mourning and Melancholia" that the features of mourning sometimes repeat the mania of melancholy. But what if mourning was not worked through? What if mourning was refused? This conjecture (and that of the secret which constitutes the crypt—some crime of a forbidden desire fulfilled) must be our starting point.

Our conjecture must start with the suspicion that the crypt was already built in 1866 and then was shaken in 1881—as the Winchester house was in 1906—with the death of her husband, William. "It should be remarked that as long as the crypt holds, there is no melancholia. It erupts when the walls are shaken, often as a result of the loss of some secondary love-object who had buttressed them. Faced with the danger of seeing the crypt crumble, the whole of the ego becomes one with the crypt, showing the concealed object of love in its own guise. Threatened with the imminent loss of its internal support—the kernel of its being—the ego will fuse with the included object, imagining that the object is bereft of its partner. Consequently, the ego begins the public display of an interminable process of mourning."[2] Sarah Winchester's discrepant responses to her two tragedies lead us to speculate that her exorbitant commemoration of William's death, with her mansion so much like Queen Victoria's monument to Prince Albert, was the mourning she denied herself after her daughter's death. The death of her secondary love object *and* subsequent inheritance provided her with the purpose and means for "the public display of an interminable process of mourning." We suspect, however, that the Winchester house was still the extravagantly false dress of a refused mourning. Sarah Winchester converted her inheritance into a monument to her dual refusal of mourning in which her husband and child figured differently. The refusal of mourning for her husband complicated that for her daughter, forcing her to refurbish the crypt and figure a new demand in the ongoing building of her mansion.

Sarah Winchester's first period of grieving after her daughter's death demonstrated the common characteristics of mourning: withdrawal, lack of interest in object love, creative inertia. Her second mourning, however, contradictorily manifested itself as an efflorescence of creativity. Was the mania of her mansion a surreptitious recovery of her first and only object love: her daughter? Did the non-stop building fulfill her desire for something supposedly lost to death, already buried in a crypt that the Winchester house was then deceptively built around as the so-called commemoration of another death?[3]

The crypt is constructed from traumatic circumstances that date and place it. The trauma of loss does not mournfully inscribe itself as two dates, one after the other, on a family tomb. Dates are refused in the denial of mourning, but the circumstances they commemorate constitute the crypt differently. Sarah's husband originally helped buttress the crypt's construction, but at his death he too was incorporated into it through a crisis that shook its walls. The traumatic circumstances that his incorporation commemorates exceed the tragedy of his death as a preceding shame attached to Sarah's first refusal. Constituted differently, then implicated in each other in such a way that disturbed the crypt, the two incorporations needed further constraints to contain the disruptive forces of their contradictory cohabitation, individual encryptions already being an accommodation of contradiction. Visitation of the second incorporation on the first demanded more than a further buttressing or restoration of the tomb. It provoked a flight west and the building of another funereal enclosure. The Winchester house is a secondary effect of refused mourning: a crypt effect. It shelters an existent tomb; it extrudes to bury its crypt further. The complicated refurbishment of the original crypt in its transport west reflects itself on the exterior of its domestic housing. The building's front pressingly advocates a trauma kept silent: the violence of a second entombment that ruptured the crypt's walls, a violence that now articulates the mansion's facade. In 1866, Sarah Winchester's mourning for her daughter had no visible manifestation because of the silent, secret construction of a crypt. In 1881, a second death triggered a crisis: contradicting mourning in the extravagance of her mansion; displaying an aggression lacking in her first refusal; testifying to a violence, erected on the paranoiac fiction of persecuting spirits, but demonstrating its own counter-aggression.

How is a crypt constructed? The crypt is constituted by a crime that accompanies the death of a love object. The loss itself is not the cause of an illness of mourning, the crime is: the hallucinatory fulfillment of a desire attached to the love object that climaxes in a triumphant orgasm before the death of another. Unable to admit this horrific crime, the subject buries it along with its "exquisite corpse" and promptly forgets; mourning itself must be denied, and the undead love object must be encrypted along with the libidinal investments attached to it. Unlike the hysteric whose prohibited desires are expressed somatically, the cryptophore hides hers even from herself. Her desires are not repressed, though: an *already fulfilled* desire is housed in her crypt. The crypt maintains a double loss: the love object and the desire lost with that object. Sarah Winchester's amnesia, obscuring such a shameful crime against an innocent other, censored her for years as an abstention from procreation. With the death of her husband—a witness to her crime and implicated himself perhaps in shameful others—libidinal desire reawaked. Refusing another mourning, though offering its public display, she gave birth to the proliferating phantasmagoria of her mansion and its steady stream of hallucinations. Sheltered now from society by her wealth, she revisited her crime nightly through lone spiritualist seances and magically consummated her desire—though her amnesia transformed these repeated sessions into a hallucinated haunting by hostile spirits. After all, the crypt's purpose is to preserve the love object so that the desire buried with its "exquisite corpse" too might be revived, even though the pleasure of revival is disguised as pain. (Spiritualist seances would continue to be a refusal of mourning; their nightly "*fort/da*" reanimated the undead.)

Incorporation is failed introjection but mimes it through magic, immediately, without the delay of the work of mourning, as hallucinatory as the orgasm whose denial began the crypt's construction. Unable to acknowledge loss by introjecting it, the subject denies mourning altogether. The nature of incorporation depends on the role played by the love object at the time of loss. If introjection is complete, no breakdown will occur; if it is incomplete, the ego will undergo suffering, needing to keep the object alive with unassimilated drives still attached, in the hope that its desires will be revived with the object. Winchester's two refusals necessarily would constitute their effects differently. With her daughter innocent, the shame of increase in libido would rest with the mother, and the ensuing endocryptic identification with the lost object would be free of aggression. With the death of her husband who shared the grief of their daughter's death, the circumstances of trauma encrypted was not his loss at which Sarah feels shame for her increase in libido. The trauma was not her shame, but his, some other circumstance of disappointment, a shame, however, that must be denied due to his role as her ego-ideal. Only this denial constitutes encryption, and her husband's "innocence" was buried with him.

Entombed secrets are intrapsychic; they belong to the shame of love objects: "No crypt arises without a shared secret's having already split the subject's topography."[4] Sarah Winchester buried her daughter and her husband in the same crypt, where one secret wrapped the other. Who knows what Sarah and William witnessed of each other. Others who bear witness against the lost love object—if that object is an ego-ideal—who have complaints that the subject herself cannot name, face aggression. Her husband innocent again! Sarah Winchester's haunting spirits were such witnesses. They brought their class action suit against her as sole representative of the Winchester blood-soaked fortune. Instead of feigning innocence defending herself from prosecuting persecution, which her building protectively purported to be, she needed her spirit suitors and sought them out; her mansion was a flagrant and conspicuous advertisement. Her spirits were proxies in a covert countersuit. Their hostility redoubled her aggression and returned their tort as her retort to her husband. Her double inheritance—the "good" and "bad" objects of her wealth and its curse—were one and the same, tainted by her husband. No mourning memorial to him, Winchester house was a protest, the trance-speaking truth of her plight—her plight and complaint, her grief and grievance. She turned her husband's money and the violence she claimed was its heritage against him, using both to shield the

lost object of her first refusal of mourning—the
daughter she revived from the crypt through seances
dissembled as spirit conclaves.

Symptomatological Digression 3: The Phantom Effect

The phantom's periodic and compulsive return lies beyond the scope of symptom-formation in the sense of a return of the repressed; it works like a ventriloquist, like a stranger within the subject's own mental topography. The imaginings issuing from the presence of a stranger have nothing to do with fantasy strictly speaking. They neither preserve a topographical status quo nor announce a shift in it. Instead, by their gratuitousness in relation to the subject, they create the impression of surrealistic flights of fancy or of oulipo-*like verbal feats.*

—Nicholas Abraham, "Notes on the Phantom: A Complement to Freud's Metapsychology"

Having discovered Sarah Winchester's crypt buried within her mansion, we might now be convinced that the Winchester house is merely its dissembling shield, and that the haunting she claimed is another crypt effect: her hostile spirits were enlisted accomplices and guardians of her secret. In spite of incorporation being a sign that mourning has been refused, that it cannot be expressed, and that words associated with a forbidden pleasure are unspeakable, only to be buried, cryptophores want to communicate. Their communication differs from that of hysterical repression. Their cunning communication is an openly-hiding pleasure-pain that is manipulated without revealing its secret because the artifacts of that manipulation are detached from their secret source—the crypt that houses "the symbol of what cannot be symbolized."[1] The Winchester house is both detached and a deflection from the crypt it hides. What was its owner trying to communicate through the absurd apparatus of her mansion?

A shield that protects while it hides, the cover of the house is the crypt's prosthesis. Like the spiritualist-inflected technologies of telepresence, it is a technology invented to place a call of mourning, but one that fails in advance. The pulsing signals transmitted from the interior of its crypt through the diaphragm of its facade are an SOS—a prosthesis being a sign of some bodily disjuncture, and, moreover in this case, of a dislodging derangement.[2] No border between inside and out, between attack and defence, no division between persecution and counter-accusation, together hallucination and architecture elide these differences, a two-in-one hallucinatory fulfillment, contrarily hiding and seeking.

We dispute her overt claims. Sarah Winchester devised her mansion to cover a crypt rather than to appease good spirits or protect herself from evil ones. By continual accretion, it grew out to hide what was within. In spite of my speculation above, we will never know its secret; however, we do know that Sarah Winchester's claim to be haunted by spirits is a lie. She did not lie to divert us from a secret that, after all, was unknown even to her. Her haunting by spirits is a lie only insofar as these ghosts—these "particular" persecuting ghosts protesting her marriage inheritance—do not rise from her crypt. They are oblivious to a constructive mania that hoards precious contents. They care nothing for a crypt's treasured secret, seeking some other economy of restitution, some other substitution to appease their haunting. Pursuant from another place, they are destined to the subject, though arbitrary to her. Phantoms haunt through secondary associations linked socially to the subject: the Winchester fortune founded on a weapon of destruction, for example.

Phantom effects differ from crypt effects. They reside in the unconscious rather than in the cleft of the false unconscious where the crypt houses itself. They are not the ghosts of one's own tomb but haunt from the tombs of others, one's parents or grandparents, who maintain their own dead buried within themselves. "What haunts are not the dead, but the gaps left within us by the secrets of others."[3] If I have speculated on Sarah Winchester, it was through the evidence of her house; it is impossible to speculate further down the line on a "family's guarded secret" other than to relay the social effects of her patriarchal inheritance. Phantom effects emigrate from the real to lodge the social discord or injustice they protest in an innocent subject, then rise again as fantastic distortions that continue to modify the real. Whatever Sarah Winchester inherited, she transmitted it through her house, transforming her patrimony into something that was real and fantastic at the same time. Her haunted house was the means by which she settled her debt to her past and conveyed it to her time. This house financed by and designed for haunting articulated every social relation in which she participated through her money. Her mansion is a haunted *social* artifact through which she negotiated exchanges with un-repaid spirits *and* paid labourers (paying one what was due the other), one relation no different than the other in that the grounds of each are equally real and fantastic.

Deep Throats and detectives say, "Follow the money." There is no secret here. Sarah Winchester knew perfectly well that her inheritance was a crime of money. Her haunting derived from profit repeatedly taken from the manufacture of ghosts. She lived on the surplus value materialized mysteriously from the theft of souls disguised as the manufacture and exchange of commodities. Already phantasmagorical, the commodity transforms all social relations into a fantastic relation between things.[4] Giving birth to phantoms, the mystical character of the commodity gives it licence to speak for itself and to ventriloquize for others when it replaces and substitutes itself for the actions of men and women (who are secondary to its performance, merely players to its playwriting) as an object considered of value only in exchange. If we add murder to the commodity's theft of value, an existence, like Winchester's, dependent for its privilege on the unearned benefits of exchange, is ripe for haunting.

A subject cannot speak to an inherited phantom haunting or address the phantom haunting her. One inherits a haunting whole, as a family drama complete with stage directions; but for the unknowing, innocent subject, this drama is a meaningless pantomime. Taking resident company within the subject, a stranger personifies abject social effects. Staging its social scenes from within clefts of its host, the stranger prompts his fleeting hallucinations to mingle with the subject's own fantasies. Representations are contagious, and the inheritor of these theatrics routinely performs new social roles to audiences of new witnesses, plying contradiction on contradiction by staging the old, handed-down repertoire in grander and more opulent productions, such as the artificially extravagant Winchester house.

While her West Coast mansion was the protection demanded by Sarah Winchester's second refused mourning to house the renovated crypt of her first, we have to conclude now that it was also—but not solely—a means to expiate the haunting brought on by the curse of the Winchester rifle she always claimed its construction to be. (Phantasmagorical images *do* derive from external haunting; of fantastic source, they are not totally delusional; Sarah Winchester's haunting spirits are of social origin. Phantom effects, which merge with crypt effects, however, still emerge from the individual subject.) The spectacle of the Winchester house "constitutes an attempt at exorcism, an attempt, that is, to relieve the unconscious by placing the effects of the phantom in the social realm."[5] While conjured to this end, this exorcising gesture typically disguises something else. Through the exorbitant expenditure of her husband's wealth in the conspicuous consumption of her mansion, Sarah Winchester protested her inexpressible wounds, hidden in her crypt, through the wounds of others killed by the Winchester rifle.[6]

Sarah Winchester's staging of her protest in the building of the Winchester house is no isolated case but our own. We shall see in the conclusion of Blake's trilogy that the phantom effects she inherited still transmit their blood curdling effects in a bloody history re-enacted today. *Century 21* brings us up to the present, to the moment of 9/11, so we can judge for ourselves, in our own time, what antique violence haunts us still.[7]

Repeating Rifle: *Century 21*

But comes a new generation to sweep out even the ghosts, with these new vacuum cleaners. No ghost could stand up against a vacuum cleaner. The new generation is having no ghosts or cobwebs. It is setting up in the photography line, and is just going to make a sound financial thing out of it. For this purpose all old hates and old glooms, that belong to the antique order of Haughty Fathers, all those are swept up in the vacuum cleaner, and the vendetta-born young couple effect a perfect understanding under the black cloth of a camera and prosperity. Vivat industria!

—D.H. Lawrence, *Studies in Classic American Literature*

Flash forward. Sarah Winchester has been long dead, since 1922. Her house, a relic of the past, was immediately sold as a tourist attraction, the property later parcelled into other profit pursuits and new building projects that were parasitic on the old—and condemned unknowingly to repeat its repressed history. We have seen this pattern reproduced so many times in American fiction and film that it has become a pleasurable trope that we don't heed...or characters learn from: antique haunting is perennially dismissed by functionalist psychology as a throwback impeding rational modernization (and profit taking). Sometimes this disavowal is symbolized architecturally, as in *Psycho*'s modern Bates Motel doomed to failure by its overshadowing and over-possessive Victorian mansion. Should the Winchester grounds today escape a blood-soaked legacy? When would the shivering thrill-seeking of popular entertainment turn to the trembling of a really devastating cultural haunting: in whose haunted house?

Returning after all these years through Blake's concluding episode, we discover that, if film haunted the Winchester house, the hived-off property has now literally spawned three commercial movie houses. Constructed in the 1960s in identical futurist, domed style, they are also named optimistically for the time to come: successively Century 21, Century 22, and Century 23.

Flash forward: but to when? Three centuries have been named here. Every era imagines the future, popularly expressed through the science fiction images of Hollywood, but that future unconsciously depicts the contradictions of the present. Every era also anachronistically re-imagines the past in order more consciously to wield its conspicuous images to fight the ideological battles of the present: think of Gary Cooper's Cold Warrior gunfighter of *High Noon* from 1952.[1] Let's settle in this era, which we have inherited, divided between imagining the future and recalling the past and not so divided in planning the future that it wants to police and profit from by bringing the past as a weapon to its aid.

Recalling a constellation of real, not fictional, images of this period, we find many framed by the Cold War ideological struggle between Soviet communism and American capitalism. These warring signifiers of internal battles—Senator McCarthy's "Red Scare" witch hunt—or external actions—the Korean War, the Bay of Pigs invasion—are starkly real and unreal at the same time: Nixon and Khrushchev's 1959 "kitchen debate" plays propaganda war as theatre of the absurd. Threat was imminent, anxiety was diffuse, and conflicts were filtered through other forms of media representation, even those deemed trite. Near the close of the Korean War, in the May 2, 1953 edition of the *New Yorker*, the cartoonist Charles Addams ventured a whimsical portrayal of fantasies that underlay the anxieties of the period. With weapons raised, two boys in cowboy gear—guns, holsters, hats and kerchiefs—chase a third somewhat different lad dressed as a spaceman. After being pursued into the woods, the alien lad climbs a ladder into a tree and then, to the other youngsters' dismay, disappears into a departing spacecraft.

We could take the cartoon for what it is, chuckle, and turn the page. It expresses a more complex reality, however. Through it own gentle spin, the cartoon verges on public debate—not on whether the past should be abandoned for the future, the Wild West for the New Frontier, as if the Soviet's startling success with Sputnik a few years later would resolve Americans to saddle their horses to a new technocratic ideology but on the question of isolation versus intervention: whether the United States should assume a Great Power role to police the world beyond its borders. The cartoon marks a junction where the past would be taken into the future. The Western would be taken into space, masquerading in subsequent science fictions, such as television's *Star Trek*, and in the rhetoric of the Cold War arms race. Addams's boys are not playing; they are replaying the past through an image of it—not through the transmission of any living cultural memory but by means of the products of the cultural industry's revival of the Hollywood Western. The "Golden Age of the Western" coincides with the inauguration of the Cold War and performs a determined role within it.[2] Manufactured to the needs of the moment (which may vary according to financial interest, political coercion, or ideological collusion), industry's picture products do not duplicate the past in adequately evocative depictions, but they do reproduce patterns of behaviour in their consumers, whether children, politicians, or generals. Just as movies and television series spin off toys—the tiny-tot cowboy gear of the cartoon—so ideological rhetoric realizes itself as purchase of military toys. More pertinent than trite, the cartoon's punch line hits home when another pattern is rehearsed. Its depiction of an innocent pursuit where past and future collide replays the anxiety of dismay in the present as the "threat" of the alien other. When in the 1950s we ask who this alien is, we don't mean a spaceman. Instead, it is the Soviet communist or more likely his or her proxy: the Third World insurgent. Conveniently for national interest, the Third World insurgent could be modelled on America's original racial other, the (better dead than red) Indian.

With nuclear standoff between communism and capitalism, war must be fought covertly elsewhere through Third World proxies. A counterinsurgency must be assembled to address a threat beyond any border of this continent, in Southeast Asia or the Caribbean, but it must be raised parallel to a consensus of public opinion persuaded to pay for it.[3] The battle for consensus draws on ideological weapons when its rousing rhetoric recalls the "frontier" through a repertoire of language and images drawn from the national "myth of regeneration through violence." Of course, there is no language of the frontier, although myth is a type of speech. Its familiar invocations are scripted as sleight-of-hand resolutions to domestic political crises by preparing the way for covert operations in the Philippines, Iran, Guatemala, Cuba or Chile, or military interventions in North Korea and Vietnam, and now Iraq. Its own borders exhausted, America exported its violent myth to the Third World through a counterinsurgency that habitually applied the tactics of "savage war" to a simulacrum it imagined, whenever covert operatives, military advisers, and CIA financiers translated race and terrain into the familiar language of "cowboys and Indians." On the analogy of a frontier border that must be breached for settlement, crossed first by a regression to violence of a brave few preparing its peace and prosperity, counterinsurgency opened "free markets" whose borders America feared might be closed to the circulation of its commodities, whether these were material goods or the "value-free" messages of its cultural products, which reinforced America's own myths as universal statements.

If the "West" is a mythic space, any violent application that resorts to its language for justification elevates action to a politico-mythic space. This politico-mythic space, where myth operates as national agenda, is the familiar image-reservoir from which the American Jeremy Blake gathered the material to make his *Winchester Trilogy*, whose concluding work, *Century 21*, opens with a modified sequence of Addams's dismaying cartoon. One of the resources Blake drew upon was the monumental research of the cultural historian Richard Slotkin, whose three-volume indictment comprehensively documents the morally and politically corrosive effects of the Frontier myth repeated and promulgated by America's cultural artifacts. These mass-market products are not escapist fantasy or pure fiction; they are manufactured responses to a class-driven political agenda. They are not passive reflections but complicit promotions of American nationality, an ideology of imperial reach with deadly consequences:

> *Regeneration Through Violence* (1973) showed how the experience of life and warfare on the colonial and early national frontiers (1600-1820) was transformed into a body of narrative lore, which in its turn was codified as a language of myth and symbol by several generations of historians and fiction writers. *The Fatal Environment* (1985) showed how that mythological system was adapted to suit the ideological needs of a nation in the process of transformation from an agrarian republic to a fully developed industrial nation-state. *Gunfighter Nation* begins in 1890, at the moment when the landed frontier of the United States was declared "closed," the moment when "Frontier" became primarily a term of ideological rather than geographical reference.[4]

The geographical closing of the frontier—which maintained a reserve, nonetheless, for internal violence—is the moment our story begins with Sarah Winchester's migration west. At the end of the line on the California coast, she staged her expiation of violence, recapitulating in the spirit world what "Buffalo Bill's Wild West" spectacle would contemporaneously perform—with the consent of the good Indians on its payroll—as paying entertainment in the real one.[5]

Regeneration through violence is *the* Frontier myth. At its core "is the symbol of 'savage war', which was both a mythic trope and an operative strategy of military doctrine," and which had its origin in the exterminating designs of early settlement and colonial expansion. When this bloody reality entered myth, the moral contradictions and self-duplicities of its borderline battle, where social progress meant first a violent regress, became mixed in the persona of the (yet racially pure) American hero who

> must cross the border into "Indian country" and experience a "regression" to a more primitive and natural condition of life so that the false values of the "metropolis" can be purged and a new, purified social contract enacted. Although the Indian and the Wilderness are the settler's enemy, they also provide him with a new consciousness through which he will transform the world. The heroes of this myth-historical quest must therefore be "men (or women) who know Indians"...who can teach civilized men how to defeat savagery on its native grounds—the natural wilderness, and the wilderness of the human soul.[6]

At the close of the frontier, these conditions no longer prevailed. Still, the doctrine of "savage war" was applied to the class wars that followed from the bank panics, economic collapse, and depressions of 1873 and 1893, as well as to the imperialist expansionism and adventurism of the Spanish-American War. In the late nineteenth century, the logic of "savage war" was the warring means to rearticulate "the Frontier myth as a way of justifying a 'modern' distribution of social power between the managerial and laboring classes and a new balance between *force* and *consent* in the ideology and structure of republican government" and to rationalize America's Great Power role beyond its borders.[7] Belonging to this managerial class, with her dual legacy of financial benefit from its great industrial enterprises (of which she never yielded her Winchester stock) and moral complicity in laying waste to the West in order to capitalize on its destruction by the very products of these enterprises, was Sarah Winchester such an innocent victim? Partner to the female entrepreneurs of the spiritual telegraph, did she import the prerogatives of her class and the procedures of its capitalist enterprises into the spirit world in order to draw profit there? Expert in the ways of spirits—as a woman who knew (these other) Indians—was she expiating her past or re-enacting the myth of regeneration through violence by which the haunter becomes the hunted? The "fatal environment" of her haunting was the toxic ground of her own self-poisoning.[8] In America, we manufacture our ghosts, mass-produce them like guns, soap, or television serials.

"Cowboys and Indians" is boys' play, we think, a game to be outgrown. Its game is also an education. Representations are already implicit actions that communicate patterns of behaviour, whether they are consciously or unconsciously received and acted upon, or whether they stem from fictions, myths, or beliefs. Not merely child's play, "cowboys and Indians" is induction into national mythology. Myth becomes reality through the collusive reach of national agenda and industrial cultural production united in their collective transmission of social symptoms as phantom haunting. According to the artist, the first two parts of *The Winchester Trilogy* examined "how an individual (Sarah) and her environs were subject to the traumatic side effects of certain mythic constructs (the gunfighter, the outlaw, Manifest Destiny, etc.)," while *Century 21* “focuses instead on a sort of parody of the fraternities which more or less rely on the same constructs and on an examination of the way in which the mythology has been repackaged and broadcast since the end of the Victorian era.”[9]

Repackaging this scenario through the profitable medium of one of its haunted transmissions, Blake relays this story through the fiction of three movies playing consecutively in the Winchester grounds' cinemas. We have already begun this story with Charles Addams's cartoon, whose cartoon cells—grafted to the contemporary high culture symbolism and colour flourishes of the signature styles of Abstract Expressionism (as we know, with its own Gothic haunting, mythic spaces, cowboy machismo of facing the void, or pissing into it, sublimated here into light-laced jism spatters in the starry sky of this segment, and political contamination by CIA sponsorship)—now animate a movie…but, actually, we have not paid admission to the first theatre. Before we are there, *Century 21* opens with a shot that ends *1906*. As *Psycho* placed the Bates Motel under the pall of the past, enthralled to its antique mansion, so the establishing shot here innocently reveals the adjacency of mystery house and contemporary cinemas, one dome that surfaces in the background. To ominous music suggestive of Hitchcock's *Vertigo*, we rise to the top of a tower.[10] Will madness or masquerade prevail, we wonder?… Ah, it was from the roof of the spirit-summoning bell tower that *1906* ended! Then we are startled to witness the daylight transmission of the supernova that concluded *1906*. A signal we mistook for dissipation is telegraphed through light from the bell tower's “antenna” to one on the cinema's dome. A spirit world message is received in Century 21, and the weight of Sarah Winchester's misery returns to haunt another generation who, unsuspected, takes it in like mother's milk straight from the dazzling light of the screen. Or is it the whole industry of Silicon Valley that inherits this freighted motherlode of light that secretly contaminates its info-communicational products, embedded as it is in the heart of this capital community?

There is no doubt as to the past frequenting the contemporary entertainments we religiously return to. We seek nurturance from spectacles of light that are hallucinatory fulfillments of our desire to belong. The clichéd content of movies' ideological address may feed our minds—and we assume this interpellation to be myth's capture—but the enveloping play of light, colour, and sound in cinema's darkened space is its seductive form. If it is the faith we believe in, it is the form we return to. The first two parts of *The Winchester Trilogy* could abstract this formal play, whose shimmering insubstantiality already infected their tenuous photographic references, to convey the hallucinatory capacity of myth. Only an abstraction of light transmits from *1906* to *Century 21*, recurrently pulsing to the latter's music, breaching its scenes with diminishing flashes of energy. Ghosting through other gleaming images that masquerade as figures themselves masquerading the past, these signals from the beyond do not seek to feed their fading energy, as if dissipated antique vampires, from the dazzle of new product lines; rather, they are entertainment's animating heartbeat. (As intimate a relation as blood, abstraction and representation mingle in their shared luminosity, lighting through one another like the red-tinted, blood-soaked shots of Marines descending from helicopters that periodically erupt through Kenneth Anger's 1969 Vietnam-era *Invocation of My Demon Brother.*) The return of the past is insistent in its continuing animation of the present. The past and present are locked in one reinforced rhythm.

This rhythm of "no-progression-without-regression" is the psychic mechanism operating the Frontier myth and perpetuating its borderline syndrome. It is also the repression machine that maintains a domestic population in lockstep and lockup. Homeland Security and Fortress America are but split names for what made

Winchester house, a division by which the American administration plays its fearful population, psychically swinging it back and forth from isolation to intervention. If fearful, a passive population is also passive-aggressive, receptive to the regressive language of myth, swayed to the interests of power. An inverse reflection of territorial expansion, the psychic space of reception is reductive, its reserve of individual response diminished. Propaganda is closure of the last frontier. How un-American to think that the boundless space of imagination is programmed to the repetitions of Hollywood commodities! But how haunted must this mind be to venture residence there? Blake parodies the consequences of this defeatist "endgame thinking" in the second movie screening in Century 22, which, according to the artist, "roasts the chestnut that a pioneer faced with hostile natives is well advised to save the last bullet for himself," a maxim taken by the dead man in a coach who has saved himself from "certain death at the hands of two hostile natives (straight from central casting)."[11] Propaganda always casts clichés as well as stock characters, so this movie continues with several Western ones, including musical motifs.

No less than popular culture artifacts, are artworks free of myth, especially when they are complex in their construction, multivalent in their references, appropriative of the images and codes of mass media, or based in technology—or when they consciously attempt historical intervention, or even when they are called "American-type painting." Less conscious, or resistant perhaps, of a need to fulfill an ideological role, artists are no less unaware of what is unconscious in their art—that is, realizing how myth resonates within it. "You must look through the surface of American art, and see the inner diabolism of the symbolic meaning," D.H. Lawrence recommended.[12] When, self-constructing lineages of artistic identification, artists choose their own fathers and mothers, or grandfathers and grandmothers, their act is fraught with phantom attendance. Myth seconds this nomination still, as when critic Harold Rosenberg, imagining his own needs than maybe addressing the aims of artists, wrote of the Abstract Expressionists that "the American vanguard painter took to the white expanse of the canvas as Melville's Ishmael took to the sea."[13]

Blake proposes a counter-mythology to the fraternities he parodies—a counter-cowboy mythology. In Century 23, he nominates his own ghosts to a pantheon of "Spiritual America":

> The final segment reveals the inspirations for the entire trilogy. Appearing here as phantoms are the Pop artist Richard Prince, the actor and playwright Sam Shepard, and the actress Raquel Welch. Prince's Marlboro Man transformed the American cowboy from vital to spectral, and his artwork is an important touchstone for this piece. Shepard's creative choices (he embodies both hipster playwright and laconic cowboy) suggest that being an American causes him deep anxiety at times, but that he finds other ways of life almost inconceivable. Welch, meanwhile, appears in the guise of Hannie Caulder, the heroine of the eponymous 1971 film. Her character—who learns the way of the gun after her husband's murder—appears here as a pop-culture stand-in for Sarah Winchester.[14]

While there is no disputing a personal pantheon, any identification automatically spirits individuals to the phantasmagorical realm of myth. Myth incorporates by decomposition but as no secret, it seems, rather to continuing acclaim and worship. For instance, playing the paid role, Raquel Welch was already there, ready-scripted as an icon. By equating a fictional and a historical character, suggesting Hannie Caulder as a stand-in for Sarah Winchester, Blake enlists Winchester's story to the genre of the revenge Western. He also, thus, confuses history with the phantasmal world of myth, but was not history already the myth feeding Hollywood?

A deviant version, myth *Century 21* remains. *Winchester*'s problem is also its advantage. If myth is an all-encompassing milieu, its language is commonplace. Historically, in a polyglot nation with many illiterate immigrants, Hollywood lent competence, whereby its images would bind consensus.

Ennobling elevation, a pantheon casts noble images, the reflections of which we choose to attend. A pantheon reflects the world below, but detached from it—its spectral images as distant as vital is from virtual—and acquitted of connection, cause, or complicity with its terrestrial violence. Distanced, detached, and acquitted, these images, personages really, are troubled, nonetheless, by this violence. We share this anxiety (a fascination actually) since "trouble" goes up and down the line. It goes up and down the line between the two even to trouble their separation. Fascination would say *fascination itself* is proof of detachment, anxiously so, from violence—fascination with myth of violence, not violence itself. To suggest links between image and action, fascination and reality, myth and event, to recognize their violent association, to say that images are complicit (and our attraction to them) would seem to politicize what is not in the image, as in my writing otherwise haunted here. Trouble up and down the line skips borders. Skipping borders in flight and pursuit, hunter and hunted, self and other, two become three with the now witnessing neighbour. The third raises the question of justice.[15] On the other side of this border, we others judge what for Americans seems "inconceivable." At the least, we judge that it would seem inconceivable for a chosen pantheon to escape its culture's myths. Through a chain of substitution where he has already expressed solidarity with Winchester and through her now with Caulder, Blake takes up the dreaded gun by identifying with the kill-bill victim-heroines of revenge Westerns, suggesting that if it came to this—*9/11*, perhaps—he would act, and act in revenge... and so, it seems, he closes rank with his president.

What follows from the decision to delegate revenge by an act of substitution? Would we not question the very concept of substitution, question Hannie Caulder as a "stand-in for Sarah Westchester" by which her revenge substitutes for Winchester's? Certainly, we wonder why this exchange demands that the women already be ghostly, that they *appear* in *guise*, not to act but first to *learn*, whereas the male artists of this pantheon are transformative, creative, embodied beings? What would this active-passive distinction say about the already simulacral exchangeability of women and the exchange basis of vengeance? Could we think substitution otherwise so that it would sacrifice exchange and the exchange reprisals of vengeance with it? Substitution of one woman for the other would make Sarah Winchester and Hannie Caulder as different as host is from hostage. Substitution would be the basis of learning by which Sarah Winchester, appearing in ghostly guise, would have advantage over the embodied actions and aggression of her male counterparts.

Hannie Caulder is one of a number of early-1970s alternative Westerns released during the demoralized period when the Vietnam War was winding down. In this gender-reversed revenge story that insinuates sexual politics into the genre, Caulder hires a bounty hunter to train her in gun fighting in order to track down the three men who killed her husband while raping her. Is gender-reversed revenge any different from that of Anthony Mann's 1950 *Winchester '73* or Ford's 1956 *Searchers*? Must an American artist always be implicated in national myth? Justifying Sarah Winchester's mania by Hannie Caulder's violence, whereby a victim becomes an avenging heroine, would seem to implicate Blake in this American default. Perhaps it is inconceivable to escape myth but possible to critique it, but only through ambiguously inhabiting its genres and subtly diverting the codes of its transmissive representations. Such would be the artistic aim to claim 9/11 as a revenge Western, a claim whereby we could rescue the artist. Whatever one's motivations, creating a critical allegory of national myth always runs the risk of counter-interpretation and reinvestment in it. Cheering on John Wayne in *The Searchers*, seeing him through his later propagandistic counterinsurgent role in *The Green Berets*, Hollywood's bolstering of the war in Vietnam, the Marines of Twentynine Palms cared nothing for Ford's subtle demystification of the inherent racism and implicit cycle of violence of the "captivity narrative" they were about to repeat in Afghanistan. To the command of a pleasurable repetition, which is, nonetheless, a death, destruction, or aggression drive, these soldiers would rather fight a "savage war" than heed Ford's allegorical warning of John Wayne's frontier mentality of "better dead than red" recapitulating itself then in America's Cold War confrontation.[16]

In dangerous times, when covered wagons are circled in fearful consensus, perhaps artists can only address their fellow citizens through allegories that dissent from collective myth even if they risk Ford's failure. Failure is always a risk when in fabrications as fictional as myth meaning is now untended by cliché, when the powerful draw of the founding myth confounds any critical reading, turning reassuringly familiar even deviant images.

We wonder what the *political* function of myth is when outcasts of the American dream, ghettoized in the military's welfare system, turn their resentment against the innocent poor of a country, like Afghanistan, about to be destroyed by weapons that channel soldiers' own violence manipulated by mythic identification. What is this function other than dissembling *domestic* policy—a class war against a nation's own poor? On our part, to empathize with the valiant American soldier and not the violated other is to consent to residual profit from expelling the victim from all empathy. Reserving empathy for the "victims" of myth but not victims of its violence, are we not still blinded by myth? Could the other ever interest us when myth tells us *we* are the story? Coming between us and others, the image offered by myth only reflects back, reflects us, reflecting blindness: there is no *vanitas* in the narcissistic vanity of the hallucinatory, dissolving mirrors of myth. What of the *other* would be in an allegory that speaks otherwise? *Allos agoria* would be further violence against the other when victimhood is now the possession of the perpetrator.

Yet violence must be treated at its source. We need tend our wounded in order not to perpetuate wounding others. Diagnosing sickness is one thing, but curing poisoning is another danger when dosage is a draught of poison taken against it. So it is by means of poisoned images alone, conveyed through the haunted medium of a complicit art, that Blake ventures a diagnosis and a cure. *The Winchester Trilogy* reverts to the delusional repetitions that haunt his nation's history and that continue to divide a collective consciousness enslaved to its phantom violence. Venturing viewing through the madness of images, the audience may be spooked by something eerily familiar, something threateningly dwelling.

The cure would be for those who venture this dangerous passage through the haunted house of their culture. We cannot remain spectators to images that judge our complicity. Opening ourselves to the mystery of where these images will take us, we seek more than regression into the dynamics of the exposed myth. Entrusting ourselves to the responsibility of an artist, we want our passage to feigned madness to be no symbolic descent familiar to American art, whereby re-ascent signifies succeeding into consensus with national agenda, an instant of conviction now repeated in front of the depths of CNN; no covert baptismal conversion to Christian symbolism metaphorically underpinning America's literary-politico myth; no adventure of consciousness securely reappropriating itself in a homecoming to a gated community; no re-enslaving middle passage returning profitably from hypocritically disavowing inequality. From what dungeon depths do spooks rattle their chains to communicate with ours? Entrusting ourselves to an unhinged artwork, we take responsibility for a counter-descent into a madness already inhabiting us. Only we can take charge in *our* responsibility for cure and care. We seek to come through slaughter to the other side of myth, a coming-through through no violence, *beyond* myth, but by lighting out to no new territories either. We seek no exemption by a *laissez-passer*. No return or ascent but only in exile *through*, this strenuously abandoning yet passive passage leads us trembling grateful to a place where duration has no space to conquer. We find no dread border there, no violence of a faceless other, no terrorists other than ourselves. In the haunted house of a culture, there is no spook but our own making.

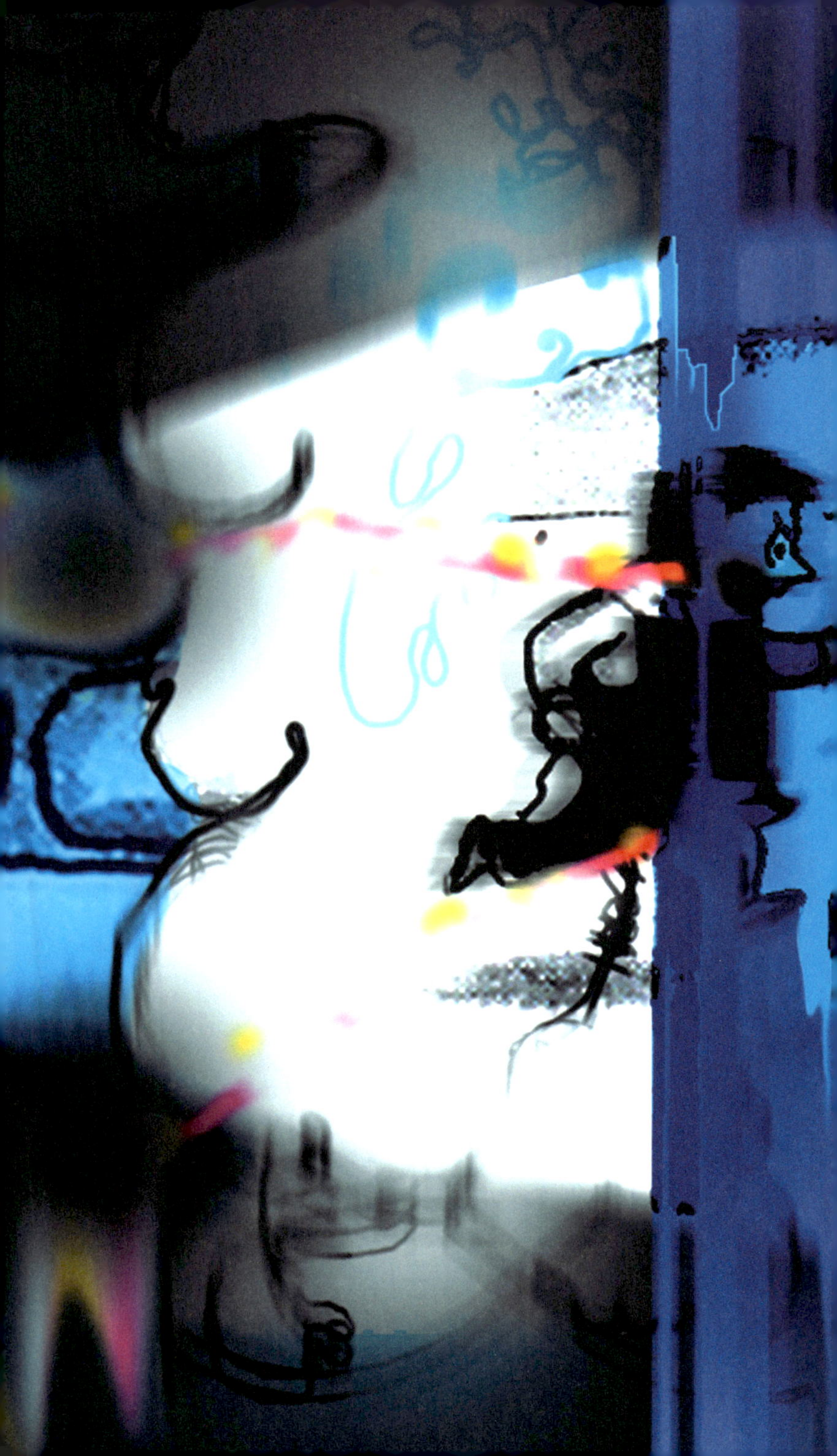

JEREMY BLAKE, *Century 21*, 2004.

START

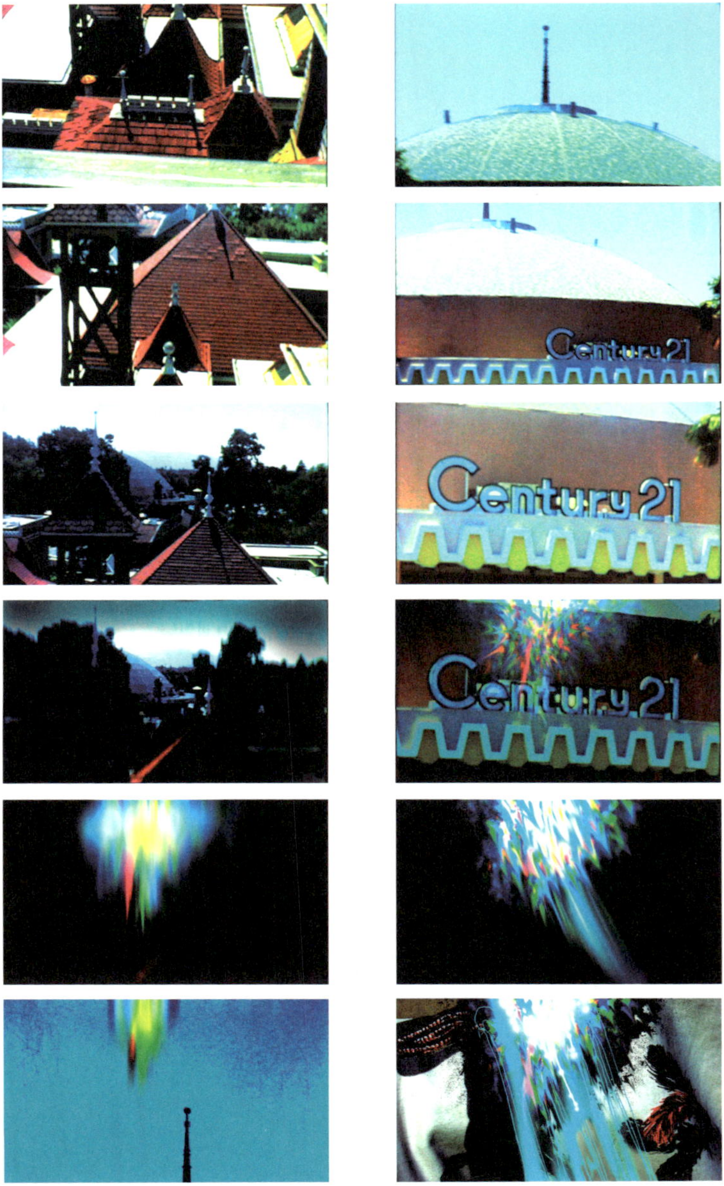

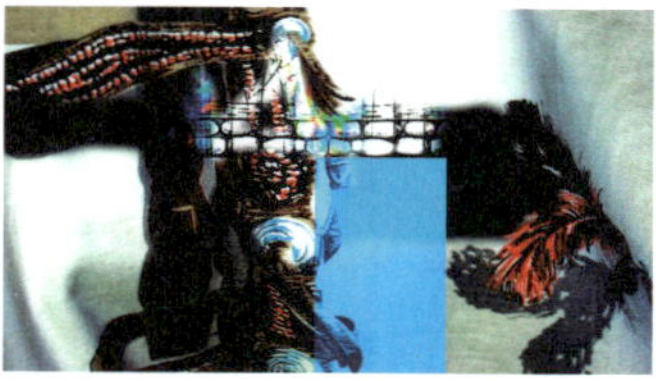
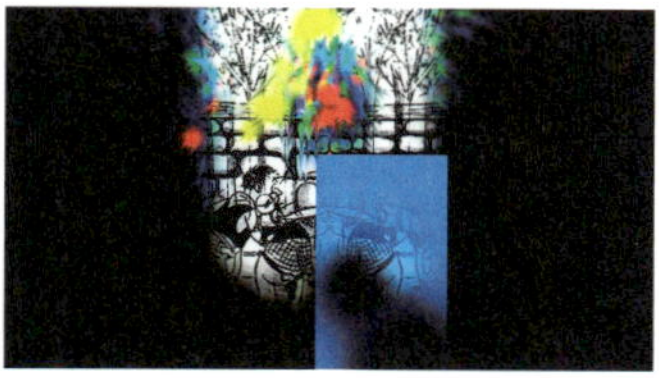
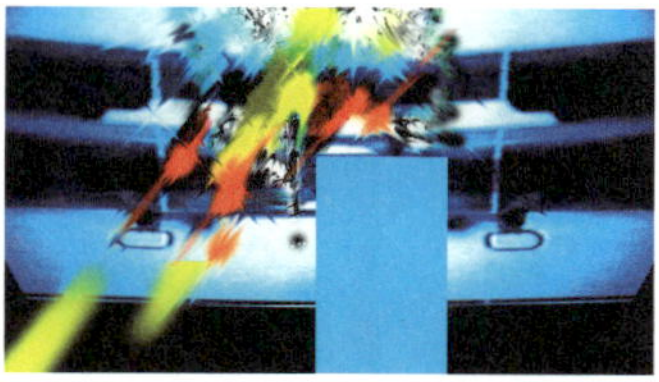
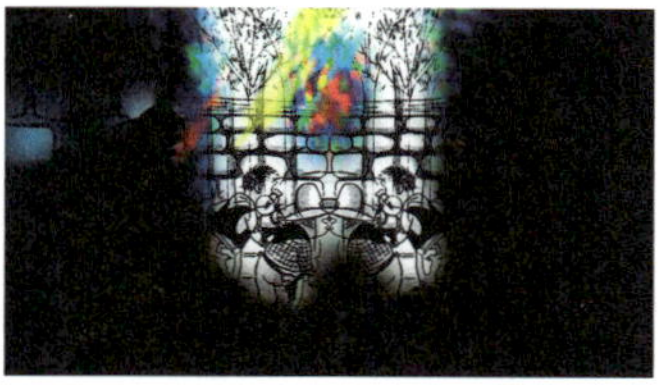
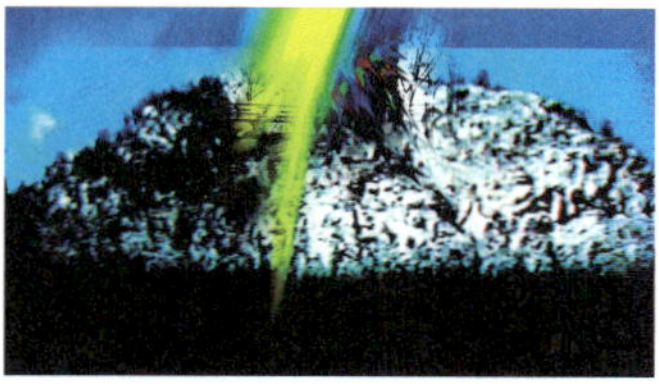
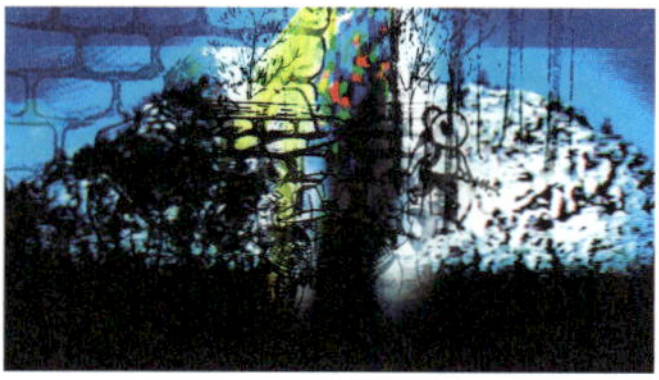
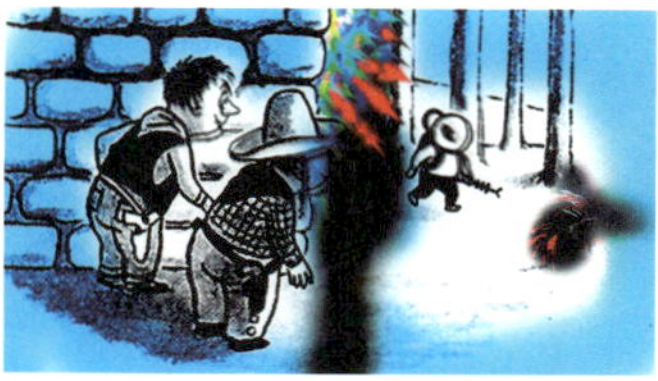
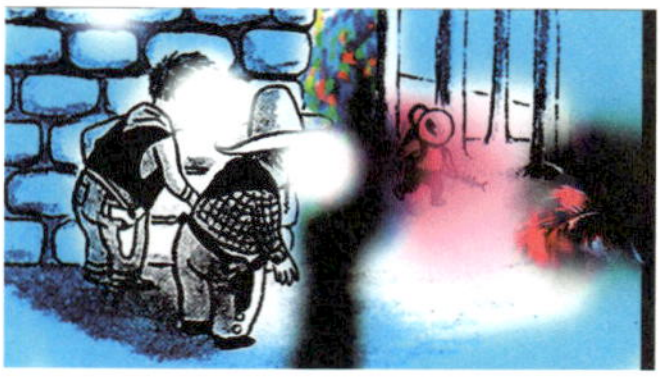
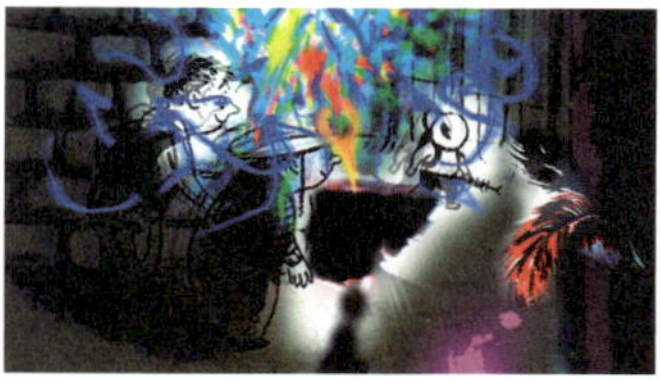
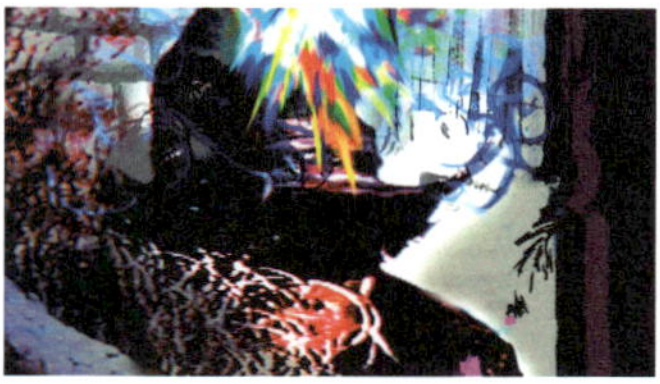
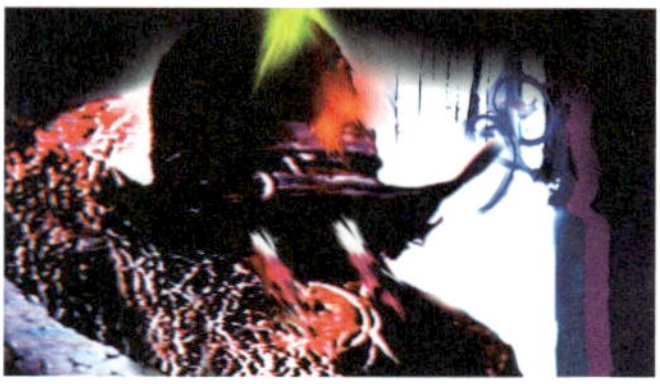
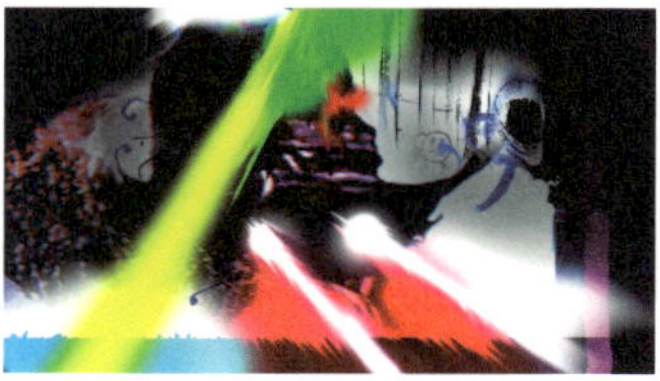

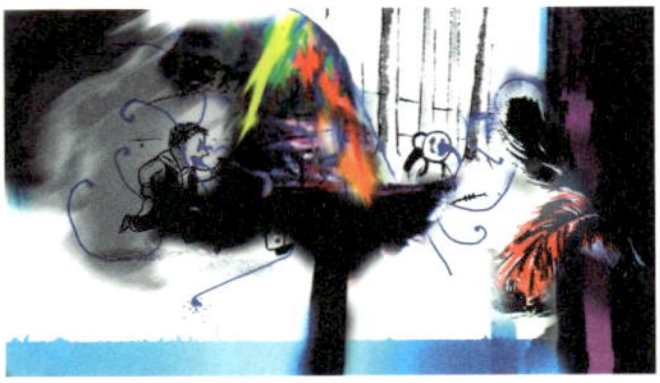
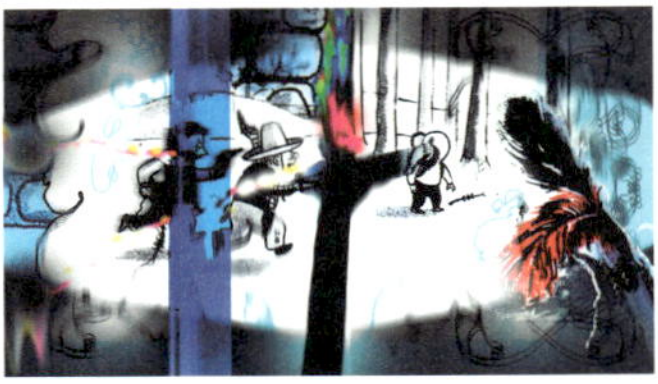
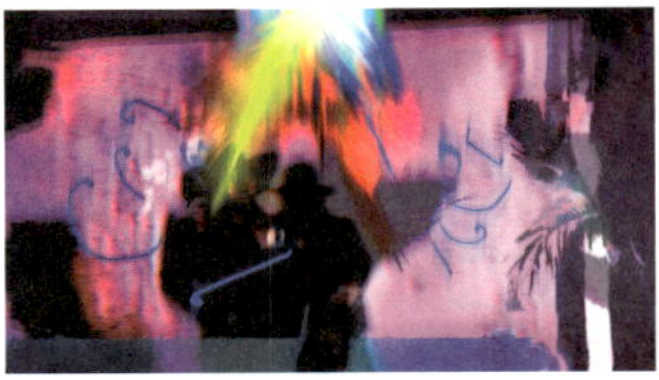
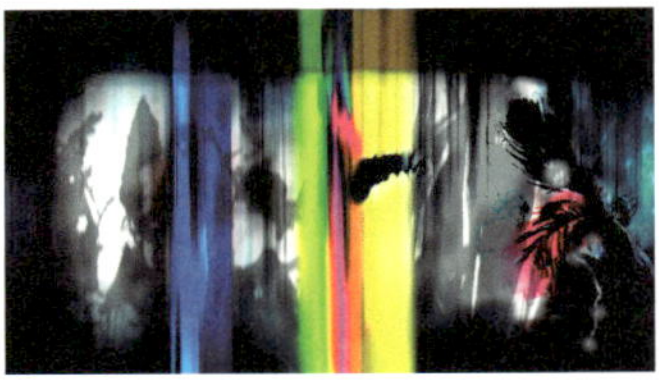
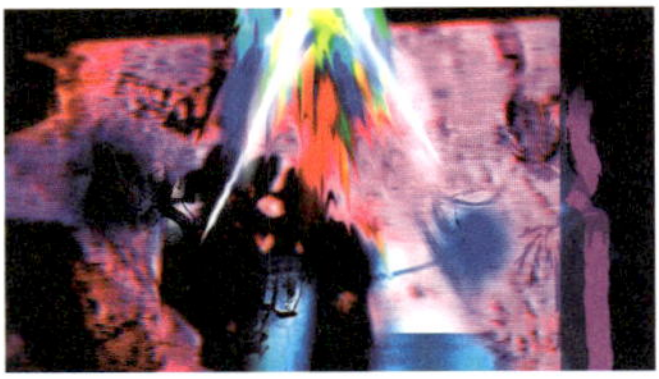
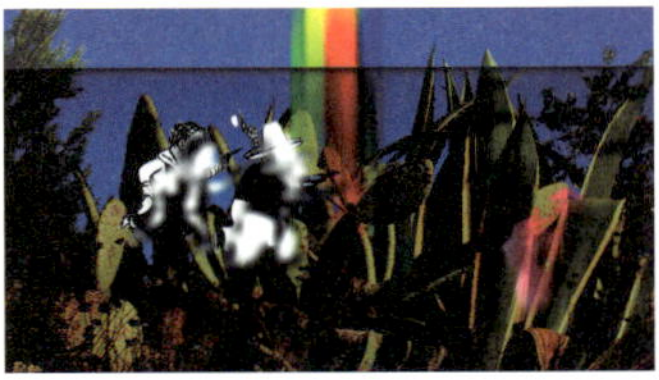
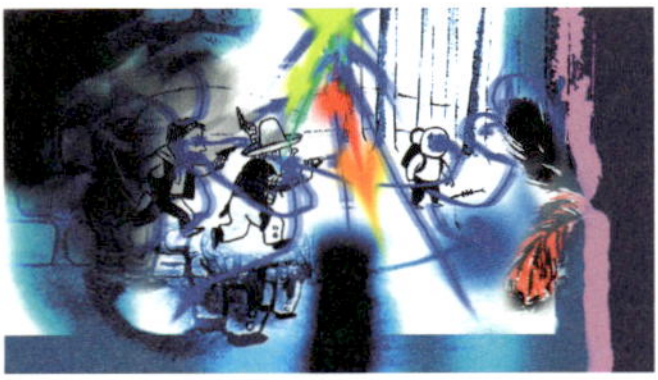
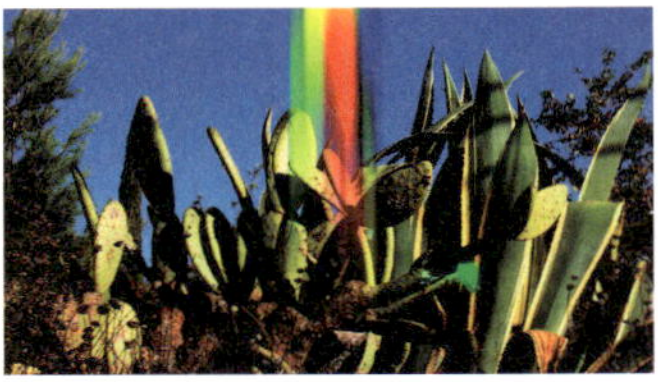
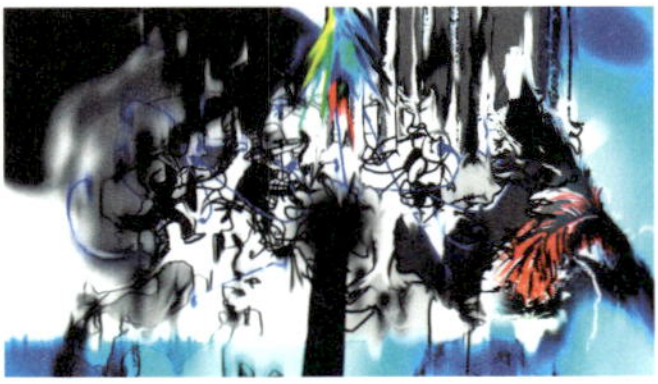
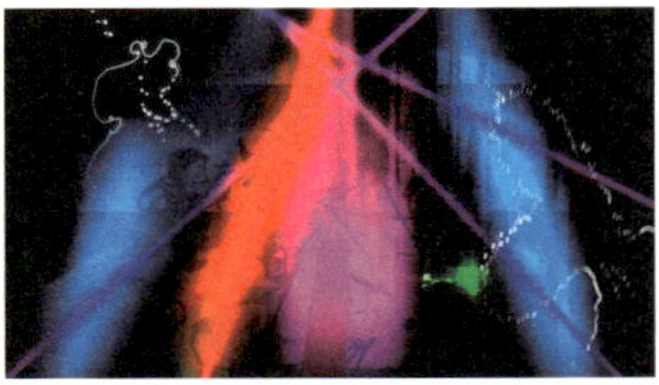
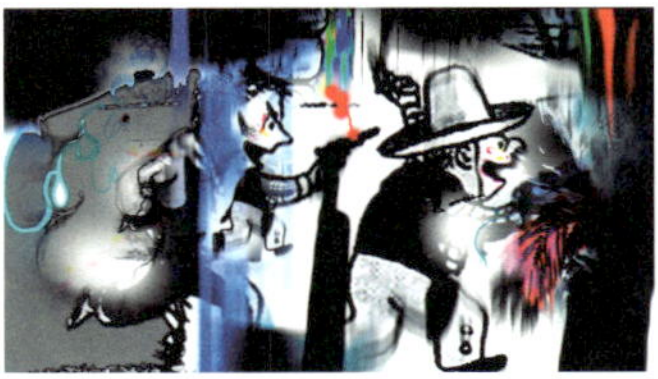
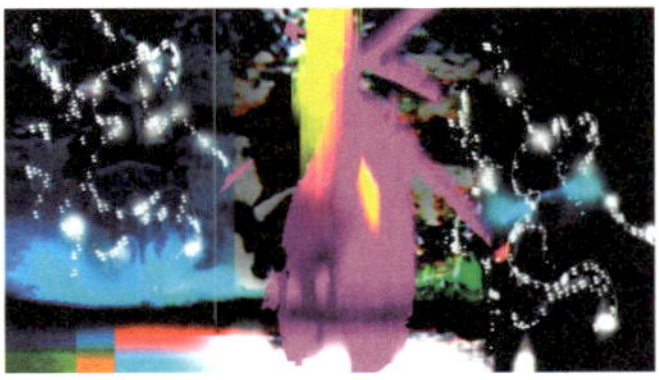

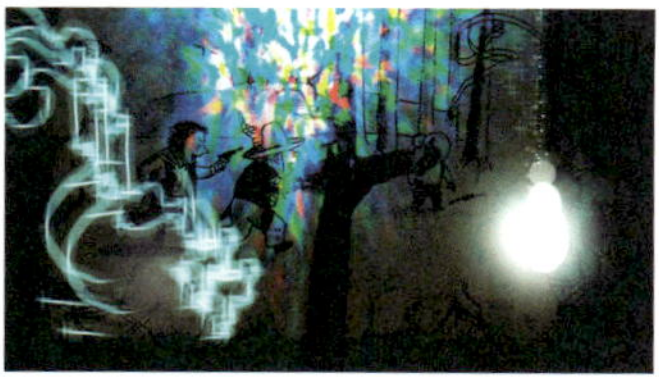
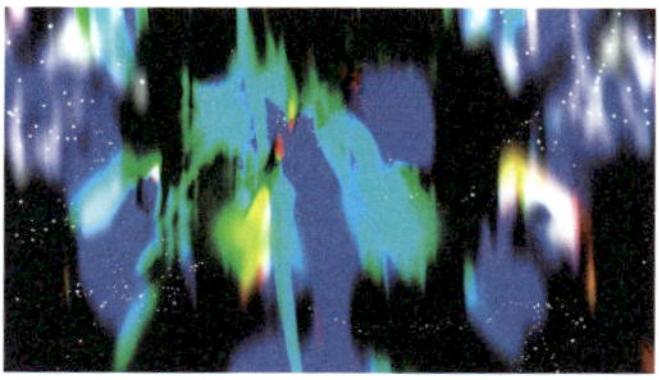
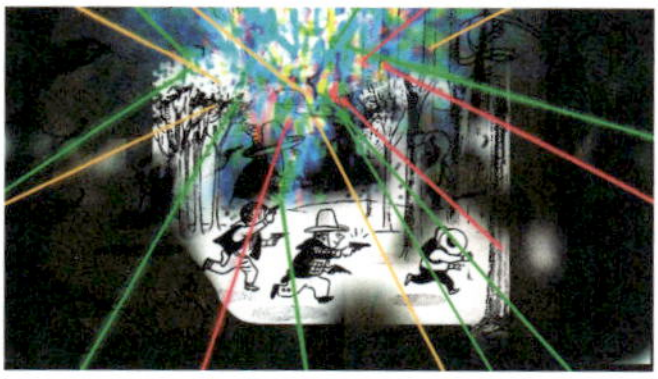
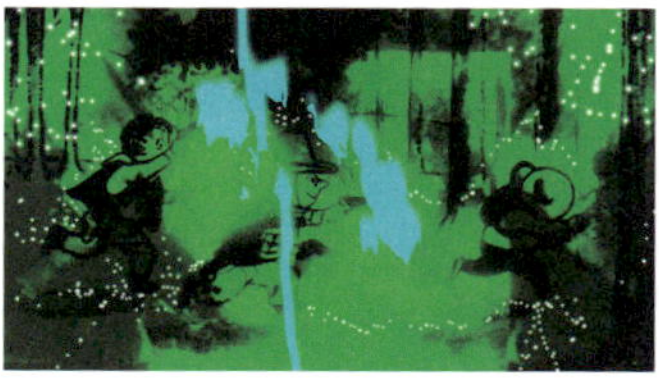
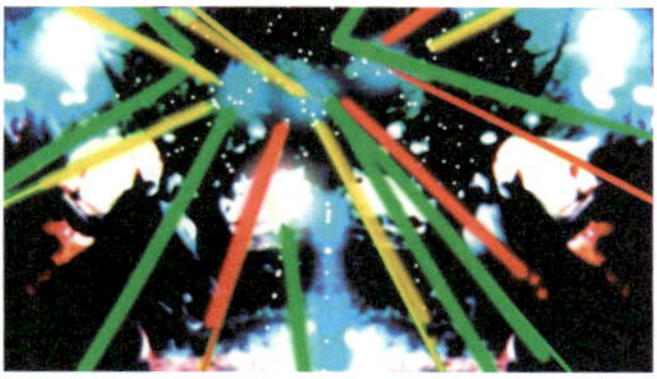
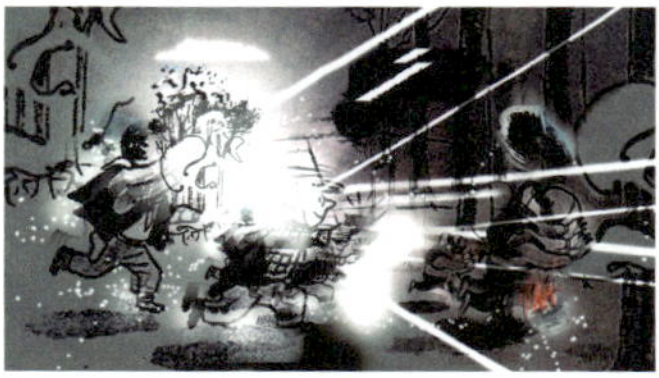
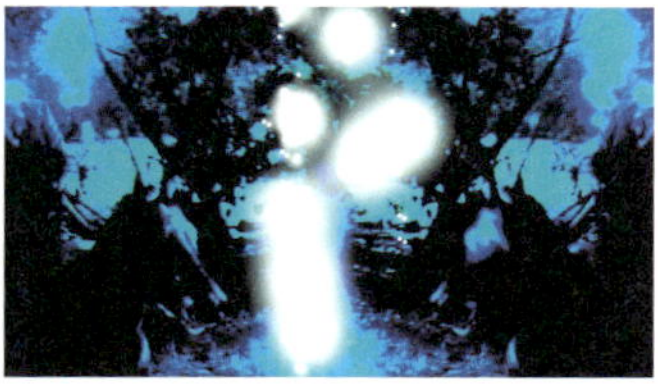
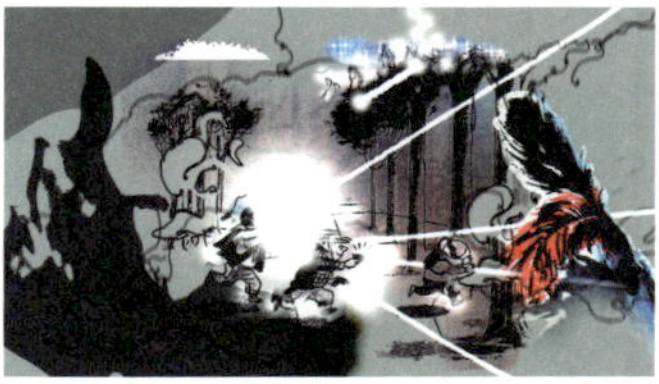
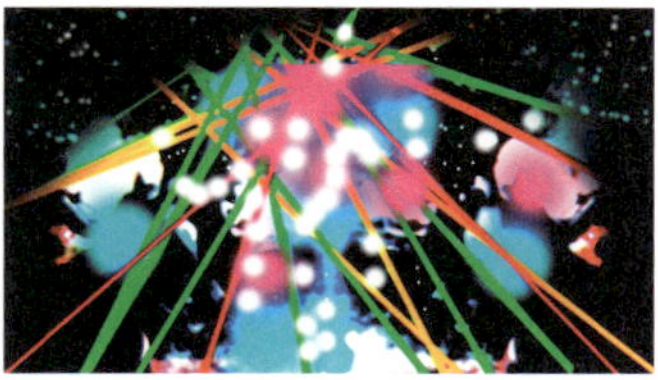
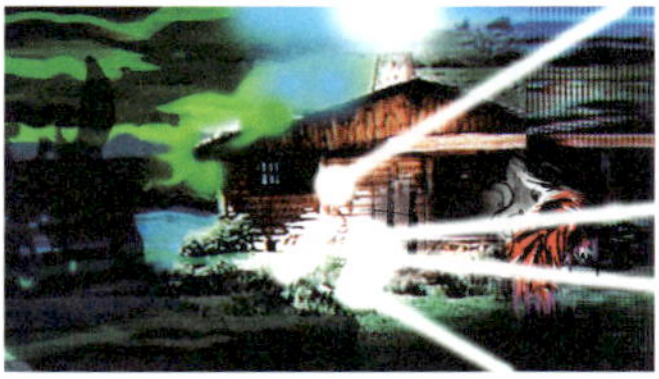
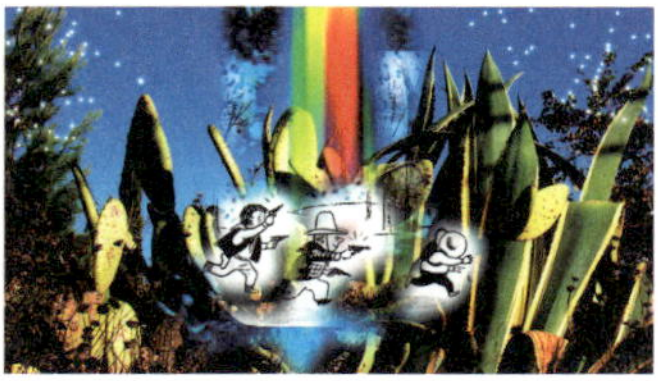
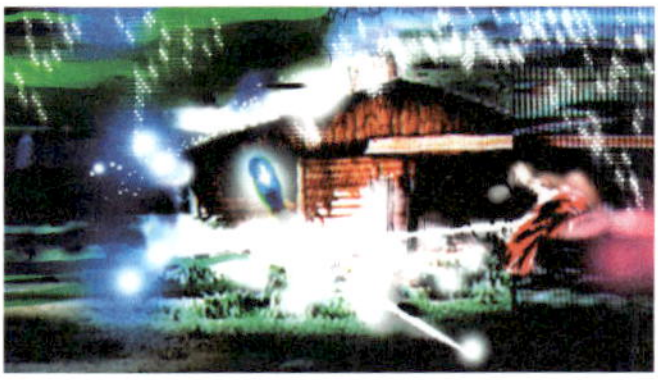

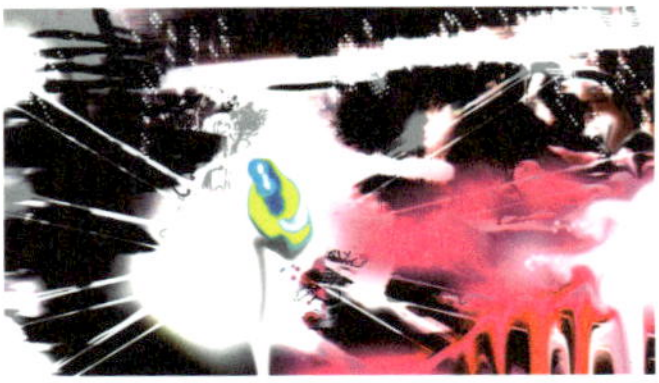
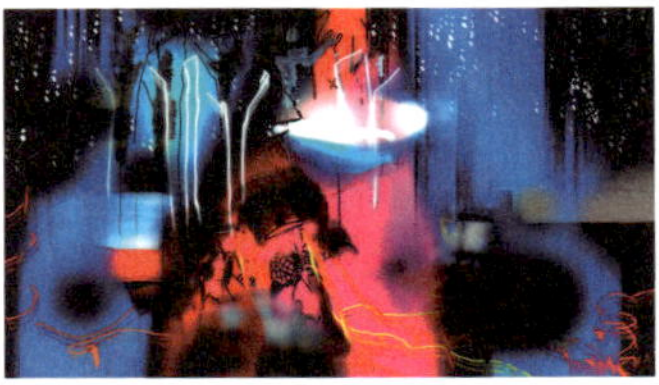
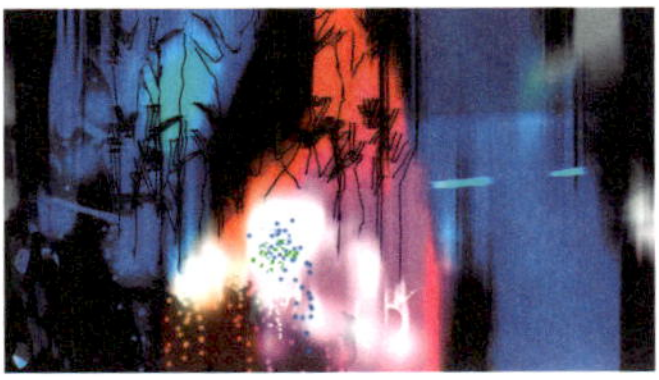
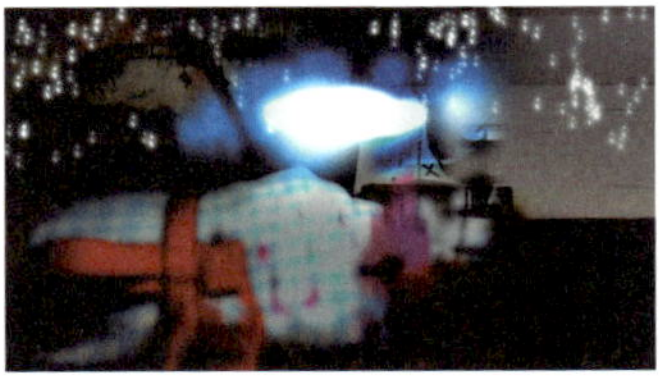
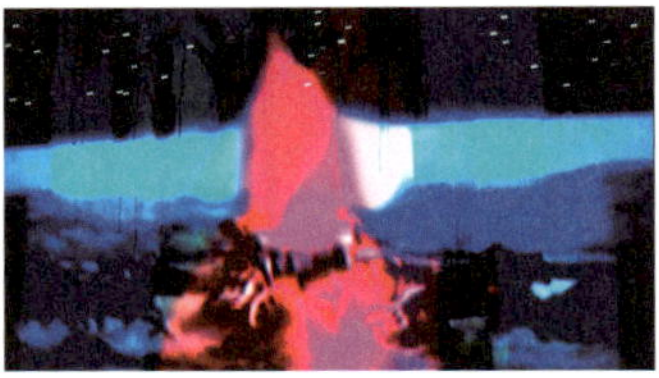
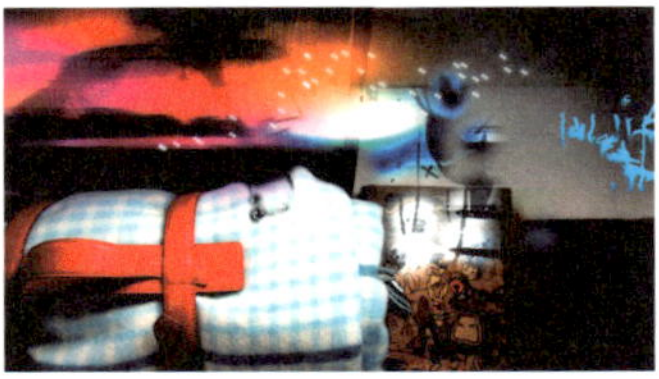
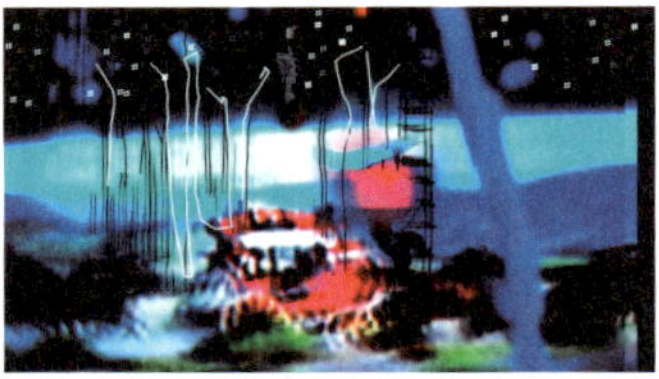
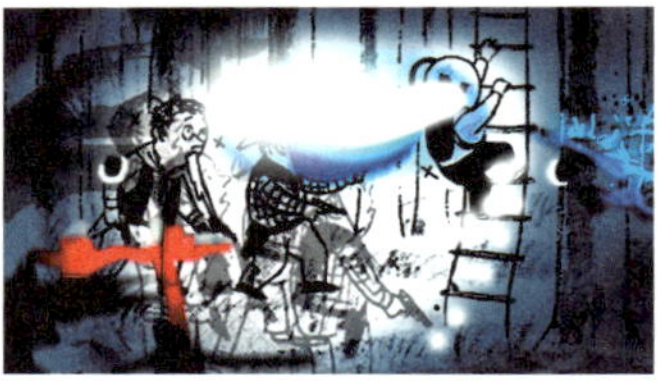
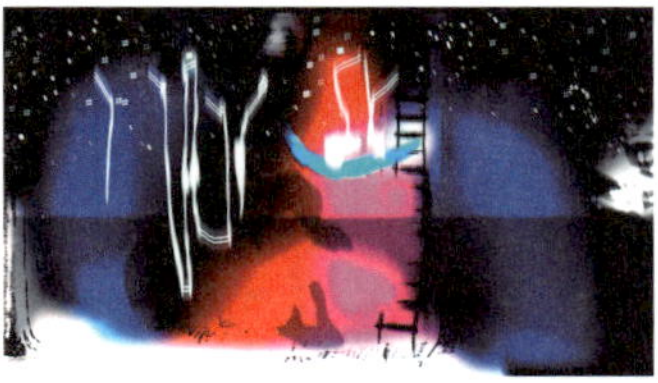
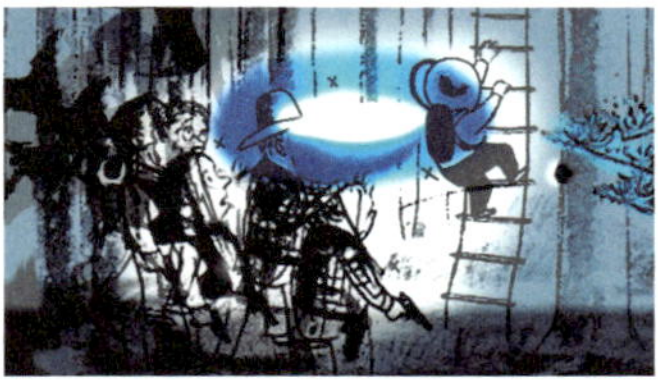
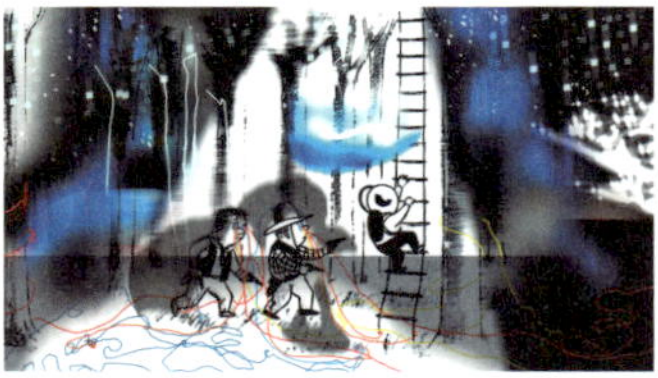
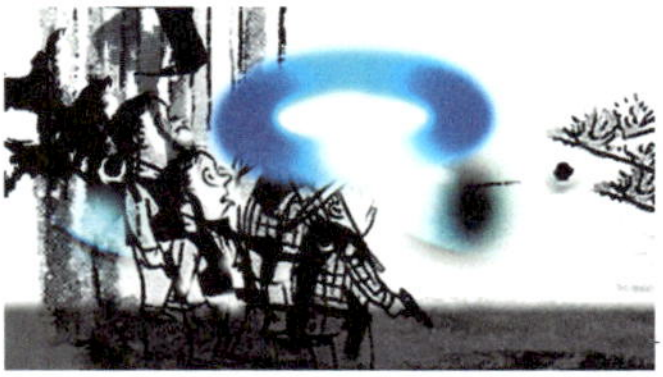

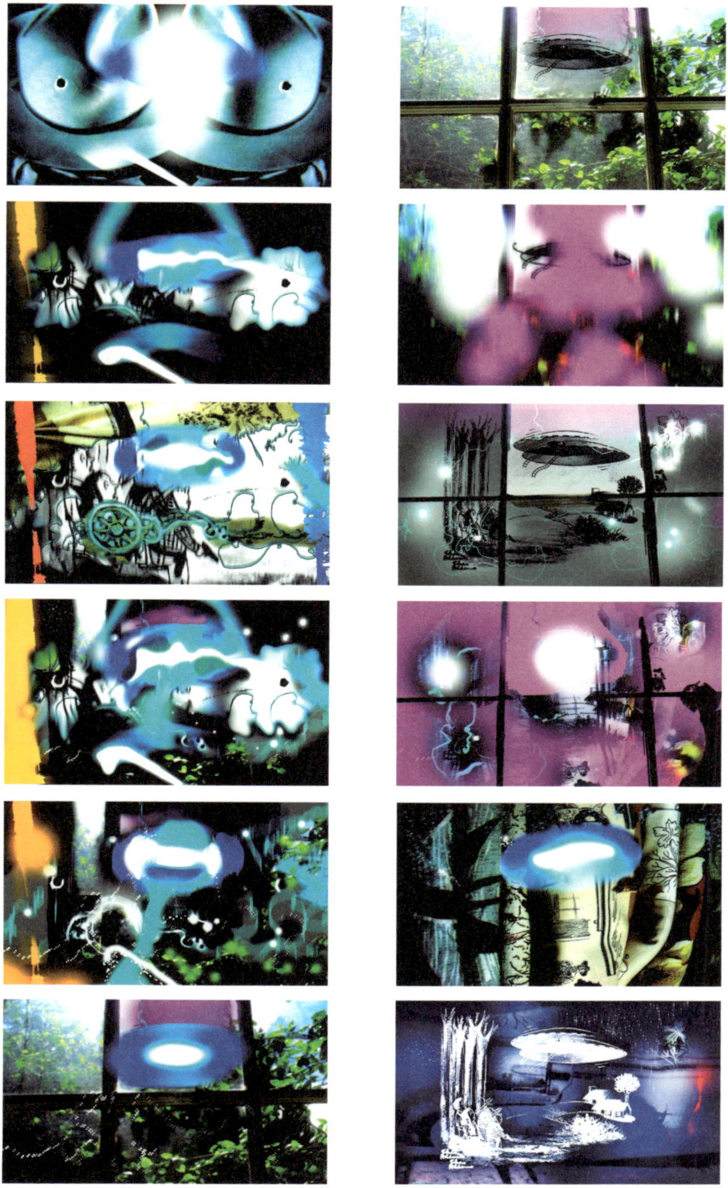

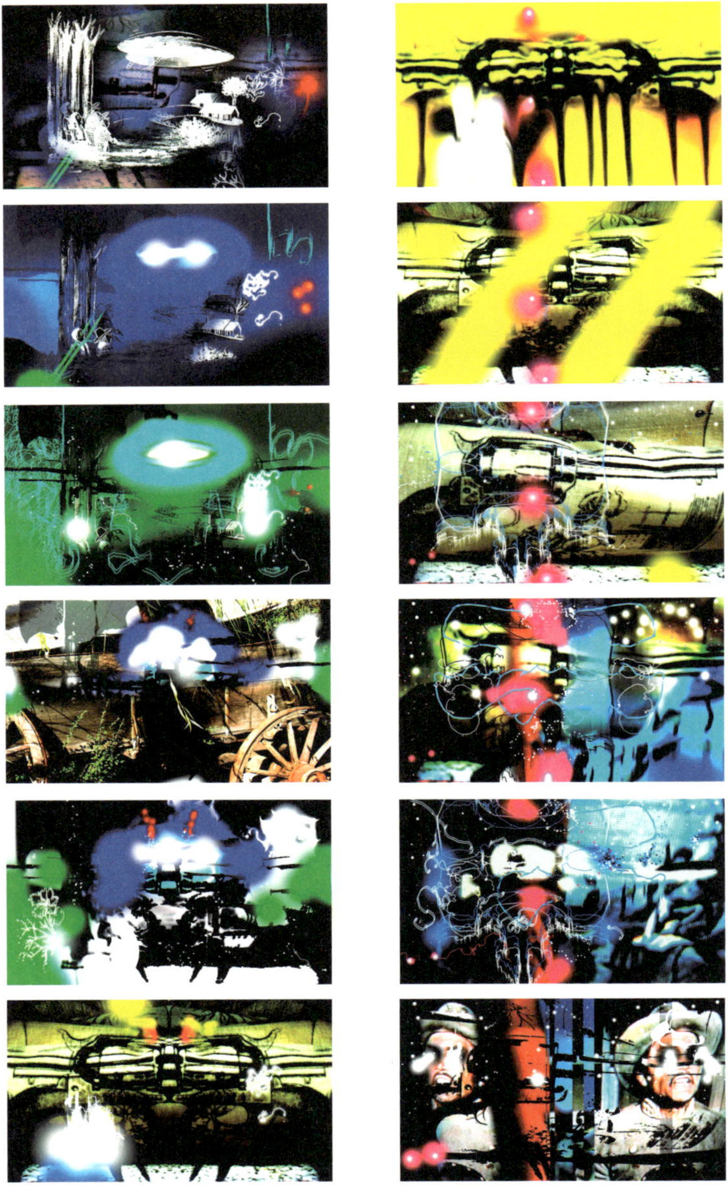

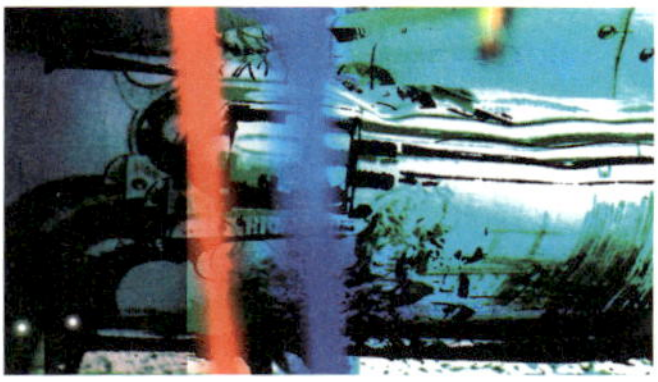

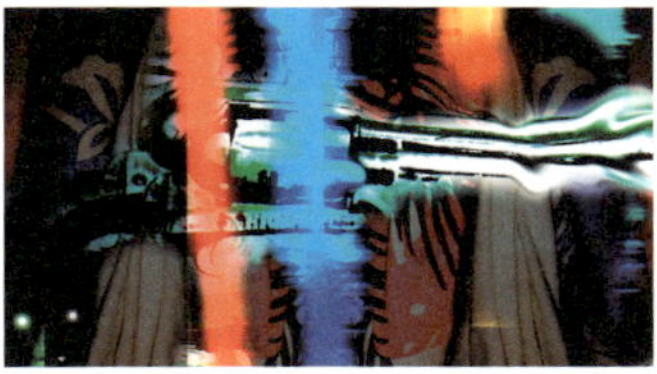

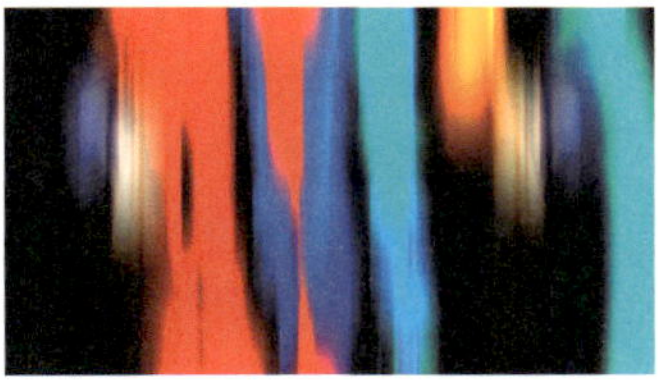

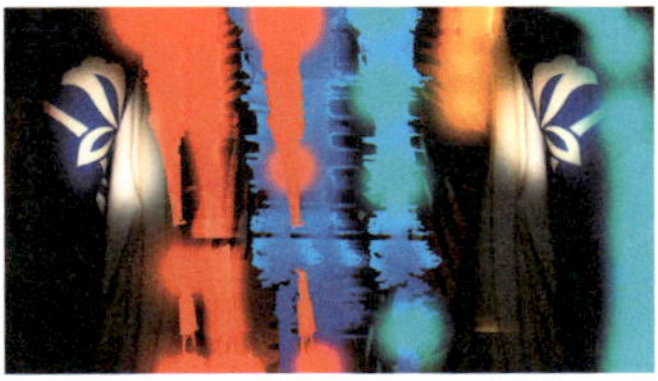

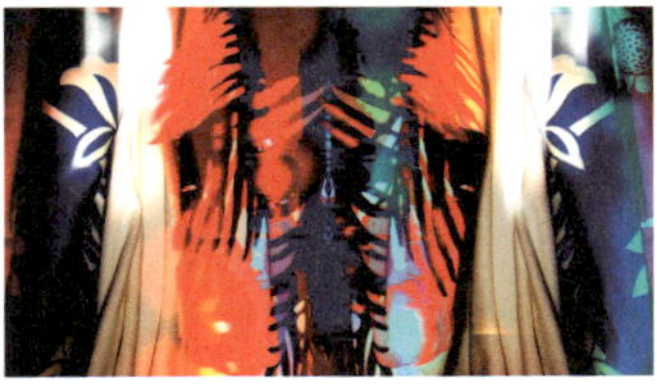

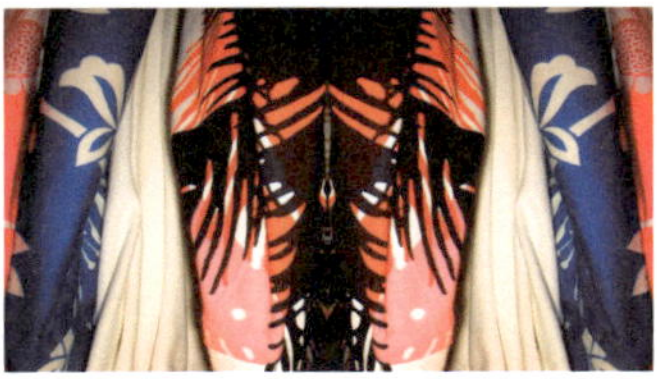

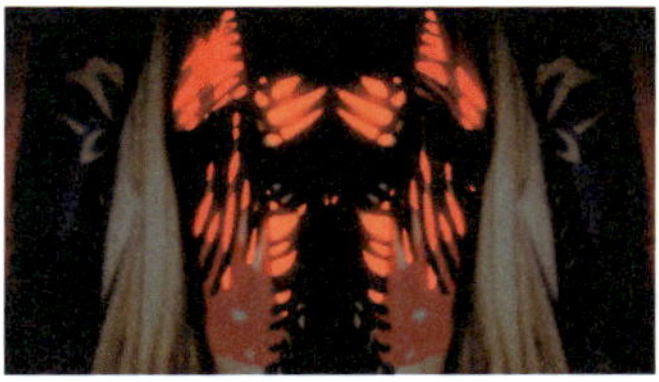

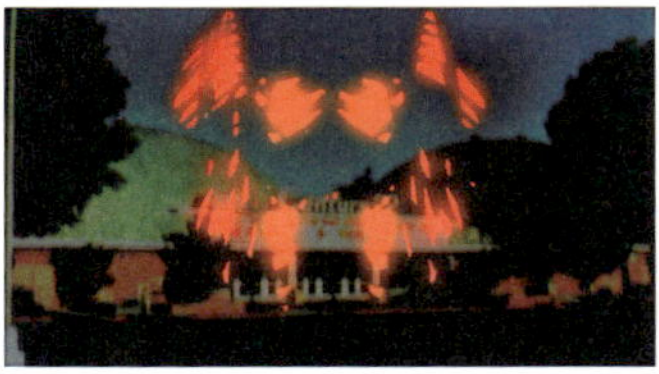

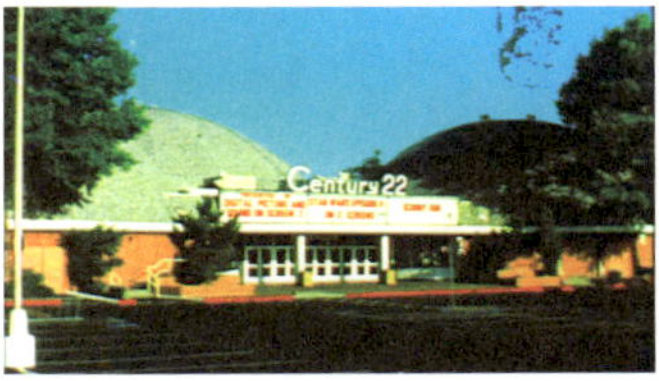
Century 22

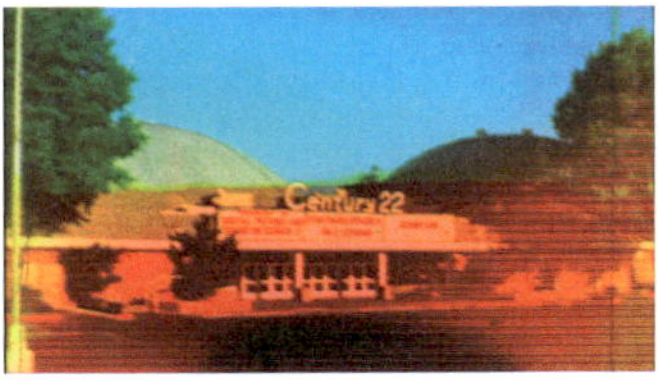
Century 22

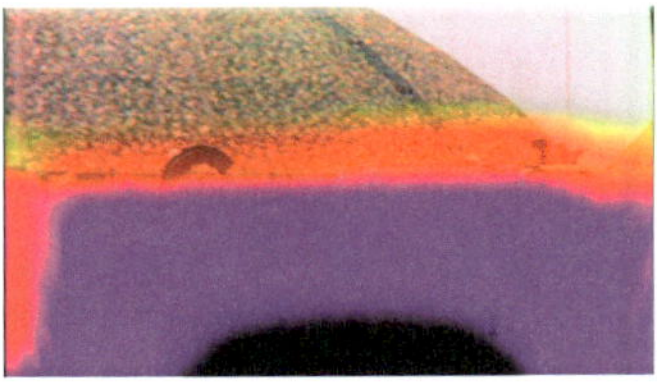

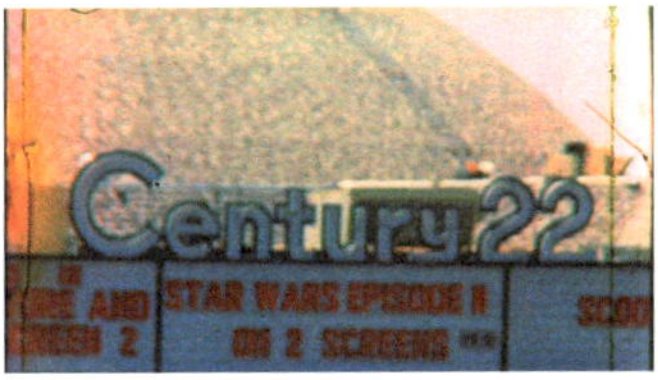
Century 22
STAR WARS EPISODE II
ON 2 SCREENS

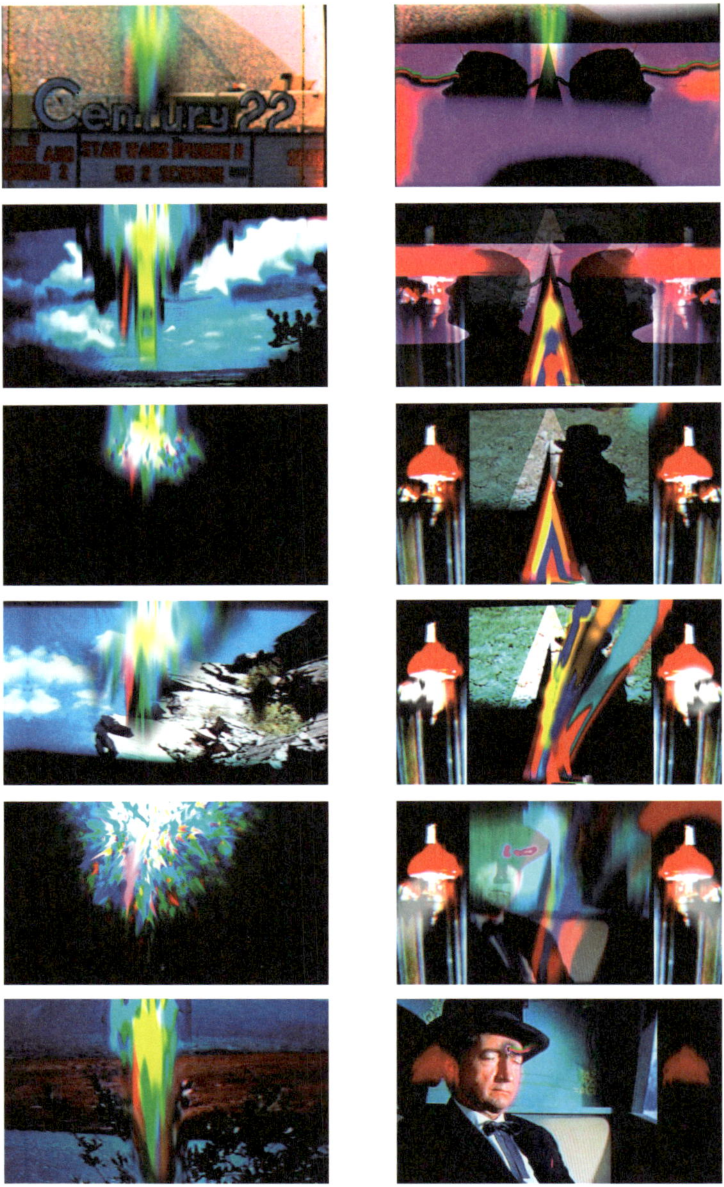
Century 22

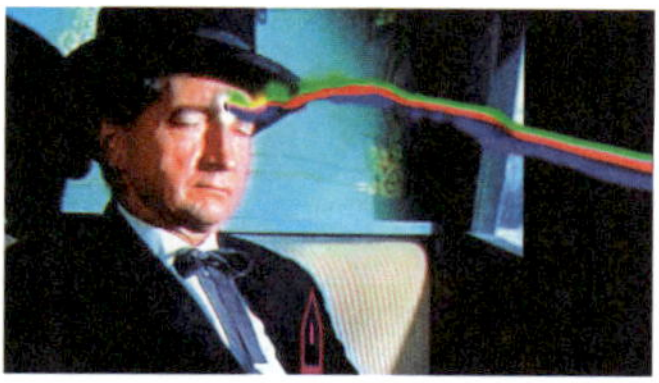
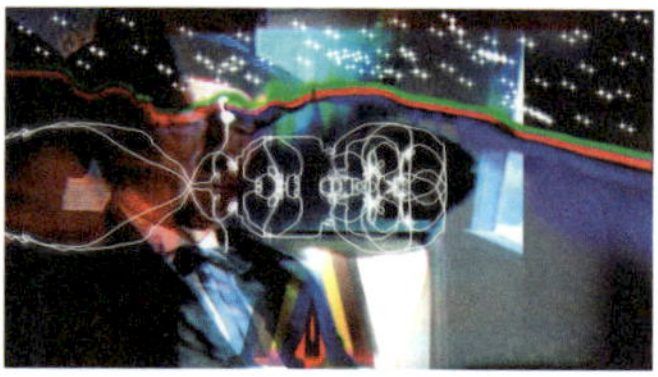
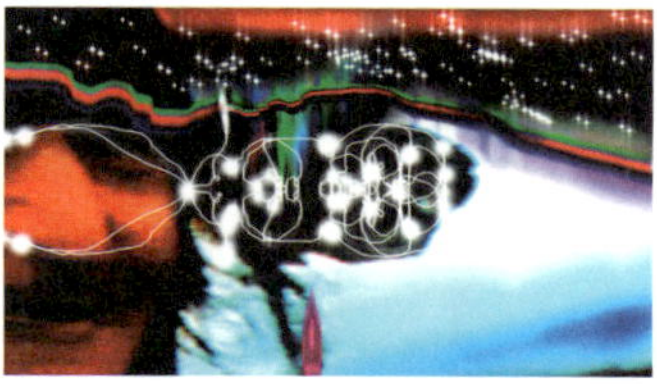
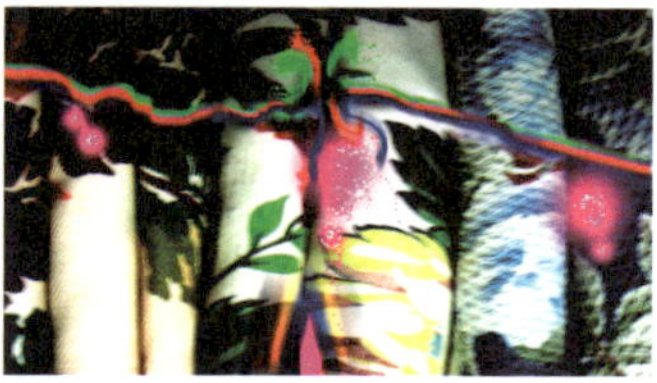
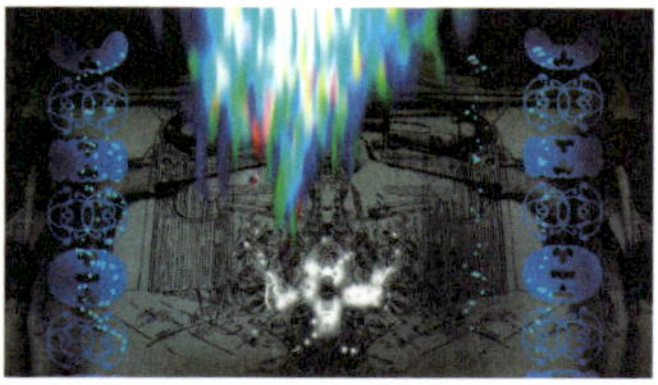
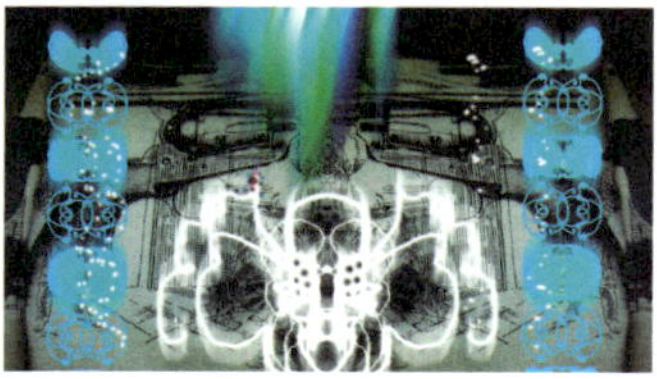
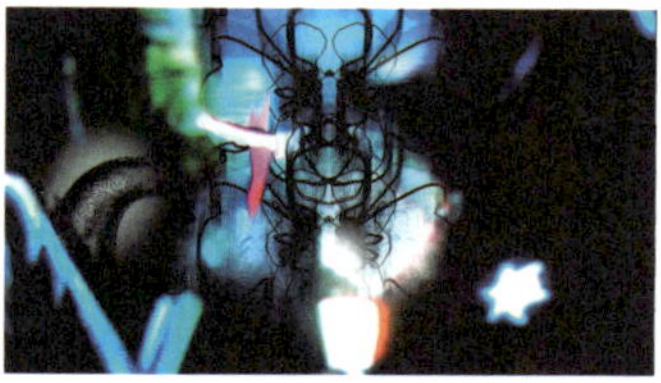
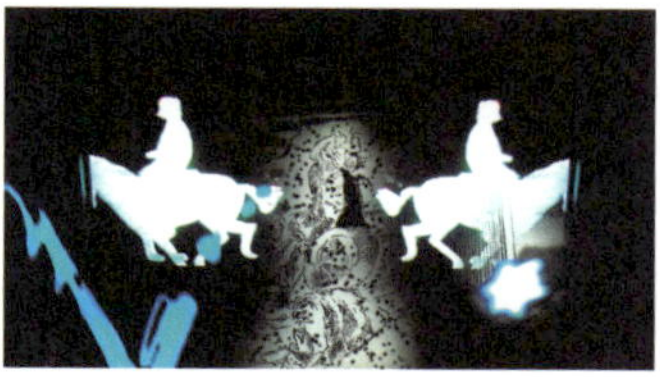
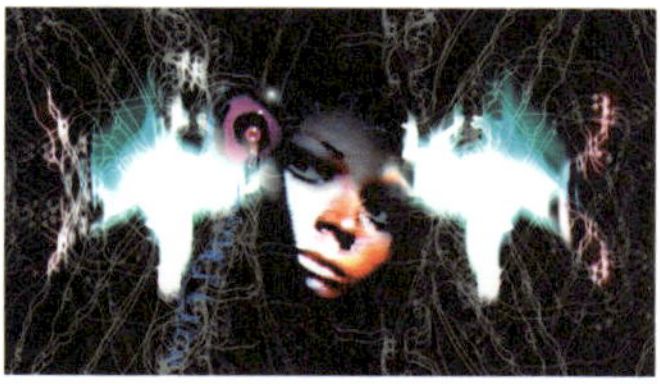
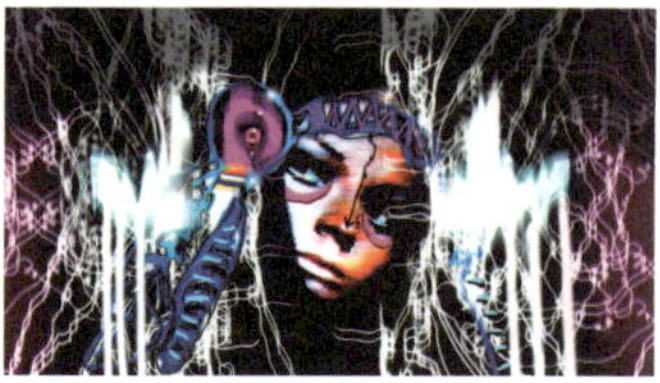
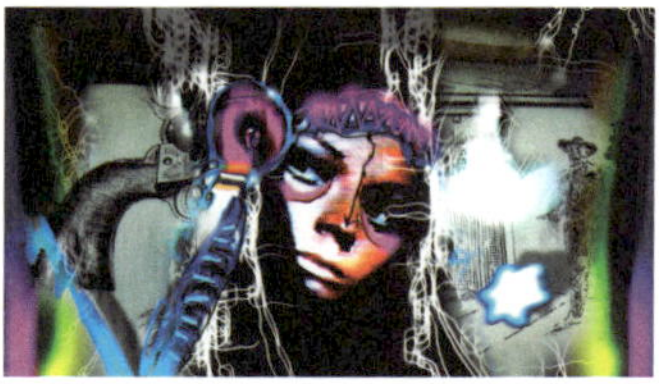
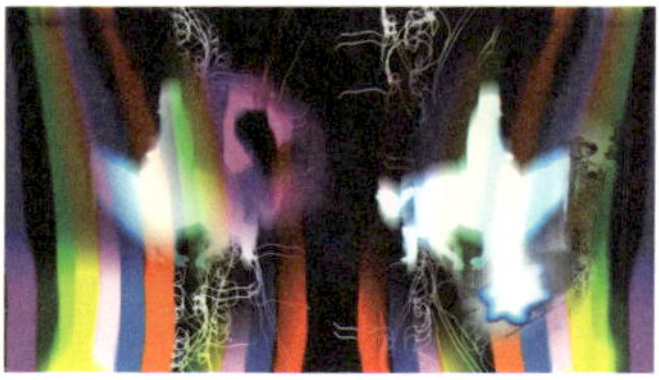

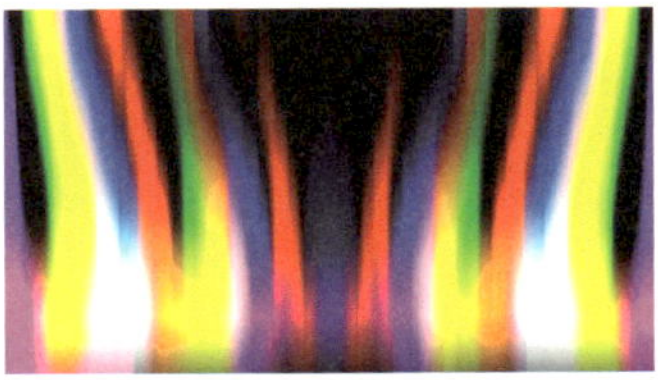
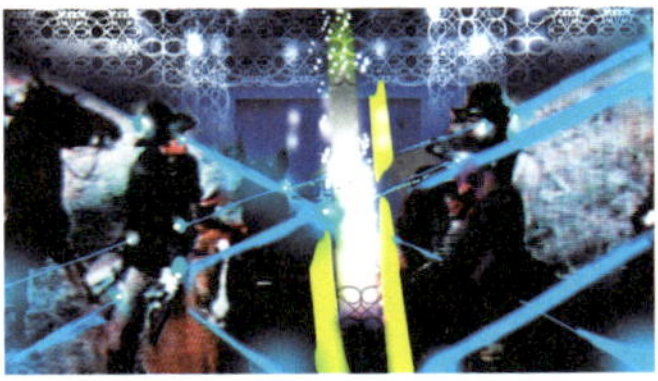
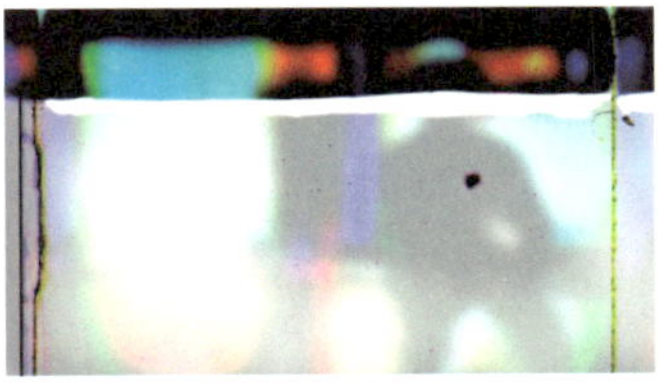
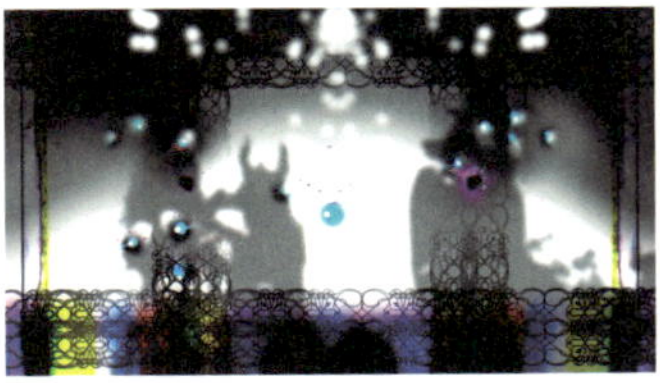
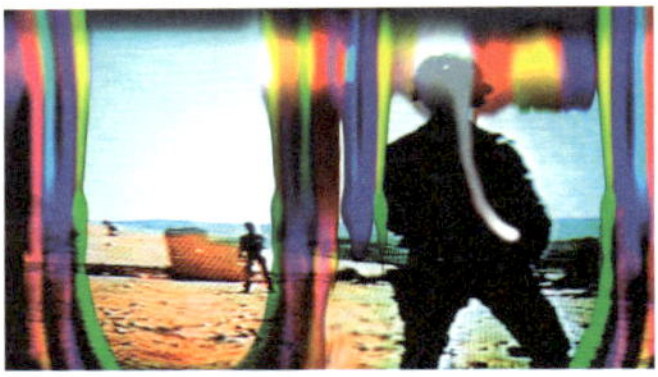
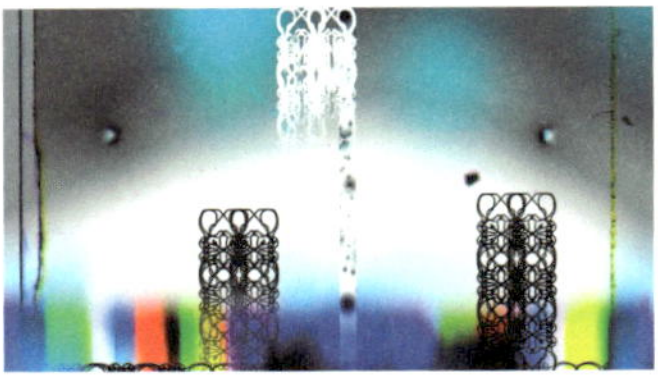
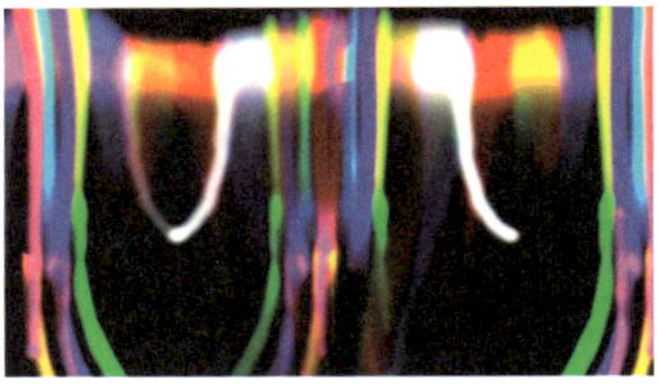
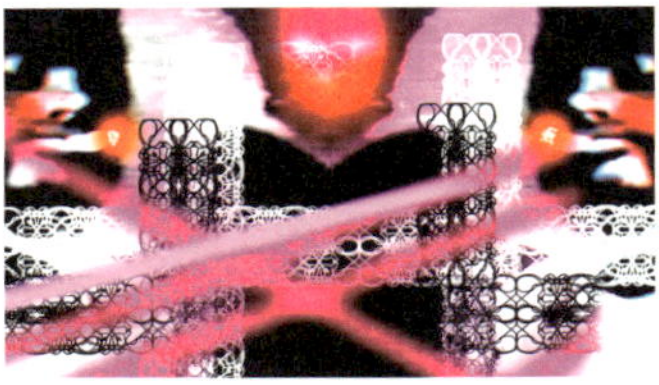
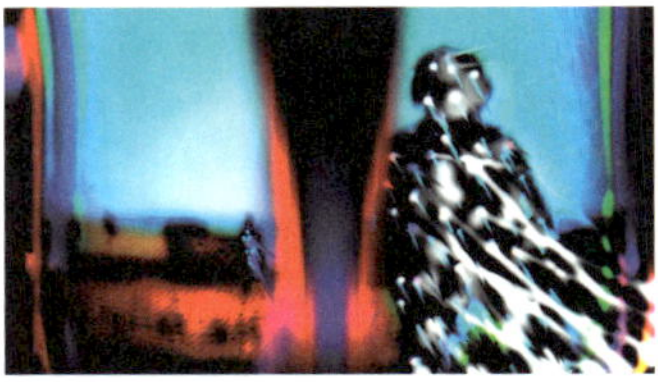
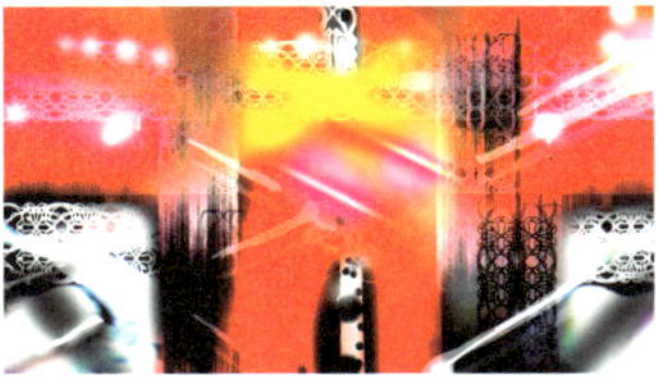
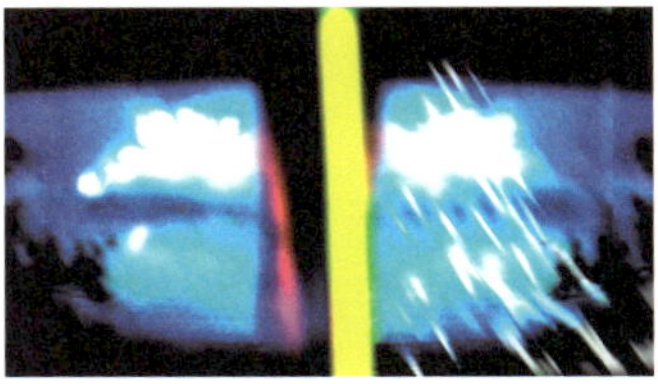
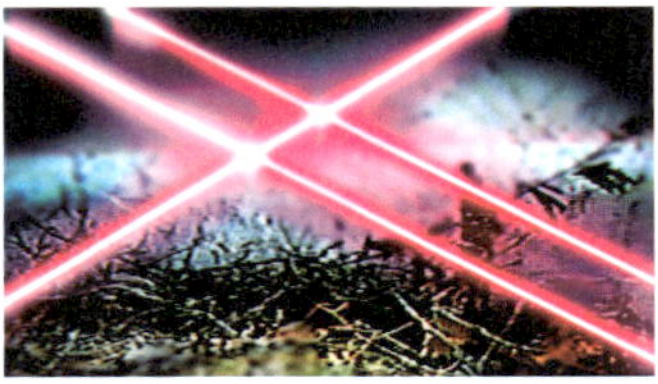

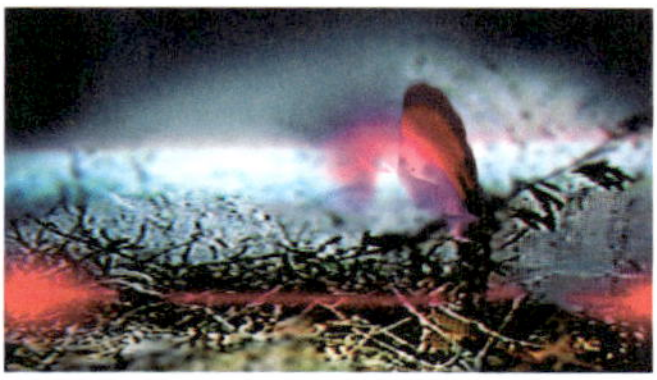
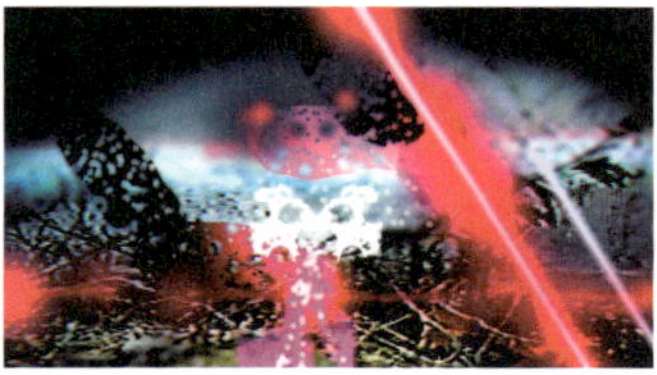
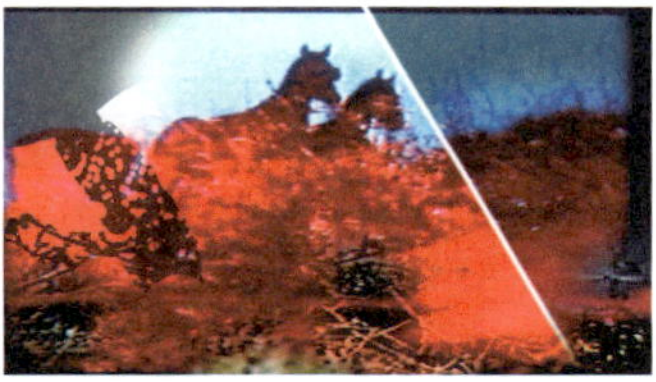
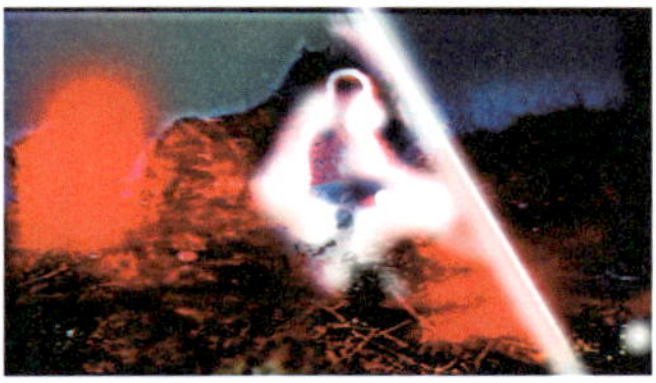
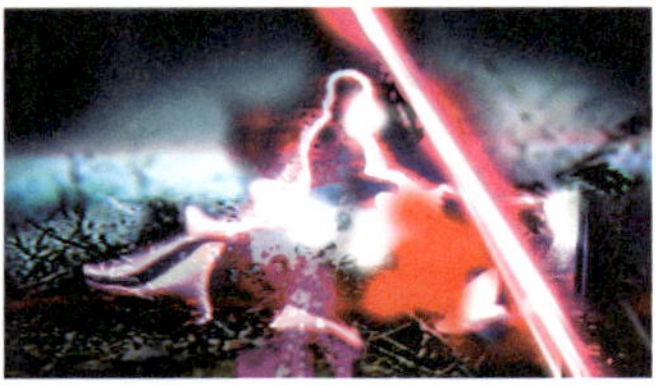
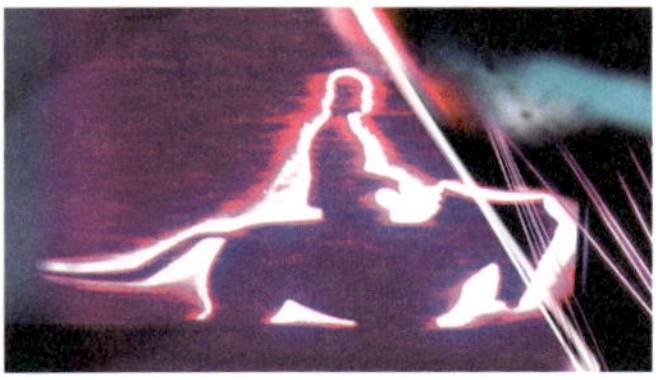
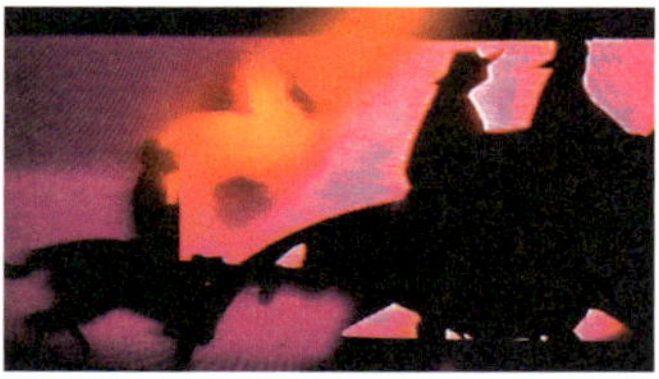
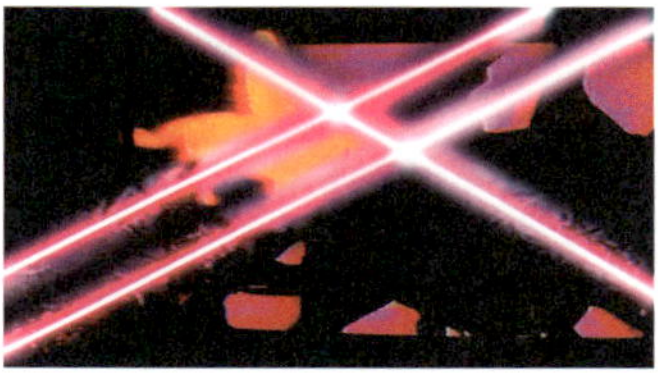
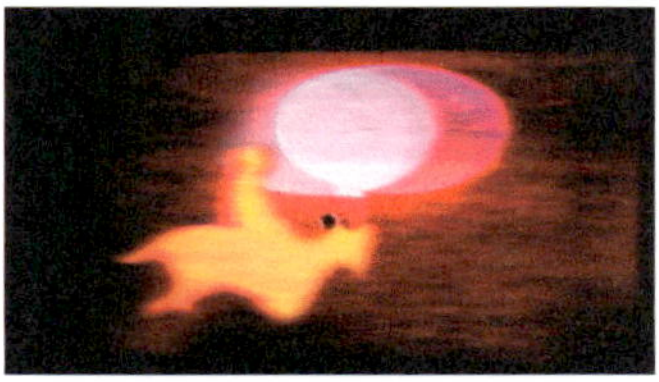
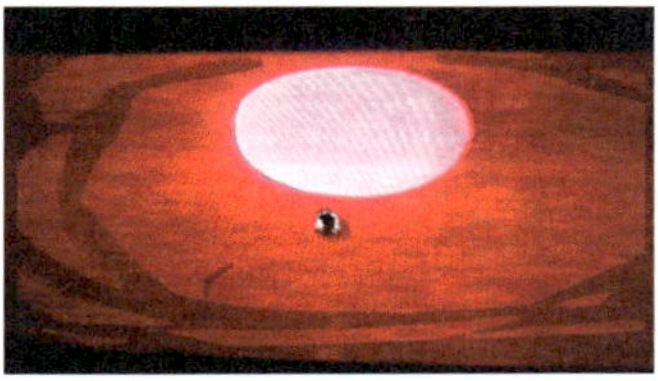
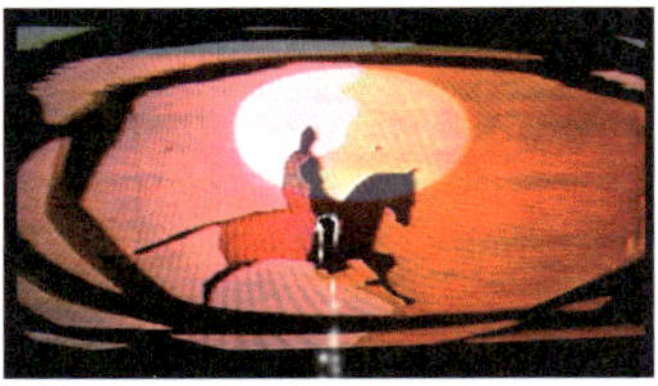
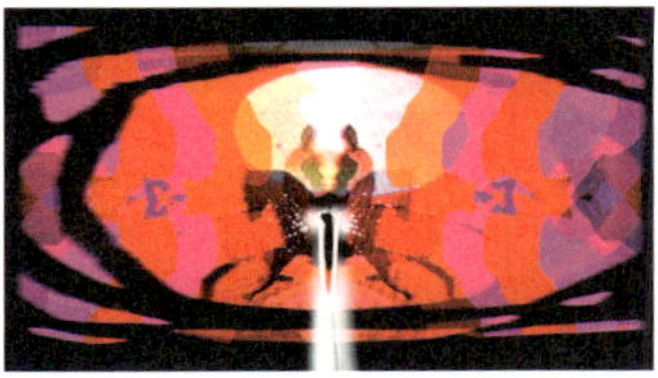

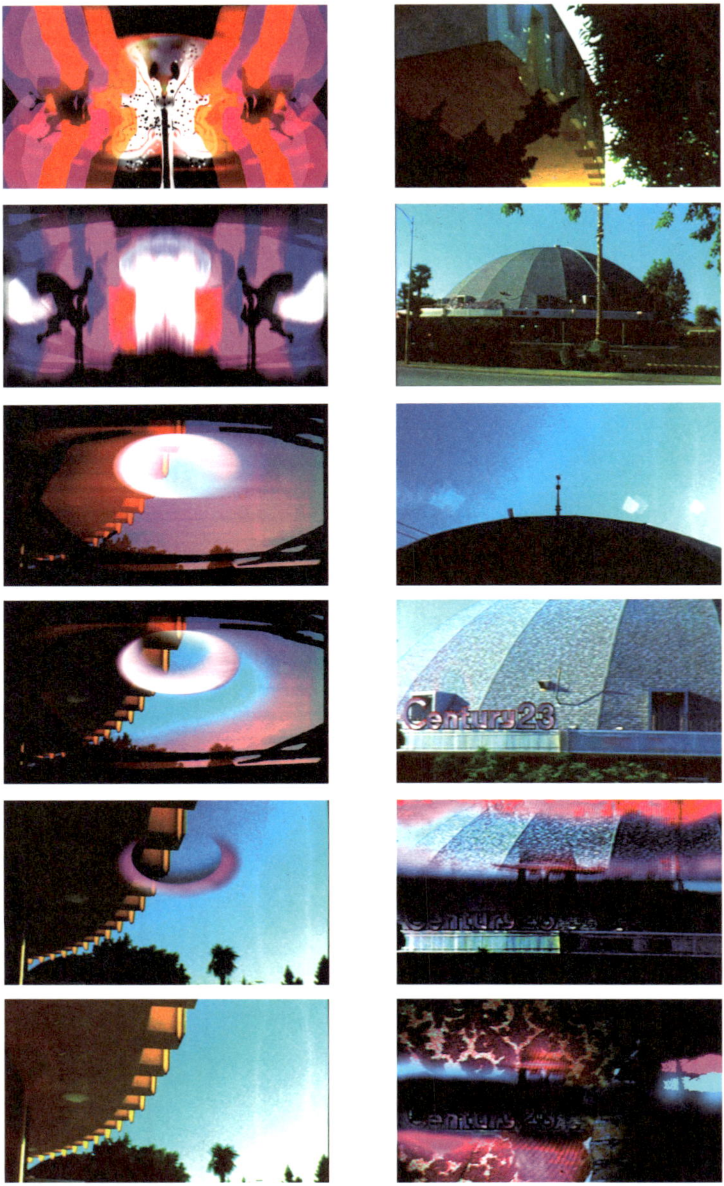
Century23

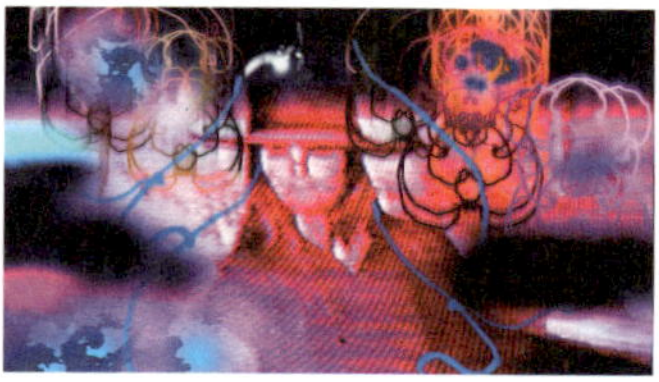
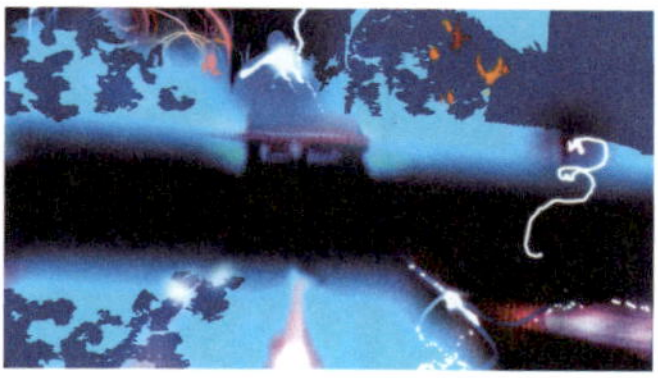
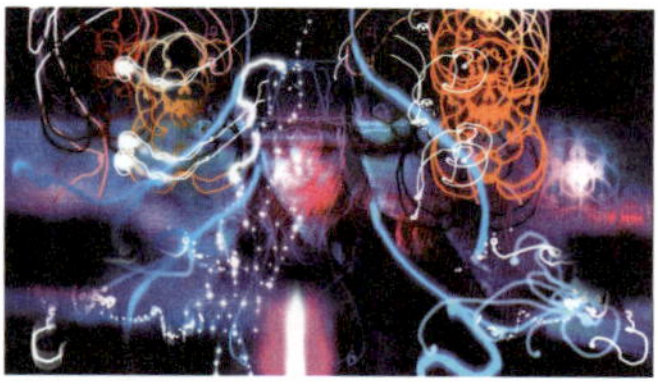
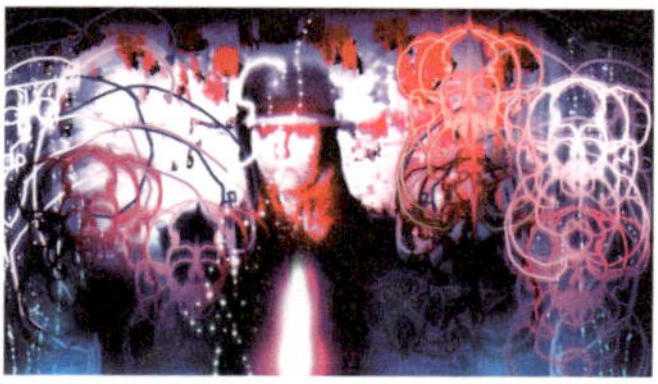
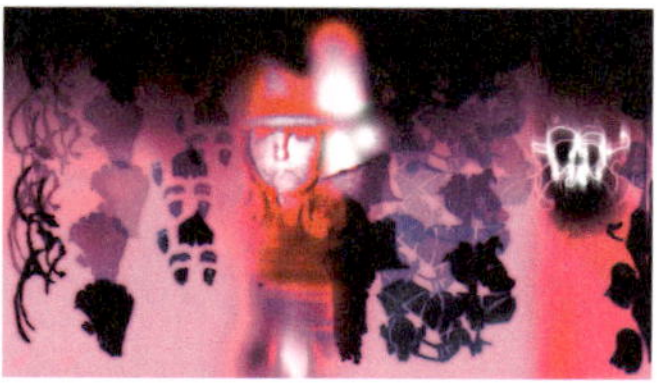
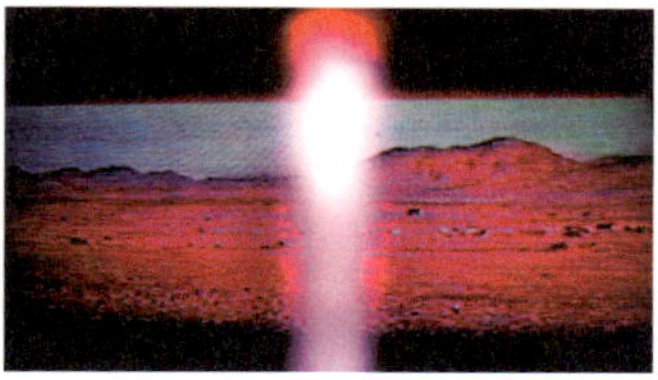
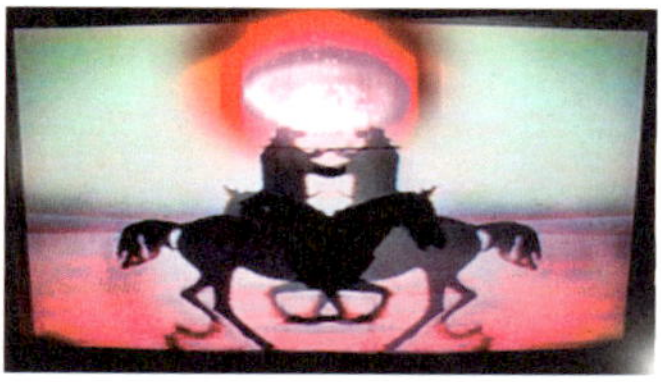
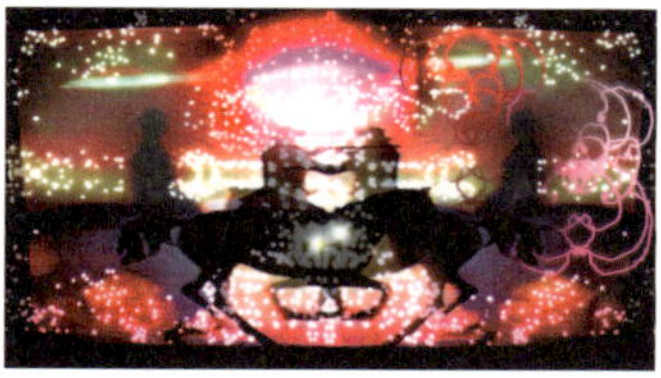
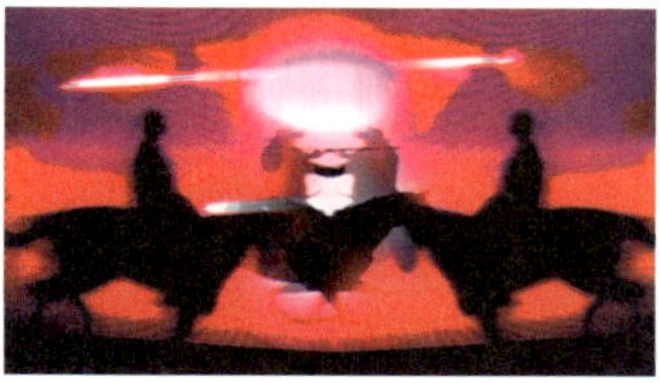
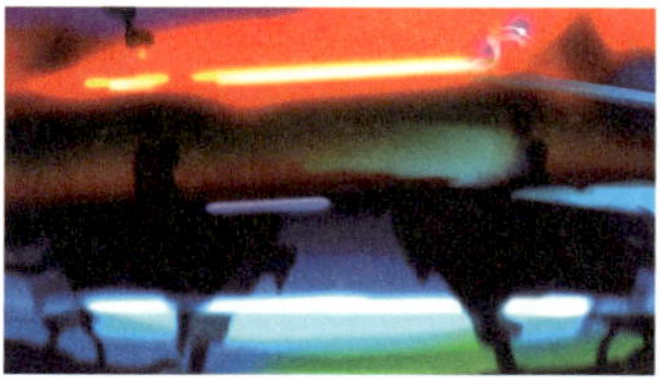
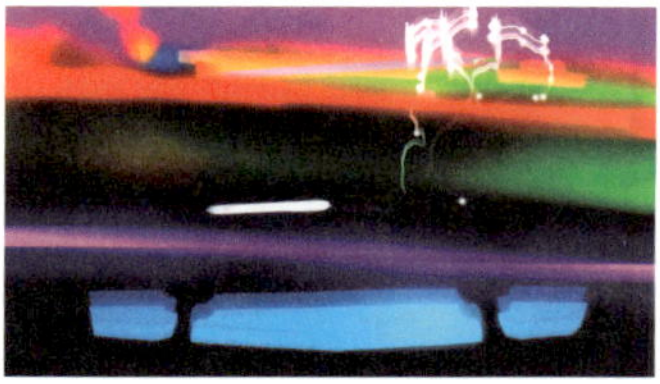
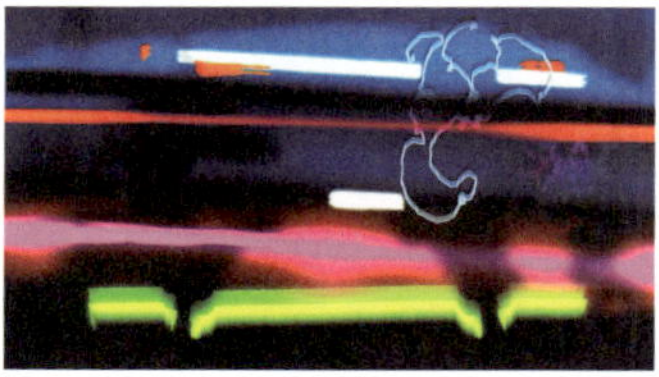

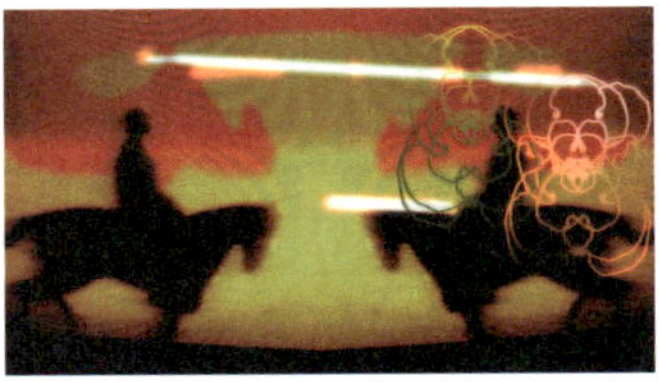
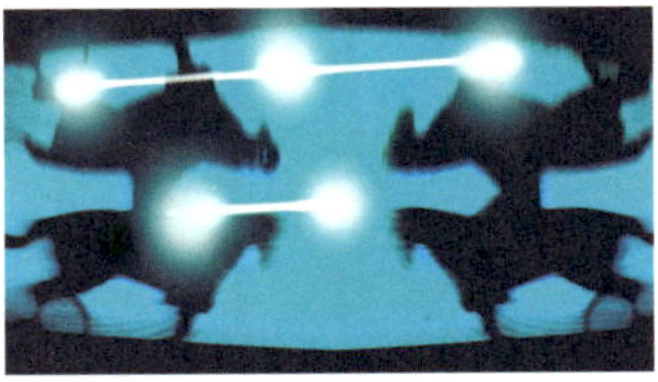
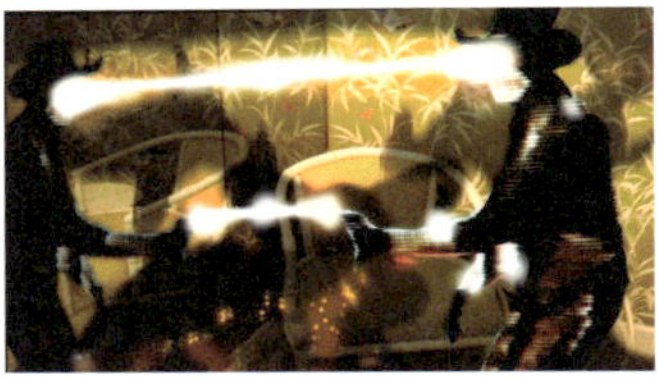
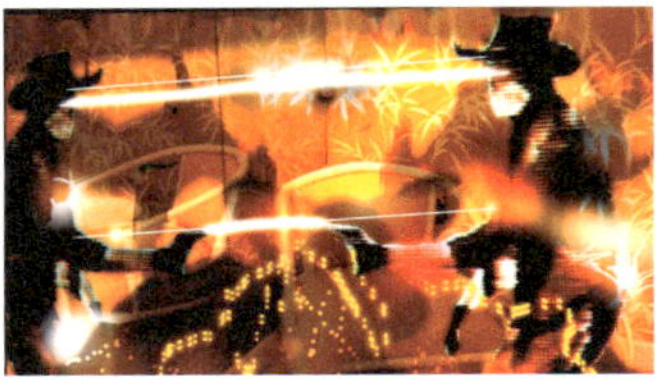
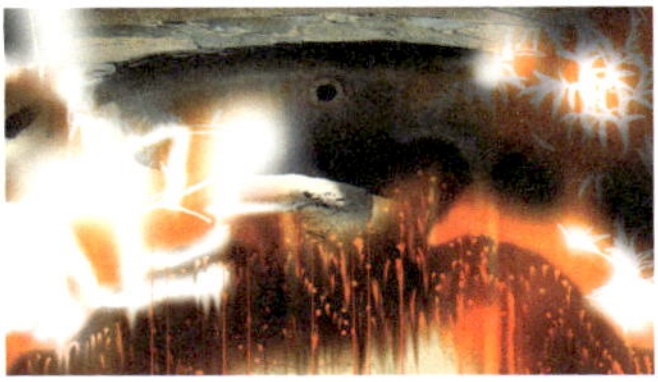
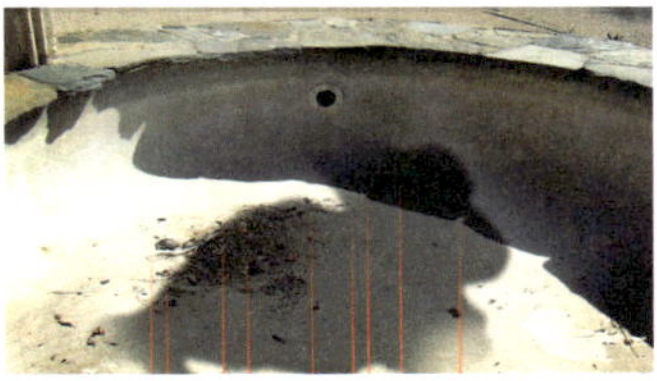
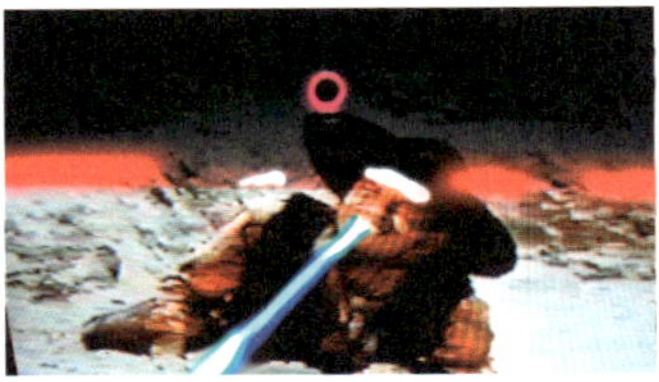
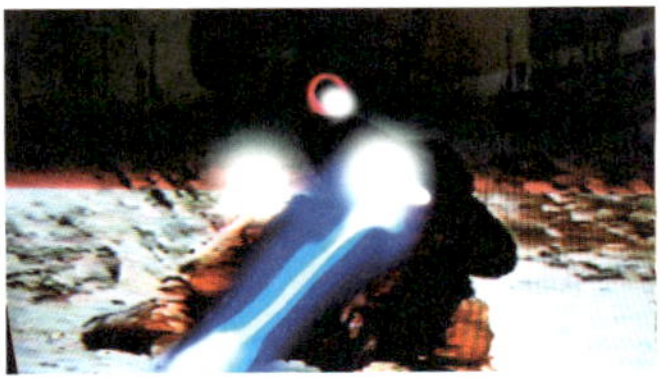
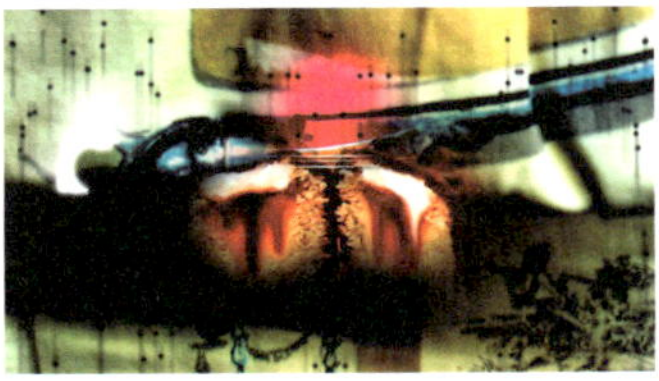
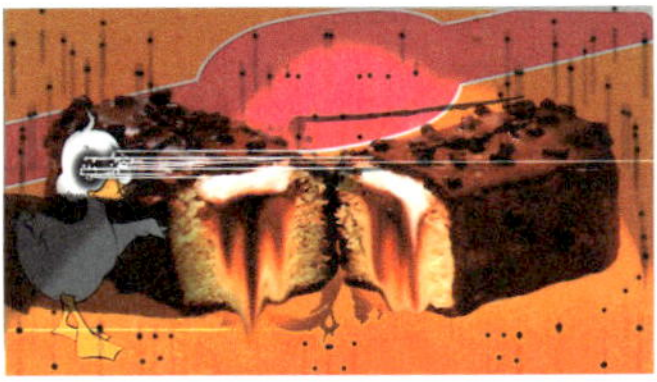
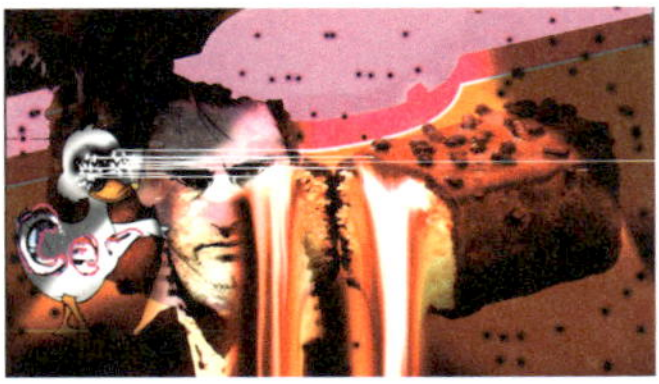
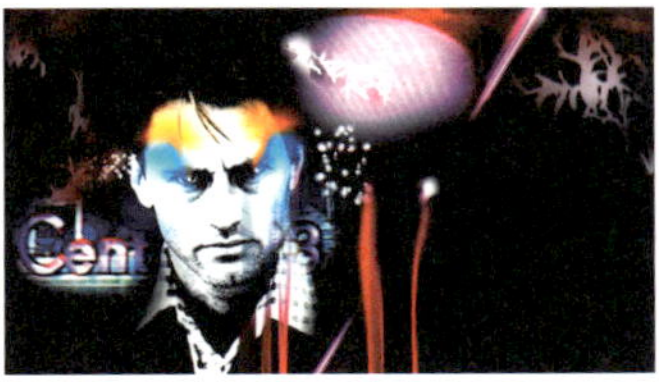

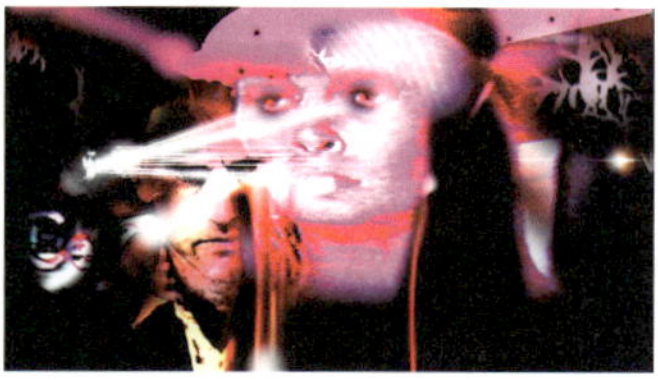
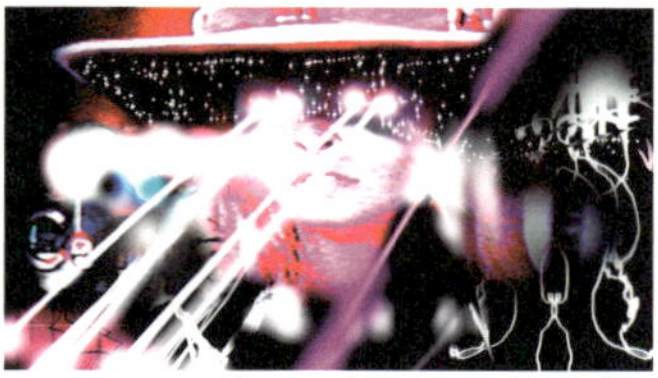
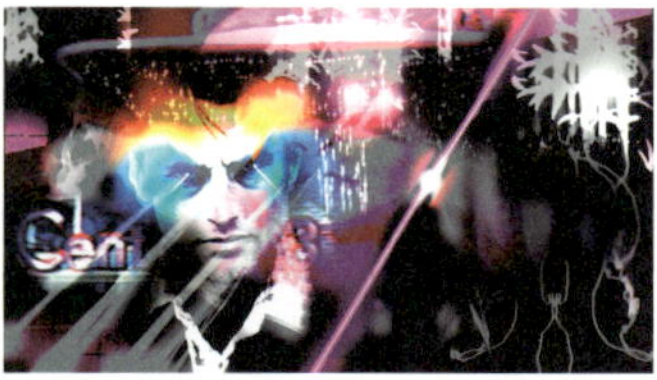
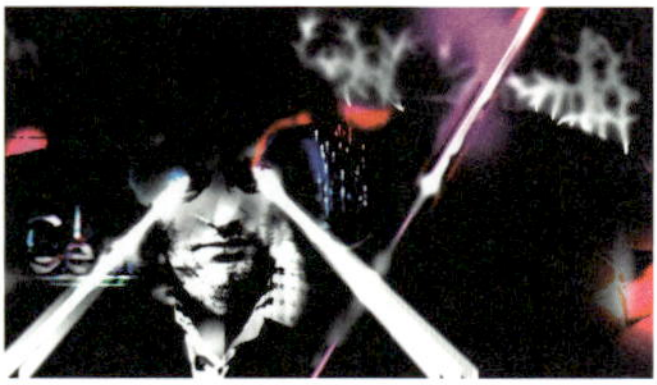
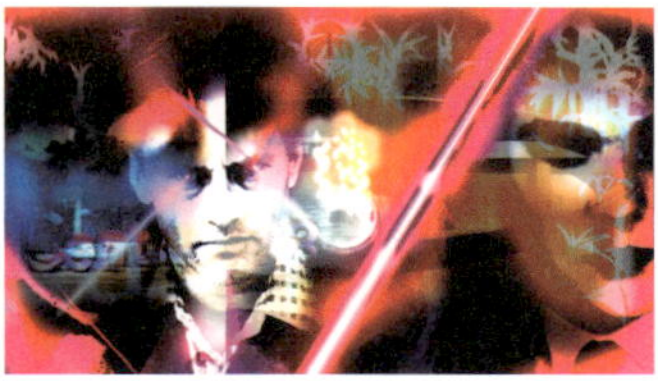
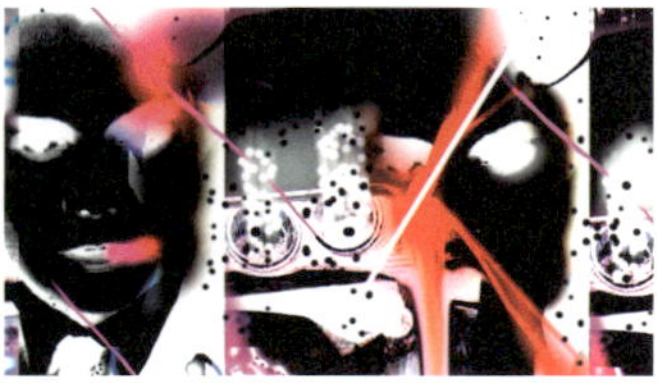
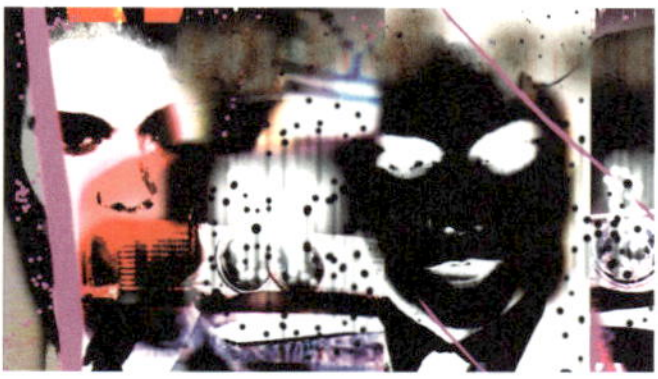
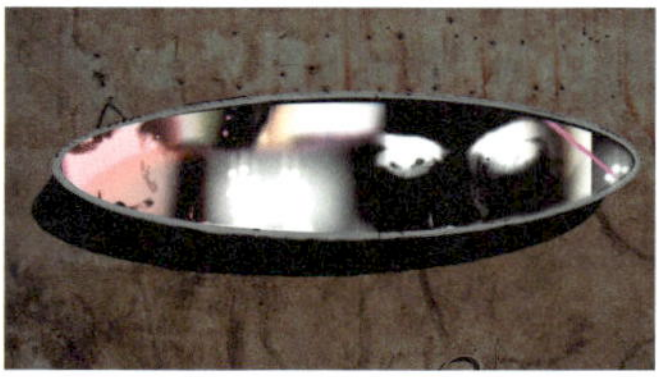
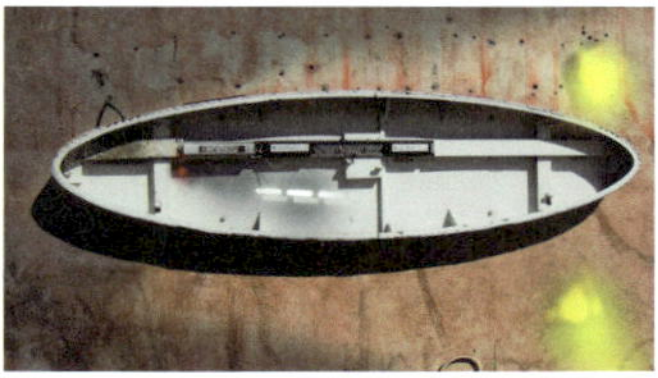
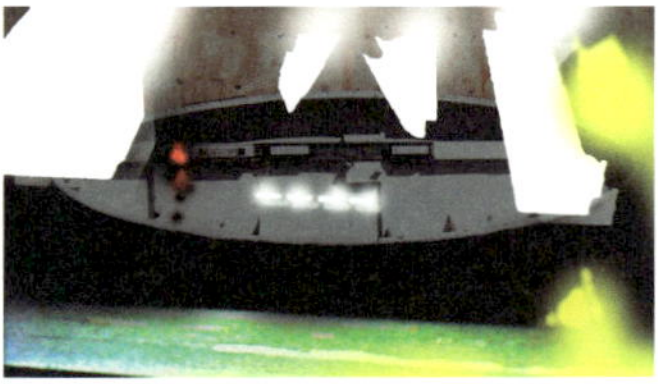
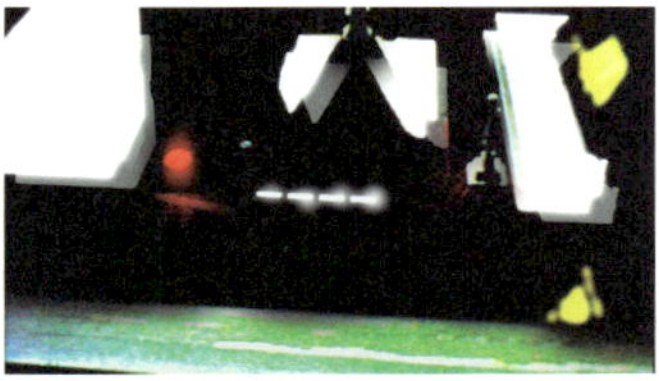
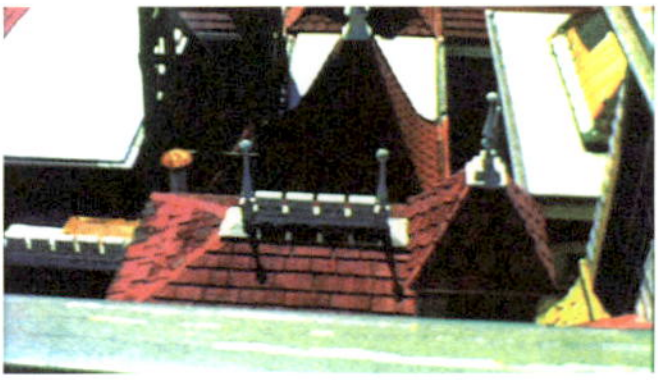

END

The Face of the Enemy

One never inherits without coming to terms with some specter, and therefore with more than one specter.

—Jacques Derrida, *Specters of Marx*

The host [hôte] *is a hostage insofar as he is a subject put into question, obsessed (and thus besieged), persecuted in the very place where he takes place, where, as emigrant, exile, stranger, a guest* [hôte] *from the very beginning, he finds himself elected to or taken up by a residence* [élu à domicile] *before himself electing or taking up one* [élire domicile].

—Jacques Derrida, *Adieu: To Emmanuel Levinas*

Is Sarah Winchester's destiny to remain the property of a tourist attraction? Is her lesson to be held hostage to its ghost stories? Paying admission over and over, can we afford not to settle Sarah Winchester's debt since it continues to mortgage us through inheritance to the profit of some and damage to others? But can we absolve Winchester of the crime of her tainted inheritance through the trick of a posthumous analytical cure in which she cannot participate, as convincing as its narrative may be? Can we force a secret that vacillates in contraries, returning one mystery after another to settle secreted in us? Anyway, could I claim authorship for discovery? How am I to know, any more than Sarah Winchester in her building mania, that mine might otherwise be a ghostwritten text, the continuing communication of haunting? Strangely, my address demands other responses as I become entangled in her story and implicated in its complicity. Winchester's story is no longer personal to her, but to the two of us: that is to say to her and me, but also me and you. Her expiation is also a matter of how we witness and testify to it.

In truth, all we can examine here are symptoms without a subject: the cinema-architecture of Winchester house. Incorporating a complex set of symptoms inherited from its surrounding culture, the house haunts once more, awakened by an artist's visit, transmitting again by way of Jeremy Blake's *Trilogy*—one cinema-architecture responding to another. A continuous parade of images and seemingly no examination, merely a spectral speculation, *The Winchester Trilogy* melds the material artifact of an eccentric architecture, Hollywood's hallucinated simulacra, and the mythic patterns of popular culture. All are social facts, together a telling mix, and each more susceptible to analysis than a secret housed within an antique relic of the past. Stemming from individual intentions, something made, something imaged, or something practiced in action, in their totality, are collective representations. We apprehend them through what they visibly present to us; however, while we respond to them, submerged within a collectivity (the condition also of myth), we assume no individual responsibility for what we share in them. Disavowed, they still lead to action. But what of an act of expiation—how do we apprehend or represent it? How does Winchester house make expiation visible, the act toward which it was built, the act it is itself? The house can neither represent it nor be its symbol. Expiation is no haunting yielding a hallucinated image; expiation is response to the call of haunting. (A direct response to the other, expiation issues no supplemental explanatory statement for the benefit of third-party witnesses.) An act, which is not just building construction, *makes* it real, makes it *this* act of expiation, makes it *real* while being something that has no visible presence. Expiation is as invisible as whatever may be there of debt, obligation, promise, or excuse in Winchester house—and they may all equally reside there. This house was the contradictory response to a demand placed on Sarah Winchester, a thirty-eight-year expiation of a debt that her marriage mortgaged her to but that explains nothing to us.

Expiation does not hide invisibly within the visibility of Winchester house the same way a secret is shielded there. It must remain secret yet admitted. Expiation is assumed in a name as an admittance of guilt and as an assumption of responsibility. Nothing visible, a name puts a face to this act. What lesson do we learn from the individual Sarah Winchester if we imagine that she took responsibility in her own name? We wonder why she felt obligated to an inherited guilt assumed by a name received in marriage for a crime that preceded her. She had every excuse to distance herself from this crime. Can we comprehend the motives behind her sacrifice to an impossible debt, which, moreover, is an individual expiation of collective responsibility? To what debt of injustice would it obligate *us*?

Winchester house may be a telling symptom, but how could it expiate a crime or cure an individual, let alone a culture? In what system of justice would this expiation be possible? Frontier justice? *American Justice*? How can we counterpoise the myth of Winchester's enterprise to an encompassing national myth that, by definition, consumes all, if indeed it was from this comparison that Jeremy Blake intended us to draw a lesson? (After all, repressively counterpoising the forces of two contradictory demands was how Sarah Winchester fabricated her crypt.) Against the fusible forces of myth, resistance is futile. Could any artist contend against its weapons of Hollywood seduction? Call this resistance? Passive resistance? Could we confront myth reasonably with a reasonable myth of our own, by a de-mystifying counter-myth? Would counter-myth absolve Sarah Winchester's spirited counteractions if told through a gender-reversed narrative that justified her revenge as rage against the patriarchy? Could any justified revenge serve justice? Must not justice instead "be removed from the fatality of vengeance" and responsibility rescued from regression to myth?[1] Would elevation to the status of popular icon exemplarily demonstrate an enlightenment beyond myth when we seem seduced here by one more spectacle? Sorting contradictions may be illuminating, but myth would still enforce its domination.

Is learning possible if it is not an individual responsibility, even though education is a generational obligation to transmit? Have we not collectively abdicated this responsibility to culture itself, by which I mean popular culture, so that any transmission automatically, indeed systematically, haunts? If Sarah Winchester had sought to teach by example, any more than she desired to explain the perverted domesticity of her haunted house, would she have locked herself silently in exile in foreign territory? Her secret is silent, her expiation, too. Explanation, similarly, is lacking in an artwork like *The Winchester Trilogy*, which is as wordlessly hallucinated as Winchester's haunting. How can we use one silent hallucination to penetrate the mystery of another when both are diffusive, when the second is a revisitation of the first, a speculative trace and inventive tracery of a prior madness? Can this madness, which has had no effect other than its residual caricature as a tourist trap, no resolution other than transmission to the future through the simulacra of an artwork, be cure to the collective, continuing madness from which its derives? Counterpoising one myth to another is no more dissolvent than when we knocked trick-or-treating on the door of Winchester's spooky mansion, a threshold across which we poised the subject's certitude to the uncertain poise of a spectre. Counterpoising is as delusory as the borderline is illusory.

Illusory does not mean without force. The borderline attracts forces and counter-forces. A divide is nothing but force. It comes into being by force, in the maintenance of force, and by a contention of forces that breach it in the war it already is.[2] Myth is never distanced fascination: myth is force. Force is undone only in the welcome of the threshold, in a disarming arrival that dissolves rather than discloses boundaries in a peace beyond the enforced aftermath of empires' wars. What cannot be counterpoised in or as a place, nevertheless, is at stake. The *threshold* is at stake, Sarah Winchester's in particular, though as no contention. What is at stake is the interpretation of the role Winchester house played in America's myth of regeneration through violence. What occurs in the decision of this door that it would become what it became, before or after our interpretation, a threshold or a border? What happens to make one and the same "place" either a threshold or a borderline but not both together? What transpires in the passage of the threshold or the crossing of the border as an opening or closing, in welcome or resistance?

When Sarah Winchester took up residence west in enemy territory, was her expiation by hospitality countermanded by hostility? What made her diverge from a mission that turned host hostage? What force of passage made her concede to national agenda to make her hostage to its violence once again, hostage to a mythic *violence* that is not a myth of violence? Or was expiation partial so that she was hostage, persecuted and besieged in the place where she was a hypocritical guest, ungenerous in return? If a man's home is his castle, was her house no welcoming domicile but actually a fortress? Whatever Winchester house was—welcome or fortification—it was no more than this door. *Only this door*. So it is at this threshold, which is not always a border, that we pose the question of individual responsibility within the fractured repose of Sarah Winchester's response: in the place where she confronted her spectral others. What was the face of Sarah Winchester's enemy? Who was she or he? Did her enemy have a face?

On the one hand, Sarah Winchester did nothing but face the enemy. The mutating facade of her Victorian mansion was her frontline. She constructed as many fronts as lines of defence. Her energy of elaboration was a perpetual positioning and retrenching of fronts. It was her obsession; she had a mania for the front, even though she perpetually fell back in order to patrol the precinct of her crypt, which her troops were unaware defending. She seemed not to care about dividing her resources by fighting on two fronts, inside and out, both of which, for all we know, were offensive and defensive manoeuvres, probably at the same time. As she was garrisoned, she did not have orders to advance; there would be no campaign like Custer's; but she did have a coordinated strategy. Hers was a strategy that combined garrison defence with guerrilla attack—even though her stated public policy was self-defence. But then, a good defence is always an offence. Tactics were covert, and, as befitting an inventor, her strategies were original (though they were founded on principles perfected on the march of Manifest Destiny west). She was a master—she assumed this mastery with her inheritance—or, you could say, she was a medium of dissimulation, dissembling her strategies and camouflaging her tactics. Her arsenal held two weapons—if one does not count dissemblance a weapon, which it is, and which her two weapons were as well; therefore, she had countless, proliferating weapons, a madness of arms. Her weapons were material and immaterial, being her house and her hallucinations, a terrifying, haunting combination. She was resourceful—if you consider that an arsenal is one's resource, which the etymological resource of language tells us an "arsenal" is, this etymology its own arms scandal, smuggling the Arabic origin of the word, which combines "art" and "house," to her aid. Cunningly, she used these domestic arts as female arts of seduction—the embroidery of her hallucinations and the domain of her home—as weapons, employing both, naturally, to simulate offence and defence. Her house was a defence, but it relentlessly marched on toward the enemy twenty-four hours day, a forced march of her carpenter army. Proceeding ahead while transmitting behind, her hallucinations entrenched and decamped a shifting redoubt. Her dissembling genius was to pose these hallucinations as the enemy's own operations, thereby confusing enemy action, dividing it by her own divisions, and then claiming territory. Of course, the dissemblance of unwarranted and unprovoked enemy assault played well at home, as the propagandist she was knew it would. Indeed, this military inventor knew how to fight the future war that would make an enemy tremble to the terrible electricity of phantom images. Moreover, she knew how well a passive and subdued home audience would consume these transmissions, spectral images no different, after all, than their routine entertainments, the profitable products of spectral media she herself had experimented developing in California as a sideline to her weapons research.

Through the tactics she advanced from strategies she had invented, yet she faced no enemy. In spite of all this technical invention and military bravado, the enemy was unseen. Her strategies were far in advance, anticipating the new "savage war" of our time, which keeps the enemy at a distance where it conveniently has no face. But was this necessary when the enemy always already is faceless, a hardly human thing to whom we owe no responsibility, obligating us to no human justice, no Geneva Convention? As effective and terrible as this strategy is, it makes us lose our human dignity in a faceless confrontation because the front evaporates along with these distant faces—it spirits away as if hallucinated from our mighty arsenal. In victory, we are left with sour defeat. Our old dismay, anxiety, and dissatisfaction haunt us still. Fighting a market war as *Lebensraum* for commodities was no salvation to the spirit. Not even the individual heroics of generic Hollywood blockbusters—for example, the propagandistic *Independence Day*, which extended American exceptionalism as an obligation to save the *world*, thank you, from the threat of the otherworldly alien—can fill this haunting hunger. No choice but to retrench and advance in some other place, some other Indian territory, against some other manufactured enemy. "*Bring 'em on!*" taunts the commander-in-chief.

Thus, the inventive laboratory of Sarah Winchester's military academy, housed in her San Jose compound, would repeat for the future what it had replayed from the past. No expiation ensues from the vainglory of its military machine, which knows only how to march its haunted troops to a regression that advances and retreats to the rhythm of a contradictory, bloody myth. There is no lesson here but obedience to the repetition of myth.

On the other hand, Sarah Winchester thought expiation due. How could a lone individual, a woman moreover, expiate a manufacture? How could one make restitution for genocide? Would not the impossibility for *one* to account for *all* alone derange an individual? How could the one named Sarah Winchester put names to serial manufacture? How could she put a face to a commodity when the commodification of death—the repeated product and profit of her family's enterprise—spirited by making a killing? Spirited profits and people, that is, equally and at the same time. Of course, the Winchester Repeating Rifle killed people; they were no more; having no earthly identity, they were spirits. Yet this repetition stole their identity, as some believe photographs spirit it away. The profitable repetition of this assembly line of death was a manufacture of ghosts. These spectral products were cast into their state: cast in, then cast out; stamped, then spirited. The ghosts haunting Sarah Winchester were phantom products manufactured by means of a tool that was just another commodity: a rifle. "*Guns don't kill people; people do.*" If the gun is not responsible, and we can hold no mere thing, no commodity, accountable, phantom products, too, would bear no responsibility—and we none to them.[3] With no responsibility of their own to bear, even to their own identity, they would all be the same, as we know them already to be serial products of manufacture. They would have no face and could appear in no mirror. The face-to-face of their haunting would have no face.[4]

This would seem to be Sarah Winchester's dilemma. Haunting would be the abyss where she could not account for the responsibility to face these spirits, face to face, to put a face and identity to them, so many, whose spectral status her family's diligence made her responsible for. To return from her profit what was proper to them, though no property, would entail the rescue of their singularity from where it was held hostage to the logic of substitution.[5] This logic had killed them two times over from a double dose of the death machine of industrial capital that transformed them—even before they were dead—into a phantom product of overkill. Even with a will to expiate all, she could not. There could be no expiation if justice was not possible. With all her wealth, Sarah Winchester could not plead this fantastic case when the forces of the capitalist economy kept it—because of the plaintiffs' ontological status being merely plaintive—inadmissible to a court of law where, after all, they could not appear in person.

She would seek restitution otherwise if, indeed, restitution was due, that is, if restitution itself was what was due. She would employ her money in the court of public opinion by no argument other than spectacle. She would conduct her case by means of entertainment, as a media, or medium, spectacle. As they are often shameful displays, indeed, the staging of celebrity shame, Sarah Winchester, too, would confess her shame. She would confess her failure to account for justice, to account for a crime that was not hers but to which no one else would confess. The crime remained hidden for no lack of evidence but for lack of admittance of it as a crime. This was the shocking truth of this secret. This was its spectral origin. The conspicuous consumption of her mansion was a public theatre protesting her failure to bring this anti-capital, class action suit to justice. She would make her mansion into a shameless mimicry of the senseless logic of capitalist production. She would spirit capital in wasteful consumption. She would expend it to no capital use, or to an end deemed mad: to serve spirits by "the commerce without commerce of ghosts." She would take on the impossible; she would parody the impossibility of justice by a cruel joke. Her revenge would be to make exchange impossible, as impossible as justice was in the world of exchange. She would exchange exchange for justice only as a sacrifice of exchange. Beyond the conspicuous consumption of her mansion, she would waste her economic patrimony by adopting the differing values of her country's enemy. She would betray ideals and principles (though not the deadly comfort of capital that maintained her in this liquidating enterprise) in order to make restitution due in a system where restitution could not, precisely, be rendered according to any calculation of exchange.[6] Emigrating from one territory to another, from one economic system to another, exiling herself in principle to destroy capital and principle, she would substitute one system for another as an expiating sacrifice to the spirit world. Her revenge would be devastation beyond the waste of capital that would expend revenge as well.

She would appease the spirit world haunting her by a sacrifice she pioneered but could not in any way take credit for. No restitution could be made out of court, out of an out-of-this-world court, by cash settlement paid through capital accrued from killing, when one already had benefit of this tainted cash. Justice could be served only by a total divestment rescinding any cash nexus. She would waste capital. She would waste the system of capitalism in a potlatch.

East Coast conspicuous consumption already mirrored West Coast potlatch but as a dissembling inversion of individual privilege.

Sarah Winchester would make her mansion a communicating vessel between the two by a potlatch that neither could rival. Her potlatch would undo the social rivalries of both by joining—despite their violent history—two peoples of contrary systems in a ceremony that would bind them other than through obligation, in a sacrifice that, although devastating, was beyond destruction as well. Their means of joining, however, would hold them together only through the discord of an unjust history that would not be dissolved in absolution but made absolute. Her potlatch would be a conspicuous wedding of disparity, an impossible union or union of the impossible whose progeny would spiritualize and harmonize a nation—but only within the disparity of discord that would be justice. Something would have to be sacrificed, indeed sacrificed to this impossibility. Her bride's gift would be this sacrifice, a sacrifice of devastation that was no violence but a *gift*.

Her transit between systems would mark her as an immigrant still in this foreign land. Her betraying dowry was no down payment justifying residence there. This perpetual bride would be carried across no threshold to any home of her own. She would never be at home in this territory, though *she* must provide welcome. Betraying herself by denying herself the benefits of obligation owed to a potlatch's donor, *she* would remain the one obligated, always subjected, persecuted, and accused. Her inverse sacrifice would passively divest the obligation demanded by potlatch. She would sacrifice any future benefit that could return to her in any way. She could not seek any obligation from those she owed a debt surpassing restitution but place herself hostage to the offer of infinite hospitality in a home where the violated were welcome, in a welcoming domicile that would be their home.

In spite of intent to face the impossible, in spite of her gift, which *was* the impossible and necessarily a secret, haunting would frequent her as an abyssal repetition of an aporia. She would mimic this abyss of accounting by a repetition of manufacture, by a counting of ciphers (a mimicry, too, of commerce's account books) of functionless chambers added endlessly—empty, unhomely rooms pressing their exterior surfaces outward to meet a null response, extruding a facade that restlessly sought the intimate front of a face-to-face. The constant divisions and partitions were her manic need to face an enemy that was now welcome (even if they were to meet through a break-in, an untimely event she anticipated with many internal fronts). Need was the mother of invention: a need, or desire, to find a face appearing on the other side of the many borders she devised. The intricacies of these serried redoubts were no defence; they were no lines of offence either, borders she wished to breach to another's territory. They were a provocation to call this face to her accounting. She answered the accusing call of her enemy's haunting by something that could not be placed or returned or restituted but could rescue *her*: by the harmony and hospitality of a line of welcome trespass. This trespass would first divide her from herself in a dispossessing expulsion that would only passively guide her to responsibility for others. This confrontation with her responsibility would put a face to her enemy who thus and then would appear to her, face to face. Unfortunately, she could not appease an enemy who was the enemy of the Easterners she had betrayed—even though the enemy of my enemy is my friend. Here was the assured and overwhelming victory of the stronghold of capital with its countless reserves of troops marching to the same myth. She could not overcome such an enemy even by allying herself to phantoms when capital could match cipher for cipher, and wastefully more, in its own too-willing sacrifice of singularity to an abstract world of profit.

Is it a wonder to know what secret Winchester house betrays after so many have been offered as interpretations—sentencing then acquitting, condemning then redeeming Sarah Winchester? So many contrarieties cancel themselves in their comings and goings, in their advancing of argument then retreat that they, too, seem to possess the insubstantiality of spirits. Secrets are unanswerable. The cover of Winchester house hides no secret, at least no *one* secret. Many assemble to dissemble disassembly within its shelter. It took all in. The house discloses itself as a medium, before we know it also as a mechanism, through which many secrets transpire, but only paired as contraries, as a conspiracy of contraries, one conjuring the other. Whether the house was a memorial or a covering crypt; whether haunting was a crypt or a phantom effect; whether Sarah Winchester was host or hostage; whether the house was to appease or offend; whether it was to attack or defend; we learn that secrets haunt—and that there is always more than one. Haunting is secrets' contagion. All these contrarieties pass through each other (host-hostage through crypt-phantom through appeasement-retribution, etc.) transpiring through this house in an interlacing that is the secret swearing of a conjuration, uniting and dividing all in a haunting that radiates out again to claim our culture. What a ball of confusion that entangles us in its knotting! Haunting, however, could be teaching. The frightful confusion facing us is a call to awake to the horror of our culture, to the slaughter at our doorstep, which was always in front of our faces.

Sarah Winchester awoke to the slaughter at her doorstep, although privilege buffered by profits kept killing at a sanitized distance. Responding, she took up residence in the killing grounds of that distant, fabled place. Her passage would be no redeeming transformation into the new American man or woman. Redemption could not be hers when responsibility was for others. She took up new residence by making her house anew. Still, her house had the appearance of the old, with the burden of all the old property relations symbolized and actualized in its protected domesticity. Could the domestic, something private, make public a secret—not some secret hidden within of Winchester's own trauma, but a secret public and private share, intimately? Winchester house would be this secret, not something sequestered, but there, *there* on its facade, on its filigreed face. But isn't a home the very emblem of tranquil reserve detached from public engagement? A house seems only a nesting of divisions retreating from the public sphere: placed behind the borderline separating the public from private property, a house facade divides exterior from interior by setting off the domestic from the social. Rather than a proper address identifying what is properly within, the facade is really a two-faced mask disguising "a topographical status quo" that binds not divides. Separation disavows that the border between public and private is a lie. Two share this secret denying that this privileging border is really a common open wound. Individual and society cannot be disjoined from the secret of social trauma that adjoins and disjoints them. Given the disproportion of power between individual and society, this is an exorbitant wound for the individual to bear. No wonder the individual condemns herself, condemns this secret to herself. No wonder we assumed that haunting issued from Sarah Winchester's sheltered secret when issuing is only the porosity of an illusory divide.

The mystery of Winchester Mystery House is no mystery if we know this secret. The mystery is its mechanism, which is no secret other than seeming instead a medium. We have seen that, although they must be distinguished from ready confusion, crypt and phantom effects are the return of social trauma manifested in individual pathology. Differing in origin, each haunts through one and the same individual or by means of one and the same social artifact: here, Winchester house. Each without the other, yet the two effects together as well, account for the mechanisms that conjure all the different haunting this house sustains itself as, that it welcomes under its roof. Although she did not consciously assemble but instituted all these divides together in her building mania, Sarah Winchester could not divorce her personal tragedy from larger social effects, even those that sustained the system. Her loved ones' deaths were no consequence of the profit of a product of killing. Still, she obsessively linked them as if they were magically associated. Whether Winchester had personal secrets that she could not acknowledge, she faced responsibility for a secret that society could not confess while conspicuously holding the smoking gun: the crime linking capital to killing. Capitalism is criminal. Winchester house was this secret admitted and denied.

According to the stories, not all spirits were enemies, not all visitations were unwelcome. Sarah Winchester sought to receive good spirits while trapping and expelling bad ones. The Winchester house's sole end would be this dual, dividing, or discriminating purpose. Perhaps this discriminating welcome was the source of her confusion whether she was host or hostage. Hostile reception would be lingering resistance to confession of criminal complicity because all spirits were now kin to her, at least those legion made in-laws through the Winchester Repeating Rifle. By admission not accusation, and outside any calculation of exchange or return, expiation is a one-sided act that puts faces and names to slaughter: naming ourselves responsible, admitting violation of another we thus identify. Expiation is one-sided, but its acts are not singular. That is, expiation is ongoing and must be repeated without notice. Expiation (which at any moment substitutes hostage for host) must admit welcome unreservedly, without conditions. When a stranger appears at her door, Sarah must welcome this stranger before she knows who he or she is, before the stranger has any qualifying properties, before she knows whether the stranger is saint or sinner, victim or killer. The shelter Sarah Winchester must offer a murderer is the welcome of her own murderous expiation. No justice is possible without this forbearance.[7] No justice is possible in a denial of hospitality that verges on revenge.

In turn, we must be generous toward Sarah Winchester's

obsession. The passion of her mission was to build a mansion of many rooms, not to capture or hunt to kill, dissembling welcome as a serial killer, but to welcome as if to a hotel or hostel or to the succour and repair of a hospice, to welcome so as well to receive, moreover to receive for herself as a learning, a learning "to live *with* ghosts, in the upkeep, the conversation, the company, or the companionship, in the commerce without commerce of ghosts."[8] Learning, indeed, is spectral.

Flight to an exile from which she never could return welcome replayed the American drama of rejection of society to seek formation of authentically truer, self-chosen communities in the far and freer distance. She was not sent off by myth but by responsibility. Departure was no regress to violent, unjust breach of a neighbour's border. Her expiatory mission was a desisting departure resisting violence in welcoming arrival, the welcome of a common habitation that differed, astonishingly, by its residence with ghosts. The enterprise of departure and invention—the departure from one community to the invention of another, the departure from conformity to the invention of the other in oneself—is persecuted in the very place of departure, which sees itself as the sole place of arrival. Sarah Winchester's departure would be suspect. But, likewise, who in the alien place of arrival would not suspect her and hold her hostage to her past and not persecute her further? In what place between two coasts would she be welcome? Any habitation *there* would be confused.

Sarah Winchester's task was impossible in so many ways. It was subjected to persecution even before it commenced. This preceding subjection preceded even the anterior crime belatedly inherited for which she owed guiltless expiation. Nonetheless, she was responsible. Subjected, she responded. A pioneer in an exile that was also a refuge to be host and hostage to the *ab*-original welcome of the aboriginal American other, Sarah Winchester, nevertheless, could not complete her mission impossible. Her order was not to decide *between* host and hostage; she was to maintain their *contrariety*; she was to be host *and* hostage. She was obligated to maintain *all* contraries together; she was "to maintain together that which does not hold together, and the disparate itself" by inhabiting the disadjustment conditional of justice.[9] Impossible perhaps, but this secret was the gift of the impossible already haunting her. Haunting was the secret, *and* the gift, *and* the impossible—or, at least, their beckoning welcome. On the edge of the abyss of welcoming the impossible, already within the welcome of the impossible and *beyond* borders, she bent back in a reversal that would become a reversed mania, returning contrary hostility for hospitality. The past would avenge her departure still by allying this reversal to what had already devastated her in that left place. Although she freely volunteered, she saw herself as hostage only, with no obligation as host—that is, a host who necessarily was hostage.

This reversal's intensity would forcibly mark any interpretation of her story, making it the one that we have chosen to believe. A "captivity narrative" makes for a better story anyway; conflict over appeasement, victory over justice is easier for Hollywood to sell. Besides, we already know the basic plot and, moreover, the comfort of consumption demands no uneasy departure on our part. And what a character to tell the story of her captivity! She could deliver. Her imagined hostage status would deliver Sarah Winchester to all the obsessions of the trauma of captivity, to hallucinating accusations and persecutions—in short, all the attributes of her haunting.[10] Unfortunately, her vast wealth protected her from rescue from a "captivity narrative" of her own devising. Her dissembling fabrications were too successfully secure for anyone to hear her appeal. The hostage status she imposed on herself would imprison her where she had regressed to hold herself captive: in a myth she had attempted to escape.

Here was the moment of the lock-down. Resisting host in her status as hostage was her decision. This decision would make her mission and mansion become what they were then to remain: the sequestering of an unwelcoming aggression. This decision would make her home become what it would be for the future: the haunted house of its own degraded myth. In the end, Sarah Winchester absolved individual responsibility by dissolving herself in the collectivity of myth. Myth cannot account for the responsibility of the face-to-face, which is exactly the effectiveness of its pledge of allegiance: as adherents, no one is responsible. Myth has an immediacy all can share, united in their individuality, righteous and without guilt in their participatory conviction. Torn between the elsewhere call of an expiatory guilt (which was a phantom haunting to which it was impossible to respond by restituting justice) and the silent call she could not bear to hear in her refused mourning (which was her own unanswered relation to death—the death of *one*, her daughter, not of all), in the end to defend herself from the wounds of these unbearable contra-dictions, Sarah Winchester counterpoised secrecy to communal myth by confusing what was common to them.[11]

Are we obligated to make the same decision as Sarah Winchester? Are we certain that victim is the status Sarah Winchester chose for herself even in her subjection as hostage (that is, host as hostage)? Can *we* so determine her status with a finality that obviates her intentions and persecuting obsessions? Because she was a victim, can we decide to avenge her by making her cause ours? By what right can we retrospectively make her enterprise this vengeance? Can we wrest the hospitality of a house, as haunted as it is by contradictions, to the sole purpose of vengeance? Would not empathy for the American victims "subject to the traumatic effects" of the mythic constructs of their culture dispense with justice, altogether denying the injustice Sarah Winchester tried to redress—justice for the violated *other*? Can we side with empathy over justice just because Winchester is one of *us*? Would empathy be cure for her or, more pertinently, us? Would it alleviate her suffering to which haunting is still testimony? Delivering the ghost of Sarah Winchester to vengeance, do we not fall victim as well—deceptively delegating the substitutive violence of a stand-in? Substituting Sarah Winchester for her stand-in Hannie Caulder would make our heiress into a sacrificial scapegoat and, at the same time, conveniently distance us from her violence, except that the substitution host-hostage is not an exchange that can be avenged. We cannot empathetically exonerate ourselves when decision is demanded of us (substitution as well)—here and now, if the current case is Iraq or any other place of military aggression. Decision here is impossible but not "inconceivable."

A door beckons. This welcoming or resistant door opens to war or peace, justice or revenge. *One and the same differing door*. It cannot be both at once, welcoming and resistant. It can no more be both-and than it can be either-or. It does not swing back and forth from one position to the other; it is not a fulcrum balancing judgement. Always open more than it is closed, this door is *immediately* open to decision. The decision what it is (or will be) is not a definition. No interpretation either. If we must sustain contradictory interpretations for Sarah Winchester's haunting, we cannot so vacillate in front of this door. Poised at this threshold, we must decide our entry. Haunting already was an entry if we opened ourselves to its rending, if we opened ourselves to its opening. Haunting was welcoming the stranger within, passively receiving the dislodging interruption of the other in us. Any one of the *Trilogy*'s fleeting hallucinations was proximate passage. Here and there, haunting dissolves divisions.[12] A ghostly event could settle justice by its ghostly unsettling, by its uncanny inhabitation in the haunted house of our soul. Welcoming of ghostly inhabitation would be expiatory justice. Haunting would call us to an ethics of the other, not force us in fearful retreat to the threat of a politics of conquest. Welcome hallucinations. Before this unhinged door that disjoints time, "the instant of decision is madness."[13]

Madness would not result from a wrong choice leading to war or to the proliferating reprisals of vengeance. *Decision* would be madness in that the moment of decision is impossible: it is an impossible moment. Not that it is impossible to choose between war and peace, vengeance and justice. As something invisible, non-present, and incomprehensible, the decisive moment itself is mad and cannot be rationally chosen. Nonetheless, obsessive expiation returns to this dilemma through the persecutions of ghostly revisitation. Why are *we* haunted? *What revenant* returns? *Who* haunts us? Derrida has meditated on Hamlet's lament that "the time is out of joint," Hamlet's complaint of his inheritance to set right disjointed justice that even dislocates time, to avenge an anterior crime, and to settle the haunting of a ghostly injunction, so analogous to Sarah Winchester's plight.[14] Derrida conjectures that disjuncture, not rendering accord, conditions the very possibility of justice. He asks, "What if disadjustment were on the contrary the condition of justice?" Redress of ghostly complaints inhabits the same disjuncture and dislocated time as haunting persecution and injustice (and risks compounding evil and injustice)—redress and complaint, justice and haunting disparately together. The address of redress is not accord. Rather, improper address is proper in the proximity of ghosts. Ourselves unhinged in the dislocated time of an impossible decision, we draw justice and the other near, near to each other and to us, proximate in our responsibility. Disadjustment is doubly conditional: Derrida adds, "Is not disjuncture the very possibility of the other?"[15]

Although poised on a threshold as *the* question, the decisive yet questionable event that is the question of the ghost bypasses the border of the *now*. The madness of the decision is the madness of this evasion. The spectral time of the haunted threshold altogether escapes the present, opening it to what evades its immediacy: the ghostly appearance of the ghostly event. Poised questionably there, ghosts beckon but also beseech by their injunctions. Pivoting on absence, opening instead to the future and to the past, this door introduces *the* question of justice:

> Of justice where it is not yet, not yet *there*, where it is no longer, let us understand where it is no longer *present*, and where it will never be, no more than the law, reducible to laws or rights. It is necessary to speak *of the* ghost, indeed *to the* ghost and *with* it, from the moment that no ethics, no politics, whether revolutionary or not, seems possible and thinkable and *just* that does not recognize in principle the respect for those others who are no longer or for those others who are not yet *there*, presently living, whether they are already dead or not yet born. No justice...seems possible or thinkable without the principle of some *responsibility*, beyond all living present, within that which disjoins the living present, before the ghosts of those who are not yet born or who are already dead.[16]

If justice is haunting, then to be just, we need always live with the enigma of ghosts—where Sarah Winchester elected to reside.

The door to Winchester house always aligned with a border—at least potentially. This was what was at stake in the decision that results in a threshold or a border, between hospitality and hostility, between peace and war, between the an-economy of the gift and the exchange of revenge. In the outcome of these, some would say dubious, oppositions, either was possible but only one was impossible. Would Sarah Winchester's exiling mission be mobilized by myth, commanded by surrender to its immersive element as dissolvent of identities as collusive capital, regressing to its dissolute and propulsive violence? The manifest destiny of a nation enthralled to myth dissolves borders only to force them ever further, even beyond its shores. (Once national borders are exhausted, the adventure of territorial expansionism may, as well, force across invisible borders by economic violence alone.) Although the "enemy" submits to violence when borders are crossed, myth transmits its wounds to its own enslaved citizens whenever it represses a collectively complicit transgression. Myth obsesses to transgress then deny. Haunting originates in this denial that represses its violence. The violence of denial splits the subject's psychic topography by a wound that sequesters it from the violated other. These wounds, however, are only supplemental to the wounding precedence that proceeds from the other. Expulsed thus from egoistic security, these nationals listlessly sojourn exiled in their ill-gotten territory. The enclosure of Winchester house would mobilize a series of transgressive crossings to serve the absolute ends of the nation, but the repeated induction to internal violence would leave traces in a serried sequence of self-imposed wounds. Dissolving myth would not in turn dissolve a nation, though the system itself is a myth. Not that the hold of myth expires when exposed to this knowledge, when force is all it is and through which it persists, but that the system is founded on a myth that it self-identifies as "regeneration through violence." The secret here is that only *myth* regenerates itself by degeneration of violence, not individuals. Allied to war, myth is the violent expropriation of the individual to absolute ends. These totalizing ends dissolve identity in a participatory vehemence that robs responsibility from one as it steals identity from the other by its exterminating violence.

In electing residence west, would Sarah Winchester herself instead be elected and "ordered toward the face of the other?"[17] Reversion from host to hostage would not trigger regression into myth. Yet expulsion would leave its own violent traces in a substitutive submission as hostage to the other. In electing expiation, Sarah Winchester would be making an open statement after all. Her home would be this statement, or rather a declaration. It would open up "hospitality by an act of force that is nothing other than a declaration of peace, the declaration of peace itself."[18] Peace would be beyond all violence and hostility. Peace would be a *beyond* beyond borders, outdistancing them altogether in a desistance that does not install their divisions otherwise. *There* would persist an inviolable violability "that prohibits violence at the very place it is exposed to it without defense."[19] *There* would be a vulnerable line, we learn, that we cannot force across, a front we only share through the apparition of the face of the other. *There* we would defer to the face-to-face. Peace would substitute a welcome threshold there, here. Peace.

NOTES

Credit obviously extends past these notes to Nicholas Abraham, Maria Torok, and Richard Slotkin. But gratitude surpassing debt must be offered to Jacques Derrida and late welcomer Emmanuel Levinas, whose ideas grace my text, indeed, sleepwalk me through it as a gift of haunting.

Given the American history that I have just recounted and the place through which I end, I imagine, in that place where it already was a resistance that was not a violence but the struggle of a passive resistance, that this essay must be dedicated (though I have no right except as author) to the exemplary spirit of the Civil Rights Movement. America's expiation was there denied.

1. Cowboys and Indians

1. Blake already had the Winchester mansion in sight as the subject of a work; current events galvanized the *Trilogy*'s production. Needless to say, the neighbourly critique of America made from the other side of what used to be called "the longest undefended border in the world" is my own, not Jeremy Blake's. No doubt it exceeds his motivations. Fortunately, I am free from the difficult demands placed on American citizens. Yet the haunting dangerously released by Blake's *Winchester Trilogy* affects the author as well, as this text is proof, being an exhibition catalogue essay that swelled into a book. The author cannot exempt himself from the continental complicity of genocide that our countries historically share, to different degrees. (Citizens of two countries, we are both captive to a system that since first settlement North America has known nothing but: the capitalism that marks us thoroughly.) No more can the author evade the demands that issue from confrontation with a haunted artwork to question him as an ethical subject. While applying a critique to others, he must assume responsibility for these unwanted and difficult questions to himself, just as together artist, author, and audience are responsible for the common ground of images, texts, and representations that we are responsive to and that we share as common cultures.

2. Spirit Hunting

1. "Like Queen Victoria, the moral emblem of the era, who assumed mourning permanently following the death of her husband, nineteenth-century women could adopt mourning as a full-time occupation. Spiritualism provided a way to show love and interest in the dead without submitting to the restrictions of one's activities that accompany mourning." Ann Braude, *Radical Spirit: Spiritualism and Women's Rights in Nineteenth Century America* (Boston: Beacon Press, 1989), 53.
2. Ibid., 51.
3. Blake cites Sarah Winchester as an "architect, inventor, and artist." She patented a carwash that is still on the grounds of her estate.
4. Jeffrey Sconce, *Haunted Media: Electronic Presence from Telegraphy to Television* (Durham & London: Duke University Press, 2000), 48. "The Spiritualists elaborated telegraphic principles into an intriguing and politically engaged theology of telepresence, weaving complex fantasies of gender and technology around the century's most celebrated electronic marvel," 27.
5. "Media always already provide the appearances of specters.... Accordingly, the invention of the Morse alphabet in 1837 was promptly followed by the tapping specters of the spiritistic seances sending their messages from the realm of the dead. Promptly as well, photographic plates —even and especially those taken with the camera shutter closed—furnished reproductions of ghosts or specters, whose black-and-white fuzziness only served to underscore the promise of resemblance. Finally, one of the ten applications Edison envisioned for his newly invented phonograph in the *North American Review* (1878) was to record 'the last words of dying persons'." Friedrich Kittler, *Gramophone, Film, Typewriter*, trans. Geoffrey Winthrop-Young and Michael Wutz (Stanford: Stanford University Press, 1999), 12.
6. Thomas De Quincey, *Suspiria de Profundis* (Oxford: Oxford University Press, 1985), 87.
7. Jacques Derrida, *Specters of Marx*, trans. Peggy Kamuf (New York & London: Routledge, 1994), 140; Herman Melville, *The Confidence-Man* (New York: The Modern Library, 2003), 10. Melville's keener hunter after these hunters, of course, refers to the confidence man, whose operation by means of sophistical simulacra would also occasion truth hunters, some whom, too, might be "hunters after hunters" such as found in Plato's *Sophist*.

3. Fluid Mechanics: *Winchester*

1. Noël Burch, "Charles Baudelaire versus Doctor Frankenstein," *Life to those Shadows* (Berkeley and Los Angeles: University of California Press, 1990), 18. He adds, "The pursuit of the fantasy of a class became the fantasy of a culture," 7.
2. The *La Poste* report is quoted in ibid., 21.
3. Avital Ronell, *The Telephone Book:*

Technology, Schizophrenia, Electric Speech (Lincoln and London: University of Nebraska Press, 1989), 4.

4. Tom Gunning, "Phantom Images and Modern Manifestations: Spirit Photography, Magic Theater, Trick Films, and Photography's Uncanny," *Fugitive Images: From Photography to Film,* ed. Patrice Petro (Bloomington and Indianapolis: Indiana University Press, 1995), 43.

5. Ibid., 60, 64.

6. Kittler, *Gramophone, Film, Typewriter*, 124. We should also note that another American arms manufacturer, Remington—the inventor of the equally famous Colt pistol—contributed to the liberation of women from domestic servitude with the demand for a new class of labour accompanying the development of the typewriter. See ibid., 252–53.

7. Derrida discusses the "paradoxical phenomenality" of the spectre, which defies semantics, psychoanalysis, philosophy, and ontology, as a return of a logic of hauntology overpowering ontology. Derrida, *Specters of Marx*, 6–7, 10.

8. "Although scientific types of multiplicity are themselves extremely diverse, they do not include the properly philosophical multiplicities for which Bergson claimed a peculiar status defined by duration, 'multiplicity of fusion', which expressed the inseparability of variations, in contrast to multiplicities of space, number, and time, which ordered mixtures and referred to the variable or to independent variables." Gilles Deleuze and Félix Guattari, *What is Philosophy*, trans. Hugh Tomlinson and Graham Burchell (New York: Columbia University Press, 1994), 127. For a discussion of the construction of temporalities in video projection—and of numeric (quantitative) and durational (qualitative) multiplicities therein—that differ from the durational art of the 1960s precisely because video projection reworks narrative structure derived from mainstream film, see the chapter "Talking en abyme," in Philip Monk, *Double-Cross: The Hollywood Films of Douglas Gordon* (Toronto: The Power Plant and Art Gallery of York University, 2003), 133–47.

9. Derrida, *Specters of Marx*, 6, 7. Besides being a (secret) conspiracy, conjuration can be either an evocation to bring forth spirits or an exorcism to expel them. See ibid. 40, 41, 47.

10. Note the soundtrack role of the music box rendition of a Sousa march (the box purchased by Blake from the gift shop to Winchester Mystery House), a standard device of horror films signifying an eerie reversion in time to some childhood trauma that continues to haunt. The music accompanies the only other image of the house that, halfway through the projection, likewise begins to bleed an aura. This is an archival photograph of the mansion at the full mania of its architectural proliferation, seven storeys high.

4. Interior Ruptures: *1906*

1. "Not able to stay in a theme, not able to appear, this invisibility which

becomes contact and obsession is due not to the nonsignifyingness of what is approached, but to a way of signifying quite different from that which connects exposition to sight. Here, beyond visibility there is exposed no signification that would still be thematized in its sign." Emmanuel Levinas, *Otherwise than Being or Beyond Essence*, trans. Alphonso Lingis (Pittsburgh: Duquesne University Press, 1998), 100.

2. See www.thespiritrealm.com. Electronic voice phenomena (EVP), apparently recorded at the Winchester Mystery House, are available at GEISTweb.

3. In 1986, Geraldo Rivera captured a large audience by hosting a live television special, *The Mystery of Al Capone's Vaults*, which after much suspense discovered only some empty bottles.

4. "A false Unconscious: the crypt in the Ego—a false 'return of the repressed', the action in the Ego of hidden thoughts from the crypt," Nicholas Abraham and Maria Torok, *The Wolf Man's Magic Word: A Cryptonymy*, trans. Nicholas Rand (Minneapolis: University of Minneapolis Press, 1986), lxxi. Unlike *Winchester*, the projector sound in *1906* is not illusory but our clue to some grounding in real materiality in contrast to the devolution to the imaginary of the computer manipulations.

5. Discussion of the anachronicity, secret diachrony, or non-contemporaneity of the present to itself is so shared between Levinas and Derrida—as are the allied ideas of the invisible null or non-place that opens in the instant of a decision that cannot be represented within the temporal present or be grasped by comprehension in language or reason—that I would not be able to identify a single source. Nevertheless, see note 13 below, The Face of the Enemy.

6. Our response to the beckoning of "other" images is only our passive surrender of the category of division as a dividing of two. Although the narrative may demand it, I do not lend "interiority" or "exteriority" priority or reality one over the other. Disinvesting visibility for an asignifying invisibility, exchanging sound for sight and inverting horizontal and vertical, Levinas has otherwise written: "The metaphor of a sound that would be audible only in its echo meant to approach this way of presenting one's passivity as an underside without a right side." Levinas, *Otherwise than Being*, 106.

7. On the animating and engineering by the Thing and its "contradiction of *automatic autonomy*," see Derrida, *Specters of Marx*, 18, 153. On the secret, see Derrida, *The Gift of Death*, trans. David Willis (Chicago: The University of Chicago Press, 1995), *On the Name*, trans., David Wood, John P. Leavey, and Ian McLeod (Stanford: Stanford University Press, 1995), and *Given Time: 1. Counterfeit Money*, trans. Peggy Kamuf (Chicago: The University of Chicago Press, 1992).

8. Freud, "The Uncanny," *Collected Papers* (New York: Basic Books, 1959), IV, 370–75.

9. "Repetition *and* first time: this is

perhaps the question of the event as question of the ghost." Derrida, *Specters of Marx*, 10.

5. *Symptomatological Digression 1: The Crypt*

1. "Whereas the paranoiac expels from his ego the impulses that have become unpleasant, the neurotic helps himself by taking into his ego as large a part of the outside world, making it the object of unconscious phantasies," Sandor Ferenczi wrote in 1909 when he proposed the term "introjection." Quoted in J. Laplanche and J. B. Pontalis, "Introjection," *The Language of Psycho-Analysis*, trans. Donald Nicholson-Smith (New York: W. W. Norton & Company, Inc., 1973), 229–30. Introjection and incorporation have become confused in psychoanalytic literature. Following Abraham and Torok here, incorporation is failed introjection. See Maria Torok, "The Illness of Mourning and the Fantasy of the Exquisite Corpse," in Nicholas Abraham and Maria Torok, *The Shell and the Kernel*, trans. Nicholas T. Rand (Chicago: The University of Chicago Press, 1994), I, 107–24.
2. Derrida, "*Fors*: The Anglish Words of Nicholas Abraham and Maria Torok," Foreword, trans. Barbara Johnson, to Abraham and Torok, *The Wolf Man's Magic Word*, xxii. "But thanks to this subterfuge, the text of the drama being written *behind* his *inner safe* will play itself out *in front*, on the *outer safe*, so to speak." Nicholas Abraham, *The Case of Jonah*, quoted in Derrida, "*Fors*," xi.
3. "Cryptophoria" is the clinical term Abraham and Torok propose for the incorporation of and identification with an encrypted object. See Abraham and Torok, "Mourning *or* Melancholia: Introjection *versus* Incorporation," *The Shell and the Kernel*, I, 131. My analysis of the crypt derives from the research of Abraham and Torok, but my unlicensed application and unwarranted extension to a non-linguistic text depart from it.
4. A search of the Web will show the appearance of the Winchester Mystery House on many haunted house sites but also a debunking by Joe Nickell, "Winchester Mystery House: Fact vs. Fancy," *Skeptical Inquirer* 26: 5 (Sept.–Oct. 2002), 20–23. Another 1997 article by Annalee Newitz, "The Winchester Mystery House and Other Ghost Stories of Industry in Silicon Valley," discusses the house haunting corporate Silicon Valley as a parody of capitalist expansion, a symbolic critique of Sarah Winchester's family by her wasteful expenditure of its death-derived fortune, and speculates on the class and race basis of Winchester's admittance of good spirits and deceit of bad ones.

6. *Symptomatological Digression 2: The Thing*

1. Torok, "The Illness of Mourning," 117.
2. Abraham and Torok, "Mourning *or* Melancholia," 136.

3. The continuation of the quotation in note 2 suggests that the second loss is not mourned, but that the "interminable process of mourning" is for the first love object. "The subject heralds the love-object's sadness, his gaping wound, his universal guilt—without ever revealing, of course, the unspeakable secret, well worth the entire universe. The only means left by which the subject can covertly revive the secret paradise taken from him is to stage the grief attributed to the subject who lost him.... Being a melancholic, I stage and let everyone else see the full extent of my love-object's grief over having lost me." Ibid., 136.
4. Ibid., 131.

7. *Symptomatological Digression 3: The Phantom Effect*

1. Abraham and Torok, "'The Lost Object—Me': Notes on Endocryptic Identification," *The Shell and the Kernel*, I, 153. The "symbol-cover" of a fetish conceals the magic word, itself the symbol of what cannot be expressed.
2. On the technical prosthesis, see Derrida, *Specters of Marx*, 8.
3. Abraham, "Notes on the Phantom," *The Shell and the Kernel*, I, 171. Saying phantom effects are different from crypt effects does not obviate the speculation of Sarah Winchester's secret or exonerate her in any way. It only verifies the haunting that has been "named" by Winchester but does not substitute in any way for the one that remains unnamed.
4. On the spectro-poetics of Marx's analysis of the commodity, see Derrida's *Specters of Marx*.
5. "It is reasonable to maintain that the 'phantom effect' progressively fades during its transmission from one generation to the next and that, finally, it disappears. Yet, this is not at all the case when shared or complementary phantoms find a way of being established as social practices along the lines of *staged words*.... We must not lose sight of the fact that to stage a word—whether metaphorically, as an alloseme, or as a cryptonym—constitutes an attempt at exorcism, an attempt, that is, to relieve the unconscious by placing the effects of the phantom in the social realm." Abraham, "Notes on the Phantom," 176.
6. While *1906* reveals damage to the interior of the house, only *Winchester* shows wounds bleeding either from the facade of the house or from the hallucinated Rorschach images of cowboys. Thus, the trilogy, from part one to part two, duplicates the dual structure of this haunting in its exterior and interior, public and private manifestations.
7. I should say, *Century 21* brings us up to the moment of 9/11... and beyond, to the present. Although subsequent to Blake's decision to take up the subject of Winchester house, the Iraq War is the test case before us now. What of myth justifies the invasion of Iraq and enables its violence? I don't ask *what* myth, since we know, but what *of* myth justifies injustice? Myth does not temporize but acts. In the wake of 9/11, Blake assumed the artistic right for an artwork to address

complex issues, in part the freedom of expression, that the political appeal to clear and present danger would rather simplify while censoring. The danger is always that the exigencies of patriotic solidarity seek to exempt the present case from examination. Worse would be the denial altogether by those whose trade is the manipulation of images (artists) or the rhetoric of language (journalists) that myth *is* violence, to suggest instead that myth is *only* myth, that America is only fascinated by images of violence that fuel Hollywood but do not motor its economy, in other words, to dispute myth's exigencies on action and its justification for it.

8. Repeating Rifle: *Century 21*

1. Slotkin suggests that *High Noon* can be read as an allegory from either the left or right. Richard Slotkin, *Gunfighter Nation: The Myth of the Frontier in Twentieth-Century America* (New York: Atheneum, 1992), 395.
2. "The rise and fall of the Western mirrors the development of the Cold War and its sustaining ideological consensus from its seedtime in 1948–54 to its fulfillment in the years of the liberal counteroffensive under Kennedy and Johnson, to its disruption by the failure of the war in Vietnam." Ibid., 347.
3. At the time of the Addams's cartoon, the Eisenhower administration was drawing up counterinsurgency scenarios that eventually gave a new covert role to the Central Intelligence Agency, whose mandate was revised after the 1954 Doolittle Report. "The Indian-war metaphor became increasingly prominent in the rhetoric of counterinsurgency after 1961, in part because of the parallels between these two kinds of fighting—both of which took place in a 'wilderness' setting against a racially and culturally alien enemy." Ibid., 493.
4. Ibid., 4. Following Blake, I derive my examples and analysis of the relation of the popular artifacts of the Western to American cultural and political history from Slotkin's extensive analyses.
5. The parallel operations of the peripatetic "Buffalo Bill's Wild West" (1883–1916) and Sarah Winchester's stationary spirit trap (1884–1922) both conceived the West as a mythic space. "Buffalo Bill's Wild West" was instrumental in the seamless transition from the myth of regeneration through violence to "regeneration through imperialism," when in 1899 it replaced its staging of "Custer's Last Fight" with the "Battle of San Juan Hill," which equally glamourized Theodore Roosevelt and his Rough Riders imperial campaign in the Spanish-American War. See ibid., 82.
6. Ibid., 12, 14. Violence is always portrayed as coming from the other side: the false report of savage extermination of white settlers; enemy fire on American ships, whether in Havana Harbour during the Spanish-American War or Tonkin Inlet during the Vietnam War.
7. Ibid., 353. The three climaxing crises of 1876–77—the collapse of

Reconstruction in race riots and Ku Klux Klan insurgence; the Great Strike of 1877; and the Sioux War of 1876 and Custer's humiliating Last Stand—were all put down by marshalling the language and techniques of the "savage war," which was then reiterated in the labour wars of 1894 and then exported a few years later to the Philippines. Ibid., 18–21, 65.

8. The title of Slotkin's second volume refers to Walt Whitman's poem "From Far Dakota's Cannons," published days after the telegraphed news of General Custer's death, where the "fatal environment" is the milieu of Custer's death. See Slotkin, *The Fatal Environment: The Myth of the Frontier in the Age of Industrialization 1800–1890* (New York: Atheneum, 1985), 10–11.

9. Communication from the artist, June 20, 2004.

10. *Vertigo*'s fictional Carlotta Valdes and her California contemporary Sarah Winchester strangely intersect through the geographic co-relation of the bell towers related to their stories and the loss to each of a child. The premise of *Vertigo*'s dissembling plot, which draws the disgraced detective Ferguson through madness to knowledge, is the generational transmission of an illness of mourning that "Madeleine Elster" inherits from Carlotta Valdes. Carlotta Valdes was the mistress of a wealthy man who built her a mansion, then abandoned her, taking her baby. Race underlies this theft repeating the Mexican loss of California to the Manifest Destiny of the United States.

11. Statement by Jeremy Blake in Benjamin Weil, Jeremy Blake, Mitchell Schwarzer, *Jeremy Blake: Winchester* (San Francisco: San Francisco Museum of Modern Art, 2005), n. p.

12. D. H. Lawrence, *Studies in Classic American Literature* (New York: The Viking Press, 1964), 83.

13. Harold Rosenberg, "The American Action Painters," *The Tradition of the New* (New York: Grove Press, Inc., 1961), 31.

14. Blake, in Weil, Blake, Schwarzer, *Jeremy Blake: Winchester*.

15. Justice arises from the arrival of a third. "It is the third party that interrupts the face to face of a welcome of the other man, interrupts the proximity or approach of the neighbor, it is the third man with which justice begins.... [The third party] is of itself the limit of responsibility and the birth of the question: What do I have to do with justice?" Levinas, *Otherwise than Being*, 150, 157.

16. Slotkin, *Gunfighter Nation*, 461–73.

9. The Face of the Enemy

1. Derrida, *Specters of Marx*, 21. Derrida adds, "Better than removed: infinitely foreign, heterogeneous at its source."

2. "We do not need obscure fragments of Heraclitus to prove that being reveals itself as war to philosophical thought, that war does not only affect it as the most patent fact, but as the very patency, or the truth, of the real. In war reality rends the words and images that dissimulate it, to obtrude in its nudity and in its hardness. Harsh

reality (this sounds like a pleonasm!), harsh object-lesson, at the very moment of its fulguration when the drapings of illusion burn war is produced as the pure experience of pure being. The ontological event that takes form in this black light is a casting into movement of beings hitherto anchored in their identity, a mobilization of absolutes, by an objective order from which there is no escape." Emmanuel Levinas, *Totality and Infinity: An Essay on Exteriority*, trans. Alphonso Lingis (Pittsburgh: Duquesne University Press, 1969), 21.

3. Is the advocacy of agency here, which acquits technology in acquitting the gun, not a magic effect, a repeating-rifle effect repeating a disavowal of one's own agency in technology?

4. On the face and the face-to-face, see Levinas, *Totality and Infinity*, *Otherwise than Being* and Derrida, *Adieu: To Emmanuel Levinas,* trans. Pascale Anne Brault and Michael Naas (Stanford: Stanford University Press, 1999). Also see note 7 below.

5. Equivalence as substitution differs from Levinas's notion of substitution as the sacrifice of the irreplaceable unique (me) for the other, a paradoxical condition that allows the subject to be both host and hostage.

6. Derrida writes that restitution cannot be calculated within an economy of vengeance (the exchange of an eye for an eye). Justice is not rendered by the accountability of restitution at all, by a calculation of what is due, but by giving *beyond* the due, the debt, or the crime thought on the basis of the gift—"justice as incalculability of the gift and singularity of the an-economic ex-position to others," this relation to others that Levinas contends is justice, a relation of gift that is "the abolition of inalienable property." The gift is "without restitution, without calculation, without accountability." One only gives what one does not have without any expectation of return because the gift "can only *come back* or belong to the other." Derrida, *Specters of Marx*, 22–27; Levinas, *Totality and Infinity*, 75. The secret, the impossible, and the gift are all implicated in one another but not in any reciprocal exchange. On the secrecy and impossibility of the gift, see Derrida, *Given Time*.

7. On the appearance of the face and the alterity of the other, without qualities, properties, or determinant ontological predicates, see Levinas, *Totality and Infinity* and *Otherwise than Being*, passim., and Derrida, *Adieu*, 111. Derrida writes here that the "absence of determinable properties, of concrete predicates, of empirical visibility, is no doubt what gives to the face of the other a spectral aura, especially if the subjectivity of the *hôte* also lets itself be announced as the visitation of a face, of a visage. *Host* or *guest* [in English], *Gastgeber* or *Gast*, the *hôte* would be not only a hostage. It would have, according to a profound necessity, at least the face or figure of a spirit or phantom (*Geist*, ghost)."

On the refuge offered the murderer, "the order to save from death a murderer haunted by the spectral return of the victim, by the revenge of the phantom, by avengers bent on dealing death in their turn," see Derrida's comments on Levinas's *Beyond the Verse*, ibid., 108, 112.

8. Derrida, *Specters of Marx*, xviii. Derrida writes, in what is the beginning of this citation, that "the time of the 'learning to live' [is] a time without tutelary present." He adds after the citation: "To live otherwise, and better. No, not better, but more justly. But *with them*. No *being-with* the other, no *socius* without this *with* that makes *being-with* in general more enigmatic than ever for us. And this being-with specters would also be, not only but also, a *politics* of memory, of inheritance, and of generations."

9. "To maintain together that which does not hold together, and the disparate itself, the same disparate, all of this can be thought...only in a dis-located time of the present, at the joining of a radically dis-jointed time, without certain conjunction.... It is easy to go from disadjusted to unjust. That is our problem: how to justify this passage from disadjustment (with its rather more technico-ontological value affecting a presence) to an injustice that would no longer be ontological? And what if disadjustment were on the contrary the condition of justice? ...Is not disjuncture the very possibility of the other? How to distinguish between two disadjustments, between the disjuncture of the unjust and the one that opens up the infinite asymmetry of the relation to the other, that is to say, the place for justice?" Derrida, Ibid., 17, 19–20, 22.

10. "Vulnerability, exposure to outrage, to wounding, passivity more passive than all patience, passivity of the accusative form, trauma of accusation suffered by a hostage to the point of persecution, implicating the identity of the hostage who substitutes himself for the others: all this is the self, a defecting or defeating of the ego's identity. And this, pushed to the limit, is sensibility, sensibility as the subjectivity of the subject. It is a substitution for another, one in the place of the other, expiation.... It is as though persecution by another were at the bottom of solidarity with another." Levinas, *Otherwise than Being*, 15, 102.

11. On the critical opposition of demonic rapture and fusion of myth to responsibility, see Derrida, *The Gift of Death*, 20.

12. The division inside/outside is a convenience that does not prioritize one over the other. The break-in by a passive falling into the beckoning inside is no different from the break out to the infinite beyond by a desisting departure. Threshold passage depends on whether we are welcomed within from our position outside or whether, there, we too welcome an outsider in. These categories are mixed when welcoming ghostly inhabitation is also a defection from the ego, an expulsion from the self, "a recurrence in which the expulsion of self outside of itself is its substitution for the other." "Obsession is a persecution where the persecution does not make up the content of a consciousness gone mad; it designates the form in which the ego is affected, a form which is a defecting from consciousness. This

inversion of consciousness is no doubt a passivity—but it is a passivity beneath all passivity." Levinas, *Otherwise than Being*, 110–11, 101.

13. "I have emphasized the word *instant*: 'the instant of decision is madness', Kierkegaard says elsewhere. The paradox cannot be grasped in time and through mediation, that is to say in language and through reason. Like the gift and the 'gift of death', it remains irreducible to presence or to presentation, it demands a temporality of the instant without ever constituting a present. If it can be said, it belongs to an atemporal temporality, to a duration that cannot be grasped: something one can neither stabilize, establish, *grasp [prendre], apprehend*, or *comprehend*." Derrida, *The Gift of Death*, 65.

14. Derrida would probably dispute my resort to "analogy" here. Although there is always "more than one specter," cases of injustice and injunctions of redress are singular. Moreover, they are singular in their demands, addressed to Hamlet or Sarah Winchester, or to you or me. This is one reason perhaps why Derrida insists that justice is irreducible to laws or rights.

15. Derrida, *Specters of Marx*, 19–20, 22.

16. Derrida, Ibid., xix.

17. Levinas, *Otherwise than Being*, 11.

18. Derrida, *Adieu*, 47.

19. Ibid., 39–40. "The face in which the other—the absolutely other—presents himself and does not negate the same, does not do violence.... It remains commensurate with him who welcomes; it remains terrestrial. This presentation is preeminently nonviolence, for instead of offending my freedom it calls it to responsibility and founds it. As nonviolence it nonetheless maintains the plurality of the same and the other. It is peace." Levinas, *Totality and Infinity*, 203.

ACKNOWLEDGEMENTS

I thank Jeremy Blake for his generosity toward my exceeding speculations derived, indeed delivered hauntingly, from his work.

Publication has been assisted by the generous financial support of Laura Rapp.

CREDITS

Jeremy Blake

Winchester, 2002
DVD with sound for plasma or projection
18:00 continuous loop

1906, 2003
DVD with sound for plasma or projection
21:00 continuous loop

Century 21, 2004
DVD with sound for plasma or projection
12:00 continuous loop

Courtesy the artist and Feigen Contemporary, New York

The Winchester Trilogy was exhibited at the Art Gallery of York University: *Winchester* and *1906*, May 12–June 27, 2004; *Century 21*, July 10–August 13, 2004 (AGYU@Trinity Square Video).